FOOD
AND
FUEL

FOOD
AND
FUEL

Solutions for the Future

EDITED BY
Andrew Heintzman and
Evan Solomon

FOREWORD BY
Eric Schlosser

ANANSI

Essays that appear in the Food section of this volume were originally published in hardcover in 2004 and in paperback in 2006 by House of Anansi Press Inc. under the title *Feeding the Future: From Fat to Famine, How to Solve the World's Food Crises.*

Essays that appear in the Fuel section of this volume were originally published in hardcover in 2003 and in paperback in 2005 by House of Anansi Press Inc. under the title *Fueling the Future: How the Battle Over Energy Is Changing Everything.*

This edition published in 2009 by
House of Anansi Press Inc.
110 Spadina Avenue, Suite 801
Toronto, ON, M5V 2K4
Tel. 416-363-4343
Fax 416-363-1017
www.anansi.ca

Distributed in Canada by
HarperCollins Canada Ltd.
1995 Markham Road
Scarborough, ON, M1B 5M8
Toll free tel. 1-800-387-0117

Distributed in the United States by
Publishers Group West
1700 Fourth Street
Berkeley, CA 94710
Toll free tel. 1-800-788-3123

House of Anansi Press is committed to protecting our natural environment. As part of our efforts, this book is printed on paper that contains 100% post-consumer recycled fibres, is acid-free, and is processed chlorine-free.

Every reasonable effort has been made to contact the holders of copyright for materials quoted in this work. The publishers will gladly receive information that will enable them to rectify any inadvertent errors or omissions in subsequent editions.

13 12 11 10 09   1 2 3 4 5

Library and Archives Canada Cataloguing in Publication

Food and fuel : solutions for the future / edited by Andrew Heintzman and Evan Solomon.

ISBN 978-0-88784-826-1

1. Food supply. 2. Famines — Prevention. 3. Agricultural innovations. 4. Sustainable agriculture. 5. Power resources. 6. Energy development — Technological innovations. 7. Renewable energy sources. 8. Fuel. I. Heintzman, Andrew, 1967– II. Solomon, Evan, 1968–

HD9000.5.F645 2009   363.8   C2008-906017-2

Library of Congress Control Number: 2008937048

Cover design: Paul Hodgson
Text design and typesetting: Sari Naworynski

Canada Council   Conseil des Arts   ONTARIO ARTS COUNCIL
for the Arts   du Canada   CONSEIL DES ARTS DE L'ONTARIO

We acknowledge for their financial support of our publishing program the Canada Council for the Arts, the Ontario Arts Council, and the Government of Canada through the Book Publishing Industry Development Program (BPIDP).

Printed and bound in Canada

CONTENTS

Introduction

The evidence is right in front of us, spread out over thousands of kilometres. Still, no one can say definitively what it is. Is it a kind of energy? Or a food? It is a mystery that goes back over a hundred years. On June 4, 1896, a thirty-two-year-old engineer working in a tiny shed in Dearborn, Michigan, used it to power a spectacular invention. Since that moment it has, in one way or another, determined the lives of billions of people, been the cause of wars and prosperity, and now, many believe, it might determine the very fate of the planet itself. It is not just food. It is not just energy. It is, amazingly, both. Yellow gold. Corn. The crop that feeds the world. And one that might fuel the world as well.

Henry Ford, that young engineer in Dearborn, knew all about the profound connection between food and fuel. After all, he came from a farm, but loathed the back-breaking rural life. He preferred to tinker with machines, like taking apart and putting back together his father's watch. As soon as he could, Ford bolted for the big city of Detroit, where he found work at the Edison Illuminating Company. There he met Thomas Edison himself, who, in an historic moment, personally encouraged Ford to keep noodling on the invention Ford called the "Quadricycle." The Quadricycle was a motorized carriage Ford built in the cramped quarters of the shed behind his modest little house, where he and his wife and son lived. Four bicycle tires supported a wooden carriage, and a tiller was used to steer. That was the simple part. The key to the contraption was the fuel. Ford powered his combustion engine with the fuel of the day, ethanol. It was, ironically, made from the very crop grown on the farms Ford so hated: corn.

In other words, the dawn of the mass production of cars and the mass production of food were intimately intertwined, and have remained that way since. By 1906, Ford founded his own automobile company and that year, when Congress finally repealed the liquor tax, he announced that ethanol was the fuel of the future. His famous Model T was the first flex-fuel car, designed to run on a mixture of gasoline and ethanol, very much like the cars coming off the Ford plant in Dearborn today.

A century later, Henry Ford's ethanol revolution is actually happening. The record-high, volatile oil prices, combined with concerns over energy security and climate change, have made ethanol once again a popular fuel. Politicians of all stripes, including President Barack Obama, are open supporters of the idea that America can grow its energy. After all, ethanol means votes. In Iowa alone — a key state in every U.S. presidential primary season — over 50,000 jobs are dependent on the biofuel business. Governments around the world have followed suit, aggressively setting targets for increasing the percentage of ethanol mixtures in automotive fuel. (In Brazil, 30 percent of the cars run on a sugar cane–based ethanol, which is actually more efficient than corn-based ethanol.) These targets come with huge subsidies. In the U.S. the biofuel industry received government subsidies of over $8 billion a year, which has kick-started the ethanol industry explosion. Private investment in ethanol is expected to reach $100 billion by 2010 in the U.S. alone.

But there are serious questions about using food as fuel, especially the so-called yellow gold. It turns out it requires almost as much energy to produce a barrel of corn-based ethanol as one can derive from it. On the climate front, the math is even worse. Depending on the processing method, corn-based ethanol can emit more greenhouse gas emissions than a similar quantity of conventional oil. In the developing world, the turn to biofuels has another devastating effect. Converting huge tracts of land to the production of corn and sugar cane in places like Indonesia or the Amazon basin in Brazil is an environmental catastrophe. Biodiversity has been sharply reduced, and vast and valuable carbon sinks of rainforest have been eliminated. Clearly, industrializing agriculture is not an effective, long-term strategy to combat climate change.

However, the impact of the biofuel industry is felt most dramatically at the grocery store, not at the gas station. When the appetite for biofuel grows, so does the price of staple foods. It is not surprising that in 2008, when the price of oil approached $150 a barrel and the price of natural gas shot up to record highs, the price of food also skyrocketed. The amount of grain it takes to make enough ethanol to fill the tank of a single car could feed a person for a year. In a world where over 800 million people are starving, the relationship between food and fuel is not an abstract economic issue. Last year, we witnessed some more remarkable illustrations of this: there were riots in Mexico over the price of flour, which is needed for the diet staple of tortilla; protests in Italy over pasta and in France over bread; uprisings in Pakistan, Cameroon, and Haiti over basic food needs. In the last year alone, the cost of making bread around the world has doubled. When food prices rise, the one billion people in the world who spend 90 percent of their income on food suffer. That makes for one very expensive tank of "environmentally friendly" gas.

The circle that began with the promises of Henry Ford has closed. We have reached a point where we are being asked to choose between having fuel or having food. It is a terrible choice. But to make matters worse, it is now almost impossible to know where one ends and one begins. Food makes fuel and fuel makes food. They are like identical twins, separated at birth. Without either one, our society literally grinds to a halt. At the same time, our reliance on cheap energy and vast food reserves has created a host of devastating problems, the worst of which is global climate change. This book is about finding a way out of this dilemna.

For the past four years, we have been exploring the relationship between energy and food. When we first published *Fueling the Future*, talk of an energy crisis was theoretical. SUVs dominated the roads. Al Gore had yet to release his documentary. When we wrote that the need to develop a sustainable energy model was urgent, we were seen by some as alarmists. Nonetheless, many inside the energy industry knew that we were at the end of the age of abundance and at the beginning of a much more volatile age of energy scarcity. And then, just as we launched the book, 50 million North Americans were left in the darkness during the blackout of 2003. Suddenly energy security and supply became popular issues. Not long after, increasing media pressure brought to light the cascading problems of global climate change.

We also knew that if there was an energy crisis there might well be a food crisis as well. After all, everyone in the energy sector knew that food and fuel are joined at the hip, from the price of artificial, fossil fuel–based fertilizers to the cost of gasoline needed to drive tractors. But the issue was simply not being talked about in the public domain. If the public is not aware of the real problems, it cannot ask its leadership the right questions and change cannot really take place. So a few years later, we gathered together another group of experts and took a close look at the issues surrounding food. From starvation in the developing world at one end of the spectrum to obesity in the developed world at the other, we examined a diverse and at times contradictory array of problems. Once again, the idea that our food systems are dangerously unbalanced was not universally shared. If anything, critics said, there is too much food! Perhaps there was a food distribution issue, but not a food supply issue. Again, when riots over flour broke out around the world a year later, the food crisis became obvious. This is not to say that we in any way predicted the issues. Just that a deeper understanding of the dynamic of energy and food revealed something not often talked about: what happens at the oil well will show up on your dinner plate. And this relationship is going to become one of the key drivers of global change in the near future. It is — to use the political phrase of the moment — part of the fierce urgency of now.

But this book is not only about shining light on intractable problems. Rather, it is about finding practical, clearly articulated solutions to them. Solutions average people can grasp, not just experts. The truth is, most of the problems we all face are, fundamentally, solvable. Which is why exploring better models for sustainable energy and food supplies is the ultimate task of this book. Some of these solutions are technical — new inventions that will allow us to use resources more sustainably. Other solutions, though, will be social — new business relationships, new legal structures, new trade deals. In the rush to innovate, leaders too often focus exclusively on technical ingenuity, but social ingenuity is even more important. And nowhere is this more evident than in the dismal science, economics.

The economic models the world still uses to calculate value, like the GDP, do not account for damage to "natural capital" that results from human industry. This flaw in our economic model leads to many perverse results. In the classic example, the *Exxon Valdez* oil spill actually caused an increase in Alaska's GDP. The cleanup caused profitable economic activity, but the cost of the pollution was not factored in. The distortion was tragic. Who sees an oil spill as a net gain for a local economy? Apparently, we do. Throughout our economy, we almost never factor in the ecological costs into our goods and services. As a result of this gap in our calculus we never get a real understanding of the true cost of human activity. That blind spot only encourages a further degradation of our common resources. This is a phenomenon known as the Tragedy of the Commons. It was starkly illustrated by the collapse of the once great cod stocks off the Grand Banks. No one counted the cost of over-fishing to the natural environment. We counted only the cost of catching and selling the fish.

So the question remains: Why do we insist on constantly updating our technologies, but refuse to update our systems of measurement? It is a costly and retrograde error. After all, only what can be measured can be improved. We urgently need to account for the full cost of the things we use and for the costs that society bears for the use of common property, like air and water. We also must learn to account for the unintended consequences — the externalities — that have resulted from our greatest innovations of the past. That is what the authors of the chapters ahead have in mind as they propose their solutions for the food and fuel crises. After all, only when we learn to include the total cost of our actions — economic, social, and environmental — will we be in a position to use Ford's technology, and the potential of resources like yellow gold, more wisely. We will finally know the true value and cost of our actions. That is real progress.

Foreword to Food

Eric Schlosser

When you look calmly and rationally at the world's food system today, there are many reasons to feel depressed. Everywhere, farmers are being driven off the land. Agribusiness companies wield more power than at any other time in history. The supermarkets have more power. Wal-Mart has more power, squeezing producers harder and paying employees even less than many supermarkets do. The same fast-food chains sell the same food worldwide. Soda companies aggressively target children in schools. Meat-packing companies mistreat their livestock, overuse antibiotics and growth hormones, abuse their workers, pollute rivers and streams, sell meat tainted with fecal material and harmful bacteria. Farm-raised salmon are often contaminated with pesticide residues, while wild salmon are vanishing from the seas. And then there's mad cow disease, avian flu, and genetically modified foods. The wealthy, industrialized nations dump subsidized grain on the poorer, less developed ones, destroying fragile rural economies and creating famines. Modern industrialized agriculture depends upon cheap petroleum, and we're running out of that. A clear look at what's happening today is bound to overwhelm you with doom and gloom.

Some of the best things in life, however, have nothing to do with cool, calm reason. To make real change, you need other qualities, like anger, passion, and that most illogical human trait: hope. Things are bad, all right — but things didn't have to turn out this way. The more time I spend investigating how we produce and distribute our food, the more I realize that none of these problems was inevitable. Today's food system was not the inescapable result of free market forces, natural law, technological advance, or the triumph of modernity. Indeed, the "free market" had little to do with determining how and why certain foods are now produced. For years the American fast food industry has benefited from government subsidies, government-funded road construction (so essential for all those drive-throughs), and minimum wage policies that keep labour costs low. Right now in the United States more than half the money earned by corn farmers comes directly from taxpayers. This cheap, subsidized corn becomes cheap animal feed, lowering the cost of meat. And there's nothing inevitable about how the U.S. Congress frames its farm bills. Every year the large agribusiness firms and corporate farmers get what they want, family farmers get squeezed, and ordinary consumers pay the bill.

About a dozen agribusiness companies now control most of the food that Americans eat. And the powerful oligopolies that dominate nearly every commodity market are a violation of free market principles, not their fulfillment. If America's antitrust laws were enforced today the way they were fifty years ago, during the administration of President Dwight D. Eisenhower, most of our leading agribusiness companies would be dismantled. Eisenhower, hardly a left-wing activist, strongly believed in the importance of competition — and during his first year in office boldly launched an antitrust campaign against the nation's five biggest oil companies. For the past twenty-five years, government policy has encouraged unprecedented centralization and consolidation. In 1970, the four largest meat-packing companies controlled about 20 percent of the American beef market. Today the four largest control more than 80 percent. Tyson Foods — the largest producer of both chicken and beef — is now the biggest meat-packing company the world has ever seen. Its market power has huge implications for farmers, ranchers, workers, and consumers — in the United States and Canada. Fate and the free market were not the guiding forces that brought us unchecked corporate power. Every step of the way, important choices were made by politicians, chief executives, and unwitting consumers. Different choices can still be made.

In 1959, the year I was born, people of colour in much of the United States were forbidden to use the same public toilets as white people or to sleep at the same hotels. The Soviet Union oppressed its own citizens and ruled half of Europe. Blacks in South Africa were treated like serfs. In 1959, if you'd predicted that Nelson Mandela would one day be elected president of a free, multiracial South Africa, people would have said you were out of your mind. In my lifetime, I've seen segregation, the Berlin Wall, and apartheid vanish from the Earth. So I refuse to believe that the way we feed ourselves today must endure forever. Our current system won't last because it can't last. It is not sustainable. This centralized, industrialized agricultural system has been in place for just a few decades — and look at the destruction it has already caused. Look at the harm it has inflicted upon consumers, livestock, and the environment. In the final analysis, our fast, cheap food costs too much.

Yet amid the daily litany of depressing headlines, there are reasons to be cheerful. People who are well-informed about food issues — largely members of the educated, upper middle class — are changing their eating habits. They are buying organic, free-range, locally produced foods. They are rejecting fast food and supporting the Slow Food movement. They don't want anything to do with the highly processed, freeze-dried, chemical-laden foods that most people still consume. This is hardly a widespread revolution — but it could be the start of one. Change has to begin somewhere, and, like the abolition movement of the nineteenth century and the civil rights movement of the twentieth, the drive to get rid of bad food has begun mainly among the wealthy and well-educated. As awareness of the problem spreads, so will anger and disgust. Some day government policy will stop subsidizing the wrong foods and make healthy food affordable for the poor.

In Germany mad cow disease opened people's eyes. You could hardly find a nation more dedicated to reason, more obsessed with efficiency, technology, and the cool ethos of the engineer. Yet the German response to mad cow disease rejected all of that. After years of distortions and cover-ups by German agricultural officials, Renate Kuenast, a member of the Green Party, became minister of Agriculture, Nutrition, and Consumer Protection in 2001. "Things will no longer be the way they are," Kuenast declared, introducing a fundamentally new approach to food policy. The German government is now officially committed to the de-industrialization of agriculture. It vows to make 20 percent of German farmland organic within a decade. It has enacted the world's first animal bill of rights. If Germany can head down this path, so can the rest of the world.

The essays in this book suggest new agricultural technologies and new business models. Some may prove important; others, a complete waste of time. You may agree with some of the arguments made in these pages, and vehemently disagree with others. All of them, however, present us with the opportunity to make choices.

How we get our food today is by no means the only way to get it. Uniformity and conformity, a blind faith in science, a narrow measure of profit and loss, a demand for total, absolute control — these are the central values of the current food system. A new one will emerge from an opposing set. The change won't just happen, though. People will have to make it happen. Passionate anger at the way things are must replace the sense of doom and gloom. Championing the right foods, instead of the wrong ones, won't require martyrdom or violent uprising. But it will need activists to oppose the reigning food giants in the courts, the legislatures, the schools, and the realm of public opinion. Consumers can play an important role, too, just by buying foods that have been produced the right way, by supporting local farmers and ranchers. That won't take much sacrifice. To paraphrase the great Alice Waters: this revolution tastes good.

Saving Agriculture from Itself

Stuart Laidlaw

Throughout rural Manitoba there are signs of decay. Abandoned farmhouses. Overgrown railroad tracks running to closed grain elevators. Boarded-up businesses next to tattered, aging stores still open but with few cars parked outside and fewer customers inside. There are signs, too, of what was slowly creeping into the countryside in their place. Hog barns dwarf the family farms of just a decade ago. On the prairie landscape, inland grain terminals rise like mountains along the main trunk lines that left the traditional wooden grain elevators and their spur lines obsolete. Wal-Mart.

But there are also small acts of defiance: new community centres and curling rinks built with local labour and paid for with fundraising by people who believe in the future of their communities. Farmers getting together to talk about building a co-operative slaughterhouse, an alternative to the industrial food complex that has left them wondering if their farms will survive to see another generation. And, perhaps most encouragingly, gatherings of young and old to spend an evening discussing how to change two generations of farming methods for a new way.

In Pilot Mound, Manitoba, strong community loyalty and a defiant determination to keep farming viable for future generations drew seventy-five people to a night of roast beef, overhead slides, and lectures on how to break out of the industrial food system. Pilot Mound is a typical prairie town: one main street lined with wood-frame, false-front shops, and angle parking. I arrived at the community hall in October 2003, part of a group of three to lead a discussion on alternative agriculture. My job was to talk about establishing closer ties between city and country people in hopes of producing better food and giving farmers a bigger share of the grocery dollar. Fred Kirschenmann, of the University of Iowa's Aldo Leopold Center for Sustainable Agriculture, was also there. He would talk about wheat farmers who had converted their farms into bakeries. Groups of farmers who had established dairy co-operatives to sell better milk at higher prices — and were making more money than ever before. His mission, in short, was to fill the farmers with belief in the future. Ordained as a minister, Kirschenmann says his true calling has been to convert the 3,000-acre (1,200-hectare) North Dakota farm he inherited to organics, and to spread the word of sustainable agriculture. Rene Van Acker, a professor at the University of Manitoba, had brought both of us to his province for the four-town lecture tour. He was researching the appetite for change in rural Manitoba.

About an hour before our event was to begin, there was no one at the hall. The door was locked; the parking lot was empty We tried to ignore the sinking feeling that we would be speaking to an empty hall, and went for coffee. The streets, like the community centre, were empty. So, too, was the coffee shop. We made small talk, about families, work, the weather. For as long as possible we put off going back to the centre to see if anybody would show up. When finally we did, we found the kitchen busy with women preparing that night's meal, the tables set, and a lectern in place.

There's no shortage of towns in which to give such a talk. Across North America, industrialized agriculture has caused an unprecedented emptying of our rural areas as farmers are driven from the land to make way for larger operations. Economy of scale has become the driving force of farming. But when farms get big, they do so by forcing others from the industry. In 1950, 38 percent of the population in the developed world lived in the country, according to the United Nations.[1] By 1990, only 8 percent was rural, with predictions of a further drop to 2 percent by 2025 — a level already reached in Canada and the United States. In fact, the U.S.A. now has more inmates in federal penitentiaries than it has farmers.

Such statistics pushed American essayist Wendell Berry to ask, "What are people for?" Berry, like many before and since, draws a straight line between rural depopulation and the companies behind industrialized farming. "The farm-to-city migration has obviously produced advantages for the corporate economy. The absent farmers have had to be replaced by machinery, petroleum, chemicals, credit, and other expensive goods and services from the agribusiness economy, which is not to be confused with the economy of what used to be called farming."[2]

Certainly, people have always moved from the country to the city, but industrial agriculture has sped up the process, leaving small towns unsustainable, without services, schools, or businesses. Our rural areas seem destined to be little more than massive industrial parks manufacturing food away from prying eyes. Such a system is not sustainable, environmentally or economically. But it is driving urban consumers to find new sources of food. And it brought seventy-five people out to our lectures in Pilot Mound, and more to lectures in Dauphin, Riverton, and St. Pierre, to find ways to feed that market. These men and women were raised to believe that theirs was a renewable industry. The truth is, it is not. Not any more.

Through almost all of its 10,000-year history farming was, by definition, renewable. Wherever agriculture began around the world — grain in the Middle East, rice in China and India, corn in Central America, and potatoes in the Andes — it marked an end to the hunter-gatherer life that preceded it. Rather than waiting to see what nature offered, early farmers saved seeds for replanting. Each year's harvest, then, provided not only food for the rest of the year, but also seed for the following year. Manure from domesticated animals fertilized the land. No other industry has matched this level of sustainability, and saving seeds remained the foundation of farming until just the last few generations.

The beginning of the end of this ancient practice — still used widely in developing countries — came in the 1920s when Henry Wallace of Iowa began selling hybrid corn through his Pioneer Hy-Bred Corn Company. Wallace had developed a system of multi-generational crossbreeding that resulted in one, and only one, generation of high-yielding corn. Charles Darwin had explored the notion, which came to be known as "hybrid-vigour," as early as 1877, but it was Wallace who commercialized it, and changed farming forever. Previously, farmers saved part of their corn crop to sow their fields the following spring. Seeds from hybrid corn, however, do not pass their high-yielding qualities to the next generation, forcing farmers to buy new seeds each year. Seed production soon became a thriving industry separate from farming itself. In 1933, only 1 percent of corn grown in the United States was hybrid. Ten years later, hybrids had captured half the market.[3]

There's good reason for such swift market expansion. Hybrids are a big boost to production, returning in added yield about three dollars to the farmer for every dollar invested in seeds.[4] But a subtle attitude shift had taken place. "Off-farm inputs," introduced to agriculture, opened farmers to a wide array of industrial inputs over the coming years.[5] Tractors replaced horses, leading to yet another input: fuel to run the tractors. With fewer animals on the farm, farmers had less manure to use as fertilizer, and so had to buy nitrogen. They also bought chemicals to kill bugs and weeds.

Before artificial fertilizers were available, farmers had to find other ways to keep their soil productive. Manure helped replenish lost nutrients in the soil, but it was not enough. They also had to rotate crops — every year altering the crop grown in each field so the soil could replenish itself. This also kept bugs and weeds in check. With nitrogen fertilizer, such care was no longer needed. Farmers could grow the same crops in the same fields year after year, and simply apply nitrogen to restore the soil's fertility. This nitrogen fix made monoculture possible, and chemical pesticides necessary as bugs and weeds thrived in the large, uniform fields. Tractors were needed to plow and harvest the vast fields. Early potato harvesters, for instance, could clear a field of at least 80 acres (32 hectares), compared with the maximum of 30 acres (12 hectares) that a family could harvest by hand. Such mechanization soon fed on itself. A machine that can harvest 80 acres needs at least an 80-acre field to produce enough revenue to pay for the machine.

Industrial methods were introduced to farming piece by piece. Yet in the span of just one generation, farmers put the renewable heritage of their land behind and transformed their farms into assemblers of inputs from other industries — seeds from one company sprayed with chemicals from other companies using tractors and fuel from still more companies. Functions once fulfilled by on-farm inputs — animals, manure, and crop rotation — were now tied to off-farm suppliers. Bob Stirling, a rural sociologist at the University of Regina, says the farmer's job evolved from knowing his land and its needs to one of sorting through the marketing pitches of the companies supplying him. "Skill at the work of actually growing something becomes secondary in this new set of practices."[6]

The industrialization of agriculture was so gradual, and so tied to marketing pitches telling farmers how all these new inputs would make them progressive and modern, that its unsustainability would not be revealed for decades. Nitrogen, for instance, proved to be very inefficient. Use of nitrogen fertilizer increased more than tenfold in the last half of the twentieth century as depleted soils on industrial farms demanded ever-more fertilizer to keep producing. As well, only one-third to one-half of the nitrogen applied to a field is actually absorbed by the plants it is meant to help.[7] The rest simply runs off with rainwater into streams and rivers, eventually making its way to our oceans. Along the way, the nitrogen continues to fertilize speeding up algal growth in waterways. The algae use up all the oxygen, causing hypoxia — a lack of life-sustaining oxygen in the water. Nothing can live in such an environment. Where the Mississippi River empties into the Gulf of Mexico, a 20,000-square-kilometre dead zone continues to grow, fueled by nitrogen running off the farms of the American Midwest. In 1993, floods swelled the Mississippi, and an algal bloom formed in the Gulf of Mexico. The disease-ridden blob soon floated north, killing dolphins, whales, seals, and porpoises as far north as the St. Lawrence Seaway.

Farmers, however, are reluctant to give up nitrogen. For one thing, it's cheap, even with up to two-thirds of the fertilizer being wasted. Government subsidies, which encouraged the chemical-based Green Revolution, give farmers little reason to drop nitrogen use. The National Farmers Union of Canada has tracked the cost of nitrogen, relative to the price paid to farmers for corn and wheat.[8] As the grain-price fluctuates, so too does the price of nitrogen. The result is two-fold: the nitrogen companies capture any benefit that comes with better grain prices; and, by dropping their prices when grain prices fall, ensure that farmers will keep buying their inputs.

Farmers do have alternatives to artificial fertilizers. The most obvious is manure, a natural source of nitrogen. This, in fact, was once the main nitrogen source on farms. It turned a waste from one part of the farm — the livestock's manure — into a valuable input for another, the fields. But few farms today are diversified enough to have the animals needed to produce manure for the fields fertilized. One exception is Canada's dairy farms. They can stay small thanks to supply-management, which ensures farmers get a good price for their milk. The average Canadian dairy farm milks about fifty cows per day. That's small enough that the farmer can also raise most of the crops he needs to feed his cows. The cows then produce two things: milk and manure. The farmer sells the milk and spreads the manure on the land to grow crops, which are then fed back to the cows, and the cycle continues. If all farms could achieve such a balance between crops and live-stock — as they once did — there would not be such a need for artificial nitrogen fertilizer.

Other techniques could be used as well. Many come from organic farming, which does not allow farmers to use artificial fertilizers. The main practice of organic farmers is crop rota-tion. Each crop pulls different nutrients from the soil, so rotat-ing crops allows the soil to replenish itself while still producing food. While some conventional farms rotate three crops through a field, meaning a crop will only be planted in any given field once every three years, organic farmers may rotate five or more crops through their fields — giving their soil an extra chance to replenish itself. Combined rotations of nitro-gen-fixing crops such as soybeans, peas, and alfalfa, which extract nitrogen from the air and put it in the soil, eliminate the need for artificial nitrogen on organic farms. On conven-tional farms, crop rotation could reduce nitrogen use to a low enough level that farmers are no longer putting the environ-ment at risk. Such techniques would also necessitate diversify-ing our farms, and moving away from the monocultures that dominate farming today.

Our farms, however, have become addicted to nitrogen. After decades of monocultures and industrial agriculture, the soil has become so depleted of natural nutrients that it needs the boost offered by chemicals. In the summer of 2001, after visiting an organic farm in Ontario's Wellington County, I stopped by the side of the road to get a closer look at a Green Revolution farm.[9] While the soil at the organic farm down the road was rich in organic material and moist after a rainfall the night before, the soil at this farm was hard and dry and crumbled into sand. The rain had simply washed off, filling a ditch by the side of the road. In the field, the corn was maturing in full, plump cobs. Only artificial fertilizers could perform such a feat. On this farm, and millions like it, decades of monoculture had robbed the soil of its nutrients so that it now needed regular nitrogen applications to keep productive. Nitrogen also increases soil acidity, which slows biologic activity, hurting the soil's ability to produce food on its own, so even more nitrogen must yet again be applied.[10] The land is, in short, addicted to nitrogen.

And when the soil depends on nitrogen, so too do farmers. The mixed operations of the days before nitrogen offered farmers a chance to offset troubles in one sector — such as low prices — with better conditions in another. But with nitrogen-dependent monoculture, farmers have little such flexibility. Farmers need their crop to do well if they are to stay in business. As farmers took out loans to buy farmland, machinery, chemicals and seeds, farming shifted from being labour-intensive to capital-intensive. This further restricts their flexibility, according to a Don Mills, Ontario co-ordinator with the NFU. "They can't cut costs in tough times," he said.[11] "They have regular payments to make."

In such a situation, farmers are less able to take risks. They cannot gamble that their crops won't do well. With loan payments looming, the added cost of spreading nitrogen fertilizer seems a worthwhile investment, even if most of it will run off the field. A 1988 study of Mexico's Yaqui Valley, published in the journal *Science*, found that farmers could boost their profits by 12 to 17 percent by spreading nitrogen only when their wheat was best able to absorb it. This reduced the amount of nitrogen needed from 250 kilograms per hectare (kg/ha) to 180 kg/ha, cutting both farm costs and environmental impact. Armed with these numbers, researchers tried for five years to get more farmers in the Yaqui to cut their nitrogen use, but to little avail. With loans to pay and inputs to buy, farmers were unwilling to risk a new management technique that went against the teachings of the Green Revolution. "Nitrogen is cheap insurance," observed author Richard Manning. "Expecting farmers to respond to market signals now is a bit like expecting an alcoholic to order herbal tea at an open bar. This is the legacy of subsidy. Governments, including Mexico's, got in the business of making nitrogen cheap, and farmers lapped it up."[12] The result has been devastating. An August 2002 study in the journal *Nature* found that 17 percent of the world's farmland had been degraded since 1945 due to Green Revolution farming.[13]

Pesticides and herbicides used to kill insects and weeds have, if anything, made the situation worse. By killing off organic material that might otherwise fertilize the plants, they make nitrogen even more necessary. Like nitrogen, pesticide use increased tenfold in the last half of the last century, and is very inefficient in its application.[14] An Environment Canada study found that less than 1 percent of the pesticides sprayed on a field actually reach the targeted pests, and that up to 40 percent blows away on the wind as it is sprayed.[15] And, also like nitrogen, pesticides run off the land with the rain. Prince Edward Island experienced a 632-percent increase in pesticide use between 1982 and 2000 as potato production exploded. Province-wide, there have been at least 26 fish-kills since 1994 as pesticides washed into the island's 263 waterways. In one two-week period in the summer of 2002 alone, more than 12,000 fish washed up on the shores of P.E.I.'s streams and rivers.[16]

Every time pesticides flooded into a waterway, inspectors from provincial and federal ministries of the environment and agriculture were dispatched — often on overtime and on weekends. In the few cases where charges were laid, courts were tied up for up to a year sorting through the charges, and penalties were small. Afterward, Environment Canada and the province launched projects to revitalize the damaged streams and rivers. None of this comes cheap. Farmers had to spray their chemicals again, since most of what they had already applied was now damaging the water instead of the land. Such a system of ever-increasing inputs, supported by government subsidies, simply passes its environmental costs on to the rest of society. With governments struggling to keep their budgets balanced, this cannot be sustained.

Industrial agriculture can also damage local economies. Rural communities that accept massive hog barns into their midst, for instance, often do so with visions of jobs and investment coming to their communities. Industrial livestock operations tend to congregate in rural areas desperate for an infusion of cash, a United States Department of Agriculture study found. Modern hog barns were developed in North Carolina just as the tobacco industry fell into decline, and massive poultry barns were first developed in the depressed southern United States. In Canada, Manitoba communities turned to hog farming after wheat was hit by the elimination of a transportation subsidy known as the Crow Rate in the 1990s. The cruel reality for rural communities is that the new industries, rather than rebuilding local economies, slowly eat away at their financial foundations.

Numerous studies in the United States have all come to the same conclusion, that large hog barns drive down property values as neighbours complain about the smell from the barns and water wells are contaminated by manure runoff.[17] In North Carolina, property values dropped 7.1 percent on farms near a hog barn, while property values near barns in Iowa fell up to 40 percent and in Illinois up to 30 percent. All this reduces the taxes the community can collect from adjacent properties, while the barns themselves bring added costs to the community. One rural municipality in Iowa saw its gravel costs rise 40 percent as big trucks serving the hog barns tore up its roads.

Hog barns can hinder other economic development. Environmental problems may deter investment or imperil existing businesses, making the communities even more dependent on the hog barns to survive. "Their only solution is to let in more polluting activities since no other enterprises will consider locating in their area," writes Bill Weida, director of the GRACE Factory Farm Project based in New York.[18] Rather than boosting the local economy, as hoped, the introduction of factory farming can slowly destroy it — just as the fertilizers and pesticides meant to boost the productivity of soil instead slowly degrade it. One study of more than a thousand rural communities found that economic growth in areas without large hog barns was 55 percent higher than in areas with such operations.[19]

Part of the reason is that the barns themselves don't create enough jobs, either directly or indirectly, for the local economy to survive. Only three or four jobs are created for every thousand hogs on a factory farm, compared with 12.6 people needed to raise the same number of animals on traditional farms. That means fewer people earning a living and shopping at local stores. As well, large operations tend to buy their supplies outside the community, while small farms frequent local suppliers, keeping the rural economy alive. In 1994, a University of Minnesota study found that farms with incomes of $100,000 a year bought 90 percent of their inputs locally, while those with sales of $900,000 or more bought only 20 percent locally.[20] This is because large operations are tied to vertically integrated food processors that not only slaughter animals, but also sell farmers feed and dictate the breeds of animals they will raise. With such a top-down system, it is cheaper for the processor to buy feed from a central location rather than at several local operations. While this can be good for the corporate bottom-line, it is bad for rural economies and communities.

With the shift from people to machines — today's farms are much too large to be farmed without massive machines — agriculture has become dependent on cheap fossil fuels to keep operating. The fuel runs the tractors that sow the seeds, spread the chemicals, and harvest the crops, the trucks that haul away the produce, and the factories that process it into grocery-store products. It is also the basic ingredient in making nitrogen fertilizer. In livestock farming, fossil fuels power the trucks that haul feed to the barns and feedlots where the animals are fattened up, then haul away the animals to slaughter. Getting food to our tables demands an ever-increasing use of fossil fuels both to produce and ship the food, especially when consumers have come to expect fresh fruits and vegetables all year round. In 1940, the average American farm produced 2.3 calories of food energy for every calorie of fossil fuel energy it used.[21] Today, the tables have more than turned, with three calories of fossil fuel needed to produce just one calorie of food.

As Brian Halweil at the environmental think-tank WorldWatch Institute says, the modern food industry "probably wouldn't be feasible without abundant and cheap oil."[22] Breakfast cereal, for instance, requires four calories of fossil fuel energy to make one calorie of food, once the milling, grinding, drying, and baking are taken into account. "A two-pound [one-kilogram] bag of breakfast cereal burns the energy of a half-gallon [two litres] of gasoline in its making," says writer Richard Manning.[23] Livestock farms can be even worse. Beef feedlots, in which cattle are penned shoulder-to-shoulder as food is brought to them, require thirty-five calories of fossil fuel to produce just one calorie of beef. Sixty-eight calories are needed to produce one calorie of pork. Burning fossil fuels so much, of course, creates greenhouse gases and environmental problems that are not borne by the farms or food companies, but are passed on to the rest of society.

It doesn't have to be this way. One of the truly marvellous things about cattle, for instance, is that they can take something we can't eat (grass) and convert it into something we can (beef). The same was once true of pigs, which turned farm waste — slop — into pork. Modern factory farms, however, don't feed animals grass or slop. They feed them corn, because corn fattens them up quicker. More than half of the 10 billion bushels of corn grown in the United States, for instance, is fed to farm animals.[24] In Mexico, where corn was first domesticated, 45 percent of the crop goes to animals, compared with just 5 percent in 1960.[25] This is an incredibly inefficient use of one of the world's most important crops. Two kilograms of corn are needed to produce one kilogram of chicken, while four kilograms of grain are needed to produce one kilogram of pork. The cattle industry is the most inefficient, requiring eight kilograms of grain to make one kilogram of beef.[26]

All we need to raise cattle is an open field and some sun. But the industrial model of livestock farming (keeping animals penned up and bringing food to them) only works if we feed the animals grains, since grains can be harvested and stored more easily. Those grains require an enormous amount of chemicals and fossil fuels to be grown, harvested, and delivered. We have taken a renewable industry and made it dependent on outside inputs. Once all those inputs are counted in, 284 gallons (1,075 litres) of oil have been burned, on average, by the time a steer goes to market. "We have succeeded in industrializing the beef calf, transforming what was once a solar-powered ruminant into the very last thing we need: another fossil-fuel machine," writes Michael Pollan of the *New York Times*.[27]

With the world's population growing rapidly, we can no longer afford such an inefficient system of food production. We need to find more efficient ways of producing food. Today's agricultural system is very good at creating wealth for the companies at the top of the food chain, and at providing cheap food in our grocery stores, but not at creating the food itself or at providing farmers with a living wage.

In fact, Kirschenmann told the farmers on our tour, there is a limit to how much more efficient farms get as they grow.

Economies of scale on hog farms, for instance, peak between 800 and 1,200 hogs, while soybeans and corn peak at about 600 acres (240 hectares).[28] After that, economies of scale lose ground to the cost of maintaining huge operations. One North Dakota farm Kirschenmann cited tills 30,000 acres (12,000 hectares). One of its fields is sixty kilometres from the homestead, requiring the farmer to travel more than twice that distance just to get back and forth from the field. "It costs more to service that field than the one next to the farm," he said. Such farms rely on cheap fossil fuels, as well as government subsidies that drive down the cost of production, to produce food that is not sustainable either economically or environmentally.

This is what drew the men and women of rural Manitoba to Rene Van Acker's dinner and discussion sessions. The farmers who came out are part of an industrial food system that has detached them from consumers. They are at the bottom of the food supply chain, and paid poorly in keeping with their lowly status. They no longer produce food, but inputs for an industrial food system whose processing plants and profit centres are far away. Even at their local grocery store — Kirschenmann and I browsed through one in Riverton while waiting for the local curling rink to open for our talk one night — most of the food is from far away. This, of course, is not unique to rural Manitoba, though one might reasonably expect a store surrounded by farms to have some fresh, local produce.

Local food simply does not fit with the narrow definition of efficiency used by the grocery-store chains that dominate the retail food sector. For them, it makes more sense to source all their food centrally and then distribute it to their retail outlets, like the one in Riverton. As a result, food grown right outside a rural town is shipped to a central depot, then shipped back to where it came from for sale. Or it might go somewhere else. I once went into a chain grocery store in Parry Sound, Ontario, passing several women selling plump, juicy blueberries by the side of the road. At the store, the only blueberries were Californian. They were cheaper, but not as good, having travelled across the continent to get to me, deteriorating along the way. Such berries are bred more for their ability to withstand shipping than for their taste.

Brian Halweil at the WorldWatch Institute describes the "transcontinental head of lettuce." Such produce, grown in California and flown nearly 5,000 kilometres to his local grocery store in Washington, DC, burns thirty-six times as much fossil fuel energy in transport as it produces in food energy.[29] He cites a study by Kirschenmann's Leopold Centre in 2001 that found that while locally grown food travels an average of 74 kilometres to get to a dinner plate in Iowa, food shipped from outside the area travels an average of 2,577 kilometres. Besides supporting local farmers and providing fresher produce, buying locally was found to be much better for the environment. Local meals used between four and seventeen times less fossil fuels and produced five to seventeen times less carbon dioxide emissions than food bought from outside the area. Numbers like that have convinced many that locally-grown food is the answer. Not only is it better for the environment, but the food is fresher and buying it often means bypassing big chain stores and industrial farms. As well, farmers selling to local niche markets, such as organic, can command premiums from the market that increase their profits, making it easier to stay on smaller farms where industrial methods are not needed. As Manning writes, "Quality is subversive."

Tim Schmucker's Toronto shop sells hormone- and drug-free meat raised by Old Order Mennonite and Amish farmers in southwestern Ontario. He calls himself a "social entrepreneur," driven as much by a desire to do some good as to make a profit. "We're an alternative to the big chains," he says. After years of operating out of the back of his car or from the walk-in fridge at a U-brew beer shop, he and his wife Jacquie opened their own Fresh From the Farm shop in Toronto's Donlands neighbourhood, and tapped into a growing market for alternative foods. The Schmuckers deal with each of their supplying farmers individually. Tim places each order separately, and makes the two-hour drive to each farm every week to get his orders. He has been able to contract for some help to pick up orders, but just keeping his small store stocked has become a weekly logistical challenge, and some weeks he can't get everything his customers want.

He's hardly alone. Tod Murphy runs the Farmers Diner in Barre, Vermont, featuring food raised by local farmers.[30] He set up the restaurant on the small town's main street as a personal commitment, but soon found that customers were eager to support the effort. "I thought most would just see it as a diner, but they see what we're doing," he says. What he's doing is bypassing the industrial food system to buy food that's local, fresh, and sustainably grown. He soon found that it was fairly easy to get local vegetables, though sometimes his menu had to be changed to reflect what was available. Meat, however, was more difficult. He managed to find farmers he could buy from, but processing the meat was another issue. The emergence of large food companies controlling the meat industry — four companies claim three-quarters of the North American meat market — had put small meat processors out of business. Murphy had no one to convert pigs into hams and bacon. And what would a diner be without bacon? So he set up his own, very small, meat processing plant down the road from his diner. "All these food facilities that are so basic to society — the creamery, the local butcher — they're gone. You have to build them yourself." Trying to put his menu together, Murphy, like Schmucker, spends hours every week making deals with individual farmers. By contrast, the manager of a nearby Friendly's chain restaurant fills out one form online and sends it to a regional distribution centre in another state. "It takes me about five minutes," says the manager, who did not want to be named. "And then the big Friendly's truck shows up with everything."[31]

Halweil at the WorldWatch Institute says rebuilding the connection between farmers and local customers is key to establishing a viable alternative to industrial agriculture. "We need to go beyond farmers' markets," he says, and establish local infrastructures that serve more than one shop or restaurant.[32] Customers have gotten used to stores and restaurants that have full shelves and consistent menus. Back in Toronto, Schmucker is working with a few farmers to set up a sales shed where urban buyers can come to bid on fruits, vegetables, and meat once a week. They would leave with orders in hand, helping ensure the steady supply their customers demand. They would still need to get their purchases back to the city, but a sales shed would be much simpler for both the Toronto buyers and the farmers. "We need some convenience, too," says Schmucker.[33]

If the environment and adverse economic impacts are the greatest challenge to the sustainability of industrial agriculture, inconvenience may be the greatest challenge to alternative food systems. It needs to be more convenient for customers, store and restaurant owners, and, perhaps most importantly, for the farmers. They have heard the stories like the ones salting Kirschenmann's talks, but don't know how to make similar steps themselves to get out of the industrial food system. Already heavily capitalized, each year they farm hundreds, or thousands, of acres. Their marketing consists of little more than delivering their produce to the local elevator and taking whatever price has been set at the Chicago Board of Trade that day. "You can't just go to town and exchange all that for less land and smaller machines to serve the sixty people in your area," says Halweil.[34] Some farmers, he said, are simply too big, too industrial, to be turned around now. But they are the minority. Halweil endorses what Kirschenmann has dubbed "taking back the middle" — farmers too big to sell their food at farmers' markets, but who could ensure a steady supply of food to local restaurants and stores. And that means re-establishing local infrastructures such as small slaughterhouses and millers. Not only would that infrastructure ensure the steady supply retailers and their customers need, but it would give farmers somewhere else to sell their food and a way to break out of the industrial food market.

There are a few models to draw on, where local farmers and their customers are working out ways to rebuild that lost infrastructure. In Oregon, ranchers owning a total 250,000 acres (100,000 hectares) formed a group to sell their beef. They stagger production among themselves to ensure a steady supply to their customers, and bypass the big companies controlling the meat industry. "That's really the future of this," says

Weida.[35] A similar group is selling meat in Colorado. After mad cow disease was found in Alberta in the spring of 2003, a group of Manitoba farmers who could no longer ship their meat to the United States got together to set up their own small slaughterhouse to serve the local market. In our tour of Manitoba in October of that year, Kirschenmann told the story of Montana grain-farmer Dean Fallboard, who began baking his wheat into bread, then set up a retail bakery, then a deli and a store where customers could grind their own wheat into flour. Out back, his grain elevators gave other local farmers an alternative market, apart from the large grain companies, to sell their wheat.

In some cases, farmers have banded together to build a better life by working collectively. This is basically the old co-operative model that farmers have used for generations to give themselves market clout by acting together rather than bidding against each other to sell to the large corporations that dominate the food industry. But while the co-ops of bygone generations tended to organize around farmers in the same geographic area, modern co-ops often organize across wide geographic areas to corner part of a specific market. Organic Valley Farms, for instance, has 633 farmers in seventeen U.S. states from Maine to California milking 20,475 cows a day. They also produce eggs, juice, cheese, spreads, butters, creams, and meats under the Organic Valley name.

By joining together to sell their products, they can build their brand around the membership and improve the way those farmers are treated. "They want you to know that ever since they started their business, the farmers come first," Kirschenmann said during our presentation in Dauphin.[36] As he spoke, he flashed on an overhead screen graphics from the Organic Valley web site, showing how much the farmers are paid for their milk. In 2003, co-op farmers received US$20.17 per hundredweight of milk — two-thirds more than conventional farmers in the United States that year.[37] Small wonder farmers with Organic Valley can get by with farms of just thirty-two cows on average — about half the size of an average American dairy farm. In fact, they often lead better lives.

Travis Forgues joined in 1999, investing US$11,000, or 5.5 percent of his expected gross income the first year in Organic Valley. He invested the money up front, but Organic Valley does allow farmers to pay off their investments over several years if need be. Forgues readily admits he was attracted by the money, hoping to profit from the higher prices paid for his milk. "The vast majority, including myself, go into organics as a financial decision. After about a year, it changes," he says.[38] Farmers soon start to embrace the environmental aspect of organic farming, and wouldn't go back to conventional farming, with all its chemicals and artificial fertilizers, even if the prices were better. "People start thinking, 'I don't want my family around those things, I don't want it in the lake.'" For his equity stake in the co-op, Forgues is guaranteed a return of 8 percent a year, but usually gets about 14 percent, on top of the $200,000 a year he gets from milking cows. That's enough to support him, his wife, two daughters, and his parents. He's making more money with fewer cows than his father ever did when Forgues was growing up, and doing it more sustainably. "You won't see us going back," Forgues says. With stable prices offered by the co-op, he can better plan for the future, something farmers in the volatile conventional market can only dream of doing.

In his talks, Kirschenmann told the Manitoba farmers about how the co-op uses the stories of people like Forgues in its marketing. In-store posters feature the farmers' pictures and testimonials. The co-op's web site is geared to customers, with stories of how and why Forgues and other farmers joined the co-op, and with details about their farms, their families, and their cows. It tells visitors how the cows are raised, what organic standards mean, and what Organic Valley farmers do to meet and at times even exceed those standards. There is a special kids' section with games and information on where our food comes from, to build on the relationship between farmers and consumers — something that's missing in supermarkets and factory farms. Customers' children can even learn about the farmers' children and their lives. "What they want you to know is that when you buy a quart of Organic Valley milk, you are supporting these farmers, those families and those kids that you visited on their web site," Kirschenmann said. "That's part of their marketing strategy."

The co-op began in 1988 when farmer George Simeon (now Organic Valley's CEO) and seven of his neighbours banded together in Wisconsin. Within four years, its sales had topped US$2 million. Tapping into a market of consumers who want to know that their food is sustainably grown on family farms, Organic Valley has grown to be the largest co-op in the United States, with sales of more than US$150 million per year.

While not all farmers have the entrepreneurial sprit displayed by Organic Valley or Dean Fallboard, they don't need to. Fallboard's 12,000 acres (5,000 hectares) can't keep his bakery — which bakes 10,000 loaves of bread a day — and elevators fully stocked, so he buys from other area farmers looking for ways to leave the commodity market. Organic Valley and other co-ops are constantly looking for new members. In 2003, for instance, Organic Valley added 118 farmers, a 22.9 percent increase over 2002. With that kind of growth, there is plenty of room for farmers who just want to raise their cattle or grow their crops and leave the marketing to someone else. All it takes is one Dean Fallboard or one George Simeon to get things going, and before long hundreds of farmers can turn their backs on industrial agriculture and help build thriving new businesses.

That was the message Kirschenmann and I stressed the night we were speaking in Dauphin, Manitoba, where much of the audience was made up of staff from local economic development offices. Their job is to attract businesses to town to help maintain the local economy. We urged them not to fall into the trap of "smokestack chasing," and instead find ways to help local farmers stay on the land. Encouraging the kind of infrastructure Halweil says is needed for alternative food systems to take hold would also promote shopping in local stores. "The sustainable ag community must build a supply chain," Kirschenmann told them.39 "Who is in a better position to process and retain the identity of these products than micro food enterprises in our rural communities rather than a huge processing plant that's off someplace outside of our communities?" The key to such enterprises is to avoid competing with the big companies directly. Instead, micro-processors should sell specialty products with smaller markets but larger profit margins. These are markets ignored by the big companies, whose business models are based on uniformity and consistency.

Farmers supplying such enterprises tend to not take government subsidies — they don't need them — and pass on few costs to the rest of society. If they are organic, they do not use nitrogen fertilizer or chemical pesticides that poison surrounding land and waterways. By selling locally and operating smaller farms with smaller machines, they burn fewer fossil fuels. But projects such as Fresh From the Farm and the Farmers Diner have probably gone as far as they can, and risk losing market share if they can't keep up with demand. Like any growing industry, they are at a stage in their development where they need an infusion of cash to maintain their momentum. The problem is, the agriculture industry is not likely to make such an investment. Agribusiness is based on selling inputs to farmers and uniform products to consumers, and this new industry is based on selling fewer inputs and distinctive products.

The best option, then, might be for government to help by redirecting subsidy money away from industrial farming to sustainable farming and infrastructure. Economic development officers could use the money to attract and set up small processing plants and to recruit farmers to supply the enterprise. Farmers themselves could also be helped. A farmer must stop using chemicals for three years before his farm can be certified organic. During those years, production plummets while organic material is built back up in the soil, but the farmer is unable to collect the premium prices offered for certified organic crops. That can make for some difficult years, something few farmers can afford.

Subsidies to get farmers through that difficult transition would be a big help, and be more of an investment than an expense. By helping farmers go organic, governments could limit future expenditures on environmental cleanup and health problems. They could also reduce the risk of cobbling together expensive bailout packages for industrial farmers caught in yet another income crisis. Organic Valley's Forgues likes the idea of governments helping farmers switch to organic, so co-ops like his can keep up with demand.[40] But he warns against making the switch too easy. A flood of organics would drive down prices and hurt farmers like him who are already in the industry. Assistance that's high enough to tempt farmers, but low enough that they have to be serious about the transition, would likely be the best — and most cost-effective — solution.

Government subsidies got the Green Revolution started, and through research grants to our universities have kept it going. It seems only prudent — and fair — to spend some money now to clean up the environmental and social messes that revolution left behind.

BETTING THE FARM:
FOOD SAFETY AND THE BEEF COMMODITY CHAIN

Ian MacLachlan

On May 20, 2003, the discovery of a single cow infected with bovine spongiform encephalopathy (BSE) — mad cow disease — from Marwyn Peaster's farm in Peace River, Alberta, heralded an economic catastrophe for Canadian cattle producers. Over thirty-three countries closed their borders to Canadian beef exports. The potential negative impact of a $2.5-billion loss in cattle exports will translate into a $2-billion loss in GDP, a $5.7-billion decline in total output and 75,000 jobs lost.[1] BSE made the front page not because efforts to prevent the entry and transmission of BSE had been too little, too late, and not because of the potential human health risks — but largely because of the enormous disruption caused to Canada's cattle markets and regional economies. In fact, BSE was not diagnosed until over three months after the cow had been condemned as unfit for human consumption and slaughtered. Meanwhile, the carcass had already been rendered into livestock feed.

Consumers have been questioning food safety for over a century. From Upton Sinclair's *The Jungle* in 1906 — an exposé of unsanitary food handling in Chicago's meat-packing plants — to Eric Schlosser's *Fast Food Nation* in 2001, the livestock and meat-packing industries have lent themselves to alarming accounts. A century ago, the prevalence of bovine tuberculosis spurred the establishment of government-sanctioned meat inspection, while today meat is associated with a new set of diseases. The fact is, after all the science, all the guidelines, and all the exposés, we still do not understand all of the risk factors or how to respond to them. As we'll see later, the risks posed by BSE were mismanaged in the U.K. and Canada's own BSE policies are questionable.

Which explains why, despite all the headlines about BSE or *E. coli* O157:H7, the greatest contemporary challenge faced by the cattle and beef industry, its regulators, and public policy makers, is risk management. Consumers rely on their government to oversee farm-to-fork quality assurance programs. These programs span a long commodity chain that is often hidden behind closed doors and divided between federal and provincial jurisdictions. If we as consumers are to understand the risks to beef safety, and, most importantly, understand what ingenuity can be brought to the process to manage these risks, we need to understand the industry itself.

The Cattle–Beef Commodity Chain

As with all other food, the production of beef is vertically organized into a sequence of activities — the commodity chain — which adds value to basic organic ingredients: grass and cows. The first link in the chain, calf production, is found on specialist farms known as cow-calf operations, and also takes place among other activities on mixed farms. As the gestational foundation of the commodity chain, beef cows are found in every Canadian province. In 2001, 80.7 percent of beef cows originated in Prairie Canada — 43.7 percent from Alberta alone.[2] Dairy cows are concentrated mainly in Quebec and Ontario, and their bull calves are also raised for slaughter.

Within months of birth, calves are dehorned to prevent injury, vaccinated to prevent common bovine diseases, and bull calves are castrated to prevent the development of masculine characteristics. Growth hormones are commonly administered to beef calves, usually as an implant in the outer ear, a body part that never enters the human food chain. Growth hormones help cattle to reach market weight sooner and reduce feed costs by increasing feed efficiency. In North America, it is believed that the concentration of hormones in the beef of treated cattle is minute relative to the natural background level of hormones in the human body, and that they pose no health risk to consumers. Nevertheless, the European Union has banned the import of beef produced using growth hormones, effectively shutting Canada out of European beef markets.

Backgrounding, the second phase in cattle production, starts with weaned calves. Standing grass in summer and sun-cured hay in winter provides the nutrients required for them to grow out and build the skeletal frame of mature animals. It is the most land-intensive production phase of the commodity chain, and producers must manage grassland carefully to prevent overgrazing and secure sufficient winter-feed.

Grain feeding, the third phase, finishes animals to slaughter weight — about 1,200 pounds (540 kilograms) for heifers and

1,300 pounds (590 kilograms) for steers. In Ontario and eastern Canada, this is often a small-scale winter enterprise on mixed farms. In Alberta, cattle finishing takes place on specialized feedlots containing 10,000 to 20,000 head, though some are much larger. New arrivals receive a hay ration that is gradually stepped up to about 80 percent grain. In Ontario, the principal grain is corn while Alberta's cooler climate and shorter growing season make barley the feed of choice. Alberta dominates the industry; on January 1, 2003, it accounted for 63.5 percent of Canada's total beef cattle on specialized feeding operations.[3]

Finished cattle are shipped to the packinghouse by livestock trucking firms in cattle-liners, large aluminum semi-trailer

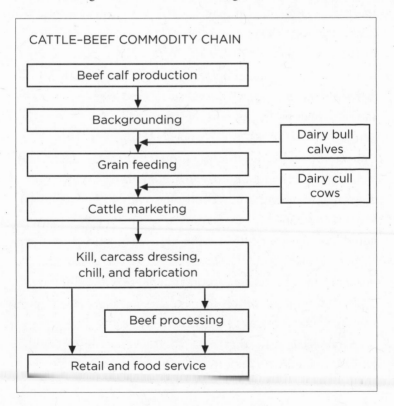

CATTLE–BEEF COMMODITY CHAIN

Beef calf production

Backgrounding

Dairy bull calves

Grain feeding

Dairy cull cows

Cattle marketing

Kill, carcass dressing, chill, and fabrication

Beef processing

Retail and food service

trucks. Most cattle are sold direct to the packer. Pricing systems are complex and may be based either on liveweight or carcass weight. Prices are often negotiated as forward delivery contracts for truckload lots, months in advance of delivery.

Slaughter plants receive cattle on a just-in-time basis, seldom holding live animals for more than a few hours, providing time for ante-mortem inspection by a veterinarian. Alberta kill plants tend to specialize in the highest-quality grain-fed steers and heifers. In Quebec, the largest packing plants process spent cows culled from the dairy herd, which are used for ground beef and processed meat products. In older and smaller plants, cattle are stunned unconscious one at a time in a traditional "knocking box." But in most large-scale facilities, there is a continuous-flow style of humane slaughter. Cattle walk calmly into the plant, gradually straddling a conveyor that lifts them gently off the floor. They glide calmly along the moving rail, oblivious to the impending blow from a pneumatically powered stunner that will cause sudden and immediate unconsciousness.[4] The insensible animal is shackled and slowly rises to the bleeding rail for exsanguination. The feet are cut off with powerful hydraulic shears and the carcass is suspended from a gambrel that slides along an overhead rail for removal of the hide and head. The abdominal cavity is opened to remove the viscera, and the carcass is then split into two sides. Conveyor tables carry pans of viscera in synch with the carcass until meat inspectors have examined the critical organs and lymph nodes and are satisfied there is no evidence of disease. Suspect and randomly selected carcasses are subject to in-plant swab tests and laboratory analysis of various tissues to identify antibiotic or hormonal residues and a variety of other contaminants.

After final trimming to remove any visible contamination, bruises, or lesions, the carcass is transferred to the cooler where Canadian Beef Grading Agency staff assign a carcass quality grade depending on age, meat texture, and marbling. Once again, Alberta dominates, accounting for 68.5 percent of Canada's reported cattle slaughter in 2002.

Large-scale beef dressing lines in state-of-the-art plants are designed to avoid the potential for cross-contamination, which has been recognized as a food safety hazard since the nineteenth century.[5] The "hide-off area" of the kill floor is seg-regated from the "hide-on area," which is prone to manure splash from dirty hooves and hides. All cutting tools must be immersed in scalding water between each animal on the line. At some workstations, direct contact with blood or viscera is unavoidable. For these workers, there are long rubber aprons and high boots. Between each animal on the line, the worker steps into a clear plastic shower booth equipped with water jets to remove all trace of the previous carcass before the next in line is handled. The largest beef dressing plants are also equipped with massive steam pasteurization chambers that use scalding steam to kill any pathogens inadvertently trans-ferred to the surface of the carcass during processing.

Fabrication or carcass-breaking divides the side of beef into smaller primal cuts (hip, sirloin, short loin, rib, and chuck), each of which is subsequently carved into subprimal cuts. The various cuts are sorted into standard lots, vacuum-sealed in plastic film and packed in cartons, labelled to indicate the name of the cut and the source of the beef. Boxed beef is shipped in refrigerated semi-trailer trucks as soon as possible to minimize the time that it must be held in the plant's cold storage warehouse. Much of the output is destined for the distribution centres of supermarket and fast food chains while the remainder is sent to manufacturers for further processing into specialty meat products and individual portion-controlled servings for institutional and commercial kitchens.

As one might expect of an intensely competitive and entrepreneurial industry, the basic commodity chain has many variants. The tendency to specialize in just one link of the chain is offset by the propensity to integrate forwards or backwards, and take some degree of control and profit over adjacent activities. Some parts of the chain have become fully integrated and co-located. For example, cow-calf producers may also background their weaned calves while Lakeside Packers of Brooks, Alberta, operates a feedlot across the highway from its kill plant, providing an in-house source for slaughter cattle.

Like many other resource processing industries, meat packing restructured dramatically in the 1980s and 1990s. Meat packing shifted westward to follow cattle production, which has become strongly concentrated in Alberta. Canada Packers and Swift Canadian, the packinghouse leaders of the mid-twentieth century, gradually withdrew from the production of fresh commodity beef as a new beef processing duopoly emerged:

- Cargill Foods of High River, Alberta, a wholly-owned subsidiary of Minnesota-based Cargill, a global food processor and grain trader.
- Lakeside Packers of Brooks, Alberta, a wholly-owned subsidiary of South Dakota–based Tyson Fresh Meats, the world's largest beef and pork supplier.

These two plants account for 80 percent of Canada's capacity for slaughtering heifers and steers.[6] While the industry leaders have changed, the meat-packing sector retains its high level of market concentration.

As trends in domestic beef consumption became uncoupled from domestic cattle slaughter, exports of boxed beef increased impressively in the 1990s with the United States accounting for 80 percent of beef exports. Canadian beef also made inroads further afield with notable success in Mexican, Japanese, and South Korean markets. Canada's beef competed favourably on quality and price while the government assured

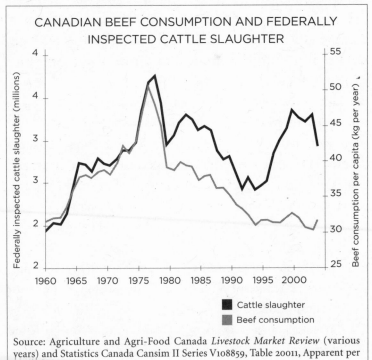

CANADIAN BEEF CONSUMPTION AND FEDERALLY INSPECTED CATTLE SLAUGHTER

Source: Agriculture and Agri-Food Canada *Livestock Market Review* (various years) and Statistics Canada Cansim II Series V108859, Table 20011, Apparent per capita food consumption in Canada (1960–2003)

consumers that Canada was free of BSE.[7] By 2003, 20–25 percent of the Canadian cattle sold in a typical week were
exported live, on the hoof for slaughter in the United States.[8]
Export markets gave leverage to producers when they bar-
gained with Canadian packers but left the producers vulnerable to U.S. trade policy on livestock. The worst-case scenario
was realized on May 20, 2003, when a single case of BSE was
confirmed and all of Canada's beef and cattle export markets
slammed shut within hours.

The graph on the previous page illustrates the divergence
and gradual uncoupling of cattle slaughter from domestic
beef consumption that began in the early 1990s. During the
1960s Canada's federally inspected cattle slaughter grew rapidly to meet the rising consumption of beef by Canadian consumers. Consumption peaked in 1976 and has since declined
almost continuously, as did cattle slaughter until about 1990
when the relationship broke down. Divergence shows that the
Canadian cattle and beef commodity chain has become
uncoupled from domestic demand while live cattle and boxed
beef exports have grown in significance. Canadian consumer
preferences were less relevant to an industry that became
increasingly reliant on exports.

The year 2003 marks a stunning discontinuity as the series
suddenly converge, a perverse outcome of the uncoupling of
slaughter from consumption. Slaughter has dropped precipi-
tously as Canada's cattle inventory rose to an all-time high.
Consumers responded enthusiastically to lower prices in a
spirit of support for cattle producers and increased their beef
consumption, highlighting the elasticity of its demand.

Bovine Tuberculosis: The Enigmatic Zoonosis

Long before the discovery of BSE, government regulation of cattle imports and the domestic meat supply was influenced by the prevalence of other zoonoses, animal diseases such as tuberculosis that can be transmitted to humans. TB was responsible for an estimated one-third of all deaths from disease in Victorian Britain.[9] It had been recognized as a killer of the urban poor for centuries but its contagious character was not grasped until 1865, and the tuberculosis bacterium was not isolated and identified until 1892. By the time of Britain's first Royal Commission on Tuberculosis in 1895, it was believed that bovine TB posed a threat to humans. But the level of risk and the procedures that should be followed when tuberculosis was detected were unclear and would become increasingly controversial. Could humans contract TB by eating beef from infected animals? What degree of tuberculous infection was tolerable in a beef carcass? If a valuable beef carcass was to be condemned in the interest of public health, should the butcher be compensated by the state? After three "science-based" Royal Commissions, there was still uncertainty. We now know that raw milk, not beef, is the major vector of bovine TB.[10]

By the 1960s, Britain's eradication program had been so effective that Britain's cow-herd was declared tuberculosis-free. However, in the mid-1990s, the incidence of bovine TB began to increase and spread. The cause of this resurgence is unclear but wild badgers are the most likely culprits. The efficacy of badger culling is questionable and hotly contested (Donnelly, 2003). Science still cannot provide the certainties that farmers and consumers would like. Britain's experience

shows that after decades of claiming that bovine TB was effectively eradicated, it has reappeared with no consensus on the
best method to control its spread.

Canada, too, has been attempting to eradicate bovine TB
for many decades. But sporadic cases still appear during post-
mortem inspection. Infected herds are typically quarantined
and the cattle destroyed. While the Riding Mountain area of
Manitoba is the only area of Canada *not* considered free of
bovine TB, isolated cases are still discovered elsewhere, and in
March 2004, bovine TB was discovered near Steinbach,
Manitoba, outside of the Riding Mountain Eradication Area.
In Canada, cervids, such as elk and mule deer, are the most
likely source of infection, but reservoirs of TB may be found in
any warm-blooded vertebrate community. It is especially difficult to control, given the spatial extent of Canada's grassland
and its availability as cervid habitat. As in Britain, cattle producers have called for an aggressive cull of the elk population,
and, as in Britain, the effectiveness of such a cull has been challenged.[11] The dynamics of bovine TB transmission are still
poorly understood,[12] but there is considerable evidence of the
growing threat to human health posed by multiple–drug
resistant strains of the TB bacterium.

Policy Failure: The Case of BSE in the United Kingdom

Given the enigmatic nature of TB after a century of research
and concerted efforts to eradicate the disease, it is no surprise
that bovine spongiform encephalopathy (BSE) is not completely understood either. The agent that causes BSE is a prion,
a self-reproducing proteinaceous infectious particle that did
not conform to any of the prevailing models of microbiology

when it was hypothesized as the cause of sheep scrapie in 1982. The prion was named and discovered by Dr. Stanley Prusiner who lost his research funding and was in danger of not being awarded tenure at the University of California at San Francisco. Virologists treated his revolutionary hypothesis with enormous skepticism when it was first proposed.[13] Fifteen years later, Dr. Prusiner was awarded the Nobel Prize in Medicine for discovering the prion, which we now know is associated with BSE. The discovery of the prion shows how recent scientific developments shape our understanding of the cause of BSE; it also underscores the contentious nature of scientific progress.

BSE was identified in November 1986 after a cow's abnormal behavioural symptoms were first recorded in December 1984. Britain's Ministry of Agriculture, Food and Fisheries (MAFF) did not know if BSE was transmissible to humans. There was no evidence. While absence of evidence is not evidence of absence, the government assured the British public, repeatedly and authoritatively, that British beef was safe, and that BSE was *not* a danger to human health. The link between BSE and variant Creutzfeldt-Jakob disease (vCJD)[14] was denied for nine years. Meanwhile, a natural experiment was in progress that would last until the incubation period (itself unknown) provided epidemiologists with sufficient data to draw a conclusion. Exponential growth in the number of reported cases of BSE in cattle was undeniable. There was a growing *apprehension* of a link between BSE and vCJD. But without a smoking gun, Britain's MAFF took little heed of the limited bits of evidence that were becoming available. Instead, the primary concern of MAFF was the negative, indeed catastrophic, impact that public knowledge of BSE would have on Britain's cattle and beef exports.[15]

Thus the British public was taken completely by surprise in March 1996 when the government made a stunning volte-face. Ten cases of vCJD in people under the age of forty-two had been confirmed, and while there was still no proof that BSE could be transmitted to humans by eating beef, the most likely explanation was that those cases were linked to exposure to BSE before specified bovine offal products (brain, spinal cord, spleen, thymus, tonsils, and intestines) were banned for human consumption in 1989. Seven days later, the European Union prohibited the export of all live cattle and beef products from the U.K. In an effort to eradicate the disease, Britain belatedly announced that no cattle over the age of thirty months would enter the food or animal feed chains.[16]

By July 30, 2004, a total of 142 deaths had been attributed (definitely or probably) to vCJD in the U.K. Annual vCJD mortality increased rapidly but epidemiological research suggests that Britain's vCJD epidemic is nearing its peak.[17] Only one death has been attributed to vCJD in Canada; it appears likely that the victim contracted the disease during multiple visits to the United Kingdom.[18]

Britain's catastrophic experience with BSE has eroded public trust in the agro-industrial commodity chain that channels the food supply to the supper table. The challenges posed by BSE were not unique — similar dilemmas were raised when the hazards of bovine tuberculosis were first recognized in the nineteenth century. Yet it seems that regulators and policy makers were no better able to manage scientific controversy and technical uncertainty in the 1990s than they were in the 1890s. Science is a process, not a pat answer with a single objective truth. Scientists do not always agree and their findings can be ambiguous or even contradictory. In the case of BSE in Britain, scientific claims-makers divided into in-groups — whose findings were declared credible and politically sound — and out-groups — who advocated precaution, but without access to research material to pursue their unpopular views.[19] Recent calls for policies, which are simply "science-based," do not recognize the complexity, uncertainty, and contingency of scientific research, let alone the awesome problem of risk in decision-making. Experience with bovine tuberculosis since the nineteenth century suggests that it may be unwise for policy makers to prevaricate until the scientific process has finally yielded complete and unambiguous answers.[20]

One in a Million: Canada's Newest Food-Borne Zoonosis

Eleven months after the detection of BSE in May 2003, the Canadian Senate's Standing Committee on Agriculture and Forestry investigated the situation, "to explore potential solutions, *with the aim of preventing the recurrence of such a disaster*." True to its agricultural mandate, it emphasized the tragic consequences of trade disruption for farm communities, but gave no attention to the challenge of risk management. The committee concluded:

> The reopening of the US border is vital to the industry's survival, and the Committee wants the government to pursue its efforts to convince the United States that it is in the best interests of North America as a whole to show leadership to the rest of the world in resuming trade *based on scientific grounds*.[21]

The Senate Committee heard from "stakeholders from the entire beef chain," including farmers, packers and retailers, the Minister of Agriculture and Agri-Food, bureaucrats from Agriculture and Agri-Food Canada and the Canadian Food Inspection Agency (CFIA), representatives from each prairie province's association of rural municipalities, and the Chief Veterinary Officer for Canada. Of twenty-seven witnesses, only *one* was a veterinarian, and not a single microbiologist, epidemiologist, animal scientist, or food scientist was identified on the witness list. Yet the Senate Committee advocated a resumption of trade *based on scientific grounds!* Like Britain's discredited MAFF, which was later restructured out of existence, the primary concern of the Senate's Standing Committee on Agriculture was the catastrophic impact of BSE, not the risk-management policies that were the ultimate cause of the crisis. Calls for science-based policy require that scientists have a seat at the table. By focusing exclusively on the economic disruption, the Senate missed the opportunity to ask more fundamental questions:

- Why did BSE appear in Canada?
- Why did the discovery of BSE take producers and consumers by surprise?

Until May 2003, the Canadian Food Inspection Agency insisted that Canada was "BSE-free." It was believed that bovine feed ingredients from domestic animals posed "no measurable BSE risk to the health of Canadians."[22] This policy was maintained even though it was well known that hundreds of cattle from BSE-infected countries were imported into

Canada between 1979 and 1993, one of which was confirmed to have BSE in 1993. Based on statistical analysis, the mean expected number of cases of BSE among the imported cattle was three, with twenty-four cases as the probable limit.[23] What were the chances that one of these imported BSE-infected animals was slaughtered or died between 1979 and 1997 (before the feed ban), its carcass subsequently rendered to produce animal feed causing another animal to became infected with BSE? The estimated probability of at least one infection of BSE occurring prior to 1997 was calculated to be 0.0073, about seven chances in a thousand.[24] The CFIA concluded that the likelihood of establishment of BSE in cattle in Canada prior to 1997 was negligible. But two cases originating in Canada were discovered in 2003. Either Canadian cattle producers were extremely unlucky or the risk factors are still not understood.

Professor William Leiss, one Canada's foremost experts in the field of risk communication, argues that the estimated probability assessment ignored the consequences — thus it was not measuring risk at all. Risk is properly calculated as the probability times the consequences. Despite the remote probability, the consequences would be catastrophic for the cattle industry. The estimation of risk should be driven by the magnitude of the consequences as much as by the remoteness of the probability. Thus Leiss argues that the risk was far from negligible — indeed, the risk was "intolerable."[25]

Canada can no longer claim to be BSE-free. Health Canada's "precautionary assumption" is that "there may be a low, previously undetected, BSE prevalence in Canada."[26] By contrast, the CFIA declares, "the incidence of BSE in Canada is equivalent to that of a minimal risk country." Based on the Terrestrial Animal

Health Code of the acknowledged authority, *l'Office interna-tional des epizooties*, the incidence of BSE in Canada is consid-ered to be less than one in a million. Only one case of BSE has been detected during the last twelve-month period in a herd of approximately 5.5 million adult cattle.[27] Nevertheless, based on the recommendations of the international panel that was com-missioned to review Canada's response to the discovery of BSE, Food and Drug Regulations were amended to ban the sale or import of specified risk materials (SRM) for food in July 2003, fourteen years after Britain had banned the human consump-tion of specified bovine offal.[28]

To maintain Canada's current international standing as a "minimal risk" country and to stand a chance of restoring export markets for live cattle and beef from animals over thirty months old, the level of BSE testing will have to be greatly increased, especially among the older and higher-risk animals. Producers are reluctant to pay for veterinary treatment when older animals with little market value appear sick, and veteri-narians may be unwilling to submit the head of euthanized livestock for testing due to the stigma attached to whoever triggers the next discovery of BSE in Canada.[29] According to the Fred Dunn, Alberta's Auditor General, "No one wants to be that number three — that third case diagnosed here," which is why some farmers may elect not to test high-risk animals for BSE and just bury their dead cows.[30] But insufficient testing of high-risk animals could itself be grounds for a further down-grading in Canada's BSE status by *l'Office international des epi-zooties*. By July 27, 2004, it was still unclear how a sufficient number of samples would be gathered to meet Alberta's 2004 test quota.[31] No one knows if a single case of BSE remains in

Canada. Cattle producers are afraid to look for it but equally afraid that no one is looking for it, betting the farm whether they like it or not. Meanwhile consumers rely on government inspection to ensure that their meat is safe.

Meat Inspection

Canada's Meat and Canned Foods Act became law in 1907, one year after publication of *The Jungle*, Upton Sinclair's sensational exposé of unsanitary food handling practices in Chicago's meat-packing plants.[32] Canada's Meat Inspection Service was created as an agency of the Department of Agriculture. Any plant wishing to ship its products across provincial or international boundaries was obliged to meet federal inspection standards.

One important lesson gleaned from Britain's BSE crisis was the need to separate the government department that promotes and supports food commodity producers from the agency responsible for monitoring and enforcing food safety standards. Britain created an autonomous Food Standards Agency (FSA) in 2000, with a mandate to represent the public interest, and an independent board, which reported to Parliament through the Health Ministers. In addition to the accountability change, Britain's FSA adopted a remarkably transparent policy on the proceedings of its expert committees, giving its scientists an unusual degree of freedom to communicate dissenting views. Unorthodox and contrary scientific views and minority opinions are considered and documented so that there is a clear audit trail showing how committees reached their decisions. By exposing scientific uncertainties and clearly identifying the very real policy dilemmas of what is both a scientific and a political process, the FSA is attempting to avoid further policy failures of the type that characterized Britain's handling of BSE.[33]

Wisely anticipating the structural problem revealed in the United Kingdom's BSE experience, Canada took pre-emptive action. The Canadian Food Inspection Agency (CFIA) was formed in 1997 to consolidate the delivery of all federal food, animal and plant health inspection programs — programs that had formerly been provided through four federal government departments: Agriculture and Agri-Food Canada, Fisheries and Oceans Canada, Health Canada, and Industry Canada. While the CFIA still reports to parliament through the Minister of Agriculture and Agri-Food, it stands at arm's length from the department that promotes agricultural output and international trade in food products.

Given the importance of its mandate and the challenging policy questions that it is likely to face, the CFIA may require even greater autonomy, with a board structure that gives science more seats at the table, as in Britain's FSA. Such a board would include private sector "stakeholders" from various agri-food sectors, but it should also have strong representation from veterinarians, and food, animal, fish, and plant scientists to bring an independent scientific perspective to bear on emerging food safety issues and the close relationships between animal and human health questions.[34] Like an auditor, the CFIA would benefit from a more independent structure. Government scientists should be given the freedom, sometimes called "whistle-blower" protection, to articulate dissenting views on the unprecedented food safety challenges emerging from industrial agriculture, innovative biotechnologies, a global food economy, and advances in health research.

Protocols for Quality Assurance

Traditional organoleptic meat inspection detects disease with the five senses, using techniques such as visual examination, incision, and palpation of various organs and lymph nodes. It is little changed since these techniques were first developed in the 1880s. Except for the grossest abnormalities, organoleptic inspection is of doubtful sensitivity, and procedures such as incision have been known to spread pathogens.[35] Considering that many recently identified bacterial and viral pathogens are not detectable by organoleptic methods, British veterinarians argue that the analysis and management of risk in the slaughter and carcass dressing process should become the key functions of meat inspection.[36] The most common technique for risk analysis in meat production is Hazard Analysis Critical Control Points (HACCP). Many of the largest meat-packing firms have already developed sophisticated new quality assurance systems based on HACCP on their own initiative. HACCP certification will eventually be mandatory in all federally inspected meat plants, as is already the case in federally registered fish and seafood plants.

The emphasis in traditional meat inspection was on ante-mortem physical condition of livestock, and post-mortem carcass dressing and meat processing — but there are possibilities that food safety may be compromised elsewhere in the commodity chain, both ante-mortem and post-packaging. Ante-mortem inspection in the pen is usually brief and arguably less important in determining suitability for slaughter than an assessment of the disease and treatment history of the animal when it was on the farm.[37] The farm is the source of many animal diseases, injuries, and other food safety hazards

Hazard Analysis Critical Control Points

Hazard Analysis Critical Control Points (HACCP, pronounced "hassip") is widely acknowledged as the standard quality assurance protocol to monitor processes for safety in the food and beverage industries. HAACP was first developed by the Pillsbury Company in 1960 to attain the 100 percent quality assurance level required to feed astronauts in NASA's space program.

To implement the procedure and become eligible to claim HACCP compliance, it is necessary to work through a seven-point process, beginning with hazard analysis and identification of the critical control points, the stages in any process where hazards exist. Procedures to measure, monitor, correct, and document the hazards and preventative actions are developed. HACCP is an unapologetically bureaucratic system that relies on measurement and documentation to integrate quality assurance into every phase of production.

While HACCP can reduce risk, it is no guarantee. For example, Excel Beef (the beef-producing arm of Cargill Foods in the United States) is HACCP accredited, but in December 2003 it had to recall 13 tons of ground beef labelled as "irradiated for food safety." For nearly three months the ground beef had not, in fact, been irradiated at all. Even in HACCP-certified plants, errors may persist for prolonged periods.

such as excessive tag,[38] broken hypodermic needles, and failure to observe specified withdrawal times after pharmaceutical treatment. Numerous critical control points in livestock production may create hazards. Feeds derived from rendered ruminants are now recognized as a serious hazard. This demands a new awareness of critical control points, both at the commercial feed mill, where rendered ingredients must be conscientiously segregated, and in the barn, where different types of feed may be stored. Post-production quality assurance is no less essential, from loading boxed beef on the reefer truck through retail and on to the restaurant or household kitchen. The *E. coli* O157:H7 bacterium originates on the farm, becomes a contaminant in the packing plant, multiplies if meat is improperly stored, but can be neutralized in the kitchen if beef is properly cooked.

The "farm-to-fork" concept refers to quality assurance programs that flow through the length of the commodity chain. To address food safety concerns, HACCP-style quality assurance systems need to be applied at every step in the commodity chain, beginning with calving, extending through ante-mortem inspection at the slaughterhouse-door, all the way to the consumer. Farm-to-fork quality assurance will be facilitated by the Canadian Cattle Identification Program, which was inaugurated in 2001. All cattle that move beyond their herds of origin must now have uniquely coded ear tags that remain in place up to the point of carcass inspection at the packing plant.[39] The ability to trace animals backward to their herd of origin, or forward when a herd becomes dispersed, provides an unprecedented level of information for tracing the spread of animal disease and meat safety hazards from farm to fork.

Many producers have accepted voluntary programs such as the Canadian Cattlemen's appropriately named "Quality Starts Here," which promotes best practice, but does not monitor it.[40] In Britain, the major supermarket chains sell only "Farm Assured British Beef and Lamb," a quality assurance certification program that requires producers to be inspected and subject to audits.[41] Mandatory compliance with on-farm quality assurance programs is the next logical step in Canada, but will be opposed by producers who guard their independence and object to HACCP as a bureaucratic burden.[42] Farmers will only accept quality assurance protocols when retailers send a clear market signal up the commodity chain, making certified and verified quality assurance a condition of market access.

Provincial Meat Inspection and the Regulatory Paradox

Provincially licensed slaughter plants may only sell meat within their home province. Cattle slaughter in provincially licensed plants amounted to 185,000 head in 2002 or about 6 percent of Canada's total reported cattle slaughter.[43] Large-scale federally inspected meat suppliers regard the provincially inspected meat plants as marginal and irrelevant to Canada's large export-oriented meat-packing sector. This is a fallacy with serious consequences. What happens in provincially inspected plants does have an impact on large-scale producers and their export markets. The "single stinking cow" that triggered the BSE crisis, according to Premier Klein, was sent to a provincially inspected plant and the animal's head languished on the laboratory shelf for over three months before it was finally examined and BSE was detected.

Since its inception in 1907, federal meat inspection legislation has excluded farm slaughter and the intraprovincial meat trade from its provisions. This had the effect of reserving the higher-quality cattle and hogs for export markets while the lowest-quality cattle went to domestic consumers. Hundreds of small slaughterhouses served local butcher shops, seldom subject to any inspection. As early as 1918, the Livestock Commission of Saskatchewan noted the problem with selective federal standards.

> At present inspection operates only in those plants which do an interprovincial business, though it covers all products of such establishments, whether sold locally or outside. The consequence is that the worst stuff is reserved for local killing and consumption. Some districts notorious for bad stock are avoided by inspected plants, only to find an outlet locally.[44]

The regulatory paradox is that when two sets of regulations are applied, the highest-quality goods, which are likely to meet the criteria, are directed to the most demanding regulator, while the lower-quality goods are dispatched to the less onerous regulatory regime. As standards in Canada's federally inspected plants rise, and plants become more comprehensively equipped to meet demands for food safety, the smaller provincially inspected plants may be left to handle the higher-risk livestock.

Dr. Temple Grandin, the leading animal scientist in the field of humane livestock handling and slaughter, audited Canadian slaughter practices in 1995, 1999, and 2003. Noting the distinction between federal and provincial plants, Grandin did not observe any sick, debilitated, or emaciated animals in federally inspected plants in 1995. She went on to argue that "downers" (livestock which cannot stand) and "cripples" have not been miraculously healed; they are simply being diverted to smaller plants, which are not federally inspected.[45] Canada's Health of Animals Regulations prohibit loading or transport of downers. But every province has its own animal health legislation, which does not always provide for the humane transportation of animals. Most provinces have only broad guidelines, so the handling of downers and sick livestock varies from province to province.[46] On January 13, 2004, the CFIA banned the slaughter of downer cattle in federally inspected plants licensed for export. This interim measure was designed to harmonize Canada's BSE risk management measures with those in the U.S.A. in an effort to maintain market access.[47] The effect of the CFIA ban is to divert downer cattle to provincially inspected plants for the domestic food chain. Thus provincial inspectors in small and sometimes remote plants may have to make a proportionally larger number of critical animal health decisions, but with less direct, onsite access to veterinary support than is the case in federally inspected plants.

In 1995, Dr. Temple Grandin expressed reservations about Canada's provincially licensed plants.

> There is a need to review practices in provincial plants that are not federally inspected or members of the Canadian Meat Council. It is likely that bad things are going on in some small provincial plants. I have learned from experience that very small plants come in two basic types. They are either excellent or disgusting.[48]

Many of the provincially inspected slaughter plants that I
have observed are cheerful family-owned businesses with con-
scientious owners and skilled workers. But few are equipped
with the state-of-the-art equipment for carcass pasteurization
and sanitation of cutting tools found in large plants. And I
have also witnessed ineptitude and inhumane practices in
provincially inspected facilities. In one case, I noted that six
bullets had to be fired from a single-shot .22 calibre rifle before
a steer was finally stunned into insensibility. While stunning
effectiveness is not a direct measure of meat safety, it is a determinant of meat quality.

The 2001 Report of the Provincial Auditor of Ontario
observed critical deficiencies in its provincially inspected meat
plants. Hazards to human health included ineffective sanitizing
equipment, carcasses transported in unrefrigerated trucks,
and unsanitary food contact surfaces. Ontario's Ministry of
Agriculture, Food and Rural Affairs was slow to verify that correc-
tive action was taken when abattoirs were not in compliance with
food safety regulations, meat inspectors' documentation was
insufficient to demonstrate that operational tasks were actually
being completed, and there was no procedure for random laboratory testing to detect evidence of contaminants in the meat
produced in provincial plants.[49] In August 2003, a provincially
inspected plant in Aylmer, Ontario, was investigated for the
alleged sale of uninspected meat, slaughtering without a provincial inspector present, and processing of dead stock. No charges
were actually laid, but the allegations were widely reported.
Between 1991 and 2003 the firm's licence was provisionally suspended five times and on two other occasions the firm was
warned about illegal slaughter and obstructing a meat inspector.[50]

These events prompted a judicial inquiry into meat regulation and inspection in Ontario. Among other problems in
the provincial inspection system, Justice Roland Haines found
evidence of nepotism in the appointment of meat inspectors,
and pointed to deficiencies in their qualifications and training
after provincial government cutbacks had replaced permanent
inspectors with part-time contractual appointees.[51] He also
identified conflict of interest as an issue. Unlike the Canadian
Food Inspection Agency, which operates at some remove from
Agriculture and Agri-Food Canada, provincial meat inspection
is typically a function within provincial ministries of agriculture.[52] Thus provincial inspection authorities may feel torn
between their responsibilities to consumers and their active
support of livestock producers. In Ontario, Justice Haines
found evidence of "a reluctance to act decisively when the
issues of public safety and client welfare collide. This only fuels
the perception that public safety is sometimes taking a back-
seat to the agricultural business."[53]

Provinces such as Ontario claim that provincial inspection
standards are equivalent to federal food standards, and that the
difference between federal and provincial inspection is primarily one of scale and scope, not food safety outcomes.[54]
Notwithstanding their equivalent inspection standards,
provincially inspected plants are typically not as well equipped
with state-of-the-art sanitation equipment, and are not as well
designed and constructed to prevent contamination. The qualifications, training, and experience of provincial inspectors
varies from one province to another, as does the frequency and
intensity of support by professional veterinarians. At the retail
meat case and in commercial or institutional dining rooms, it

is often unclear whether meat was provincially or federally inspected, and it is difficult to discover where it was slaughtered and processed.

Many Canadians prefer to buy meat from locally produced livestock, and there is growing interest in organic and natural meat products, community-supported agriculture, and alternative farming practices. This trend should reinforce the role of small-scale, locally oriented slaughter plants in the commodity chain. The friendly, small-town butcher, operating a small provincially inspected plant, provides a valued alternative to national chain stores and large scale meat-packing plants. But the friendly butcher may also be processing older livestock that are more likely to be disabled or to have some zoonotic infection. Experience with locally oriented kill plants suggests that small is not always beautiful, and provincially licensed slaughter plants may need more intensive quality assurance than is presently the case.

The smaller abattoir environment poses unique challenges to meat inspection, given the prevalence of part-time kill floors that operate only one day per week, staff who are only intermittently employed in slaughter and carcass dressing tasks, and part-time meat inspectors. Some provincially inspected abattoirs are in peripheral regions, making it difficult to provide immediate support from professional veterinarians. Given the growing importance attached to food safety, the rapid developments in the biotechnology of meat inspection, and the important role played by smaller meat plants, would Canadians be better served by one rationalized system of meat inspection instead of eleven? Can we still justify two classes of inspection, one of which is *not* eligible for export and *not* acceptable for most fast-food and supermarket chains, yet satisfactory for domestic consumers? Can more effective methods of meat hygiene and risk management be developed specifically for the needs of small plants?

Betting the Farm in Risk Society

Sociologist Anthony Giddens, Director of the London School of Economics, has identified the politics of risk as one of the most distinctive aspects of modern society. Risk is an evaluation of a hazard — often quantified as a probability — that may materialize in the future. A concern with uncertain future events, justifying institutions such as fire departments, is among the hallmarks of modernity. Why has risk become so important? Modern society has a capacity to create "manufactured risks" on an unprecedented scale. Unlike the chances of being hit by lightning (a natural hazard with an improbable but quantifiable risk), we have no idea of the likelihood of our manufactured hazards. Cassandras warn of sea level rise or bacterial resistance to antibiotics as catastrophic outcomes of anthropogenic global change. What is the risk that one of these post-modern plagues may be visited upon future generations? Civil society does not know, and scientists do not agree. Thus Giddens says that there is a new "riskiness to risk" creating "a new moral climate of politics" in our "risk society."[55] Politicians are charged with a cover-up if they elect not to take action and the worst-case scenario materializes. And if they take action against a non-existent menace, they are charged with scare-mongering. Science-based policy-making can't always win — that is the fundamental problem posed by risk society.

One way to resolve this problem is to apply the "precautionary principle," a risk management tool which states that a lack of full scientific certainty should not be used as a reason for postponing decisions.[56] The precautionary principle is written into the Treaty of Maastricht, and adopted by all member countries of the European Union. To avoid the risks posed by growth hormones, the EU applied the precautionary principle in its continuing ban on Canadian and American beef imports.[57] Among most Canadian cattle producers, this use of the precautionary principle is perceived as a hypocritical pretext for a protectionist trade policy that discriminates against Canadian beef. These trans-Atlantic differences illustrate polar opposites in the moral climate of politics described by Giddens.

The precautionary principle has also been adopted by the Canadian Food Inspection Agency and by the Canadian government at large.[58] Yet applying the principle to decision-making is challenging because there is no consensus in the public's perception and tolerance of risk. Instead there is a broad plurality of risk preferences. Risk preference plurality poses a conundrum for policy-makers trying to discern whether "risk of serious harm" is truly credible. William Leiss argues that the risk of BSE was clear:

> Trouble has been brewing for Canada's beef industry for many years, during which both political and industry leaders followed the well-known three monkeys' routine ("hear no evil . . ."). The bottom line is, Canada — with a $30 billion annual beef industry to protect — has been appallingly lax in its policies designed to minimize BSE risk. In more technical

language, we have been insufficiently precautionary,
by a wide margin, in response to the economic risk
represented by BSE.[59]

In the area of BSE policy, Canadians behaved as daring
risk-takers. Canadians bet the farm, counting on denial and
long odds to escape calamity. Canada came up short, and all
Canadians are paying the price. If Canadians are fundamentally risk-averse, given that the stakes are so high, then we
need to recognize that we are living in risk society and start
applying the precautionary principle more consistently from
farm to fork.

Glib assertions that policy decisions should be "science-
based" ignore the essentially political character of risk assessment. Science and politics must interact, so that the ambiguities
of scientific findings and the subtleties of scientific judgment
may be communicated and shared with consumers in the climate of uncertainty that characterizes our risk society.

In coping with challenges at every stage in the commodity
chain, cattle producers, beef packers, and government regulators have already demonstrated enormous ingenuity, showing
evidence of innovation at every step. This chapter points to
some areas where further innovation seems warranted and
likely in the near term. None of these proposals is truly novel,
and initiatives are already underway to address each of them;
however, progress has been glacial.

• Give the CFIA and provincial meat inspection agencies
  greater autonomy both in their relationship to agricultural
  interests and internally, perhaps with a board structure

that brings scientific perspectives to bear on "science-based" regulatory questions.

• Examine provincial meat inspection from a nationwide perspective and consider some nationwide benchmarks. Consider creative ways to implement higher national standards yet retain the essential character of small-scale meat plants.

• Extend quality assurance programs from "farm to fork."

• Use the precautionary principle, and assess risk as the product of probability and consequences to avoid future zoonotic catastrophes.

While food safety issues are changing rapidly, the challenges and ambiguities of decision-making under uncertainty will always be with us. To manage food safety risks wisely, in a dynamic policy environment, we must involve scientists more directly in decision-making processes. And we must avoid simplistic calls for science-based policy when there is disagreement, using appeals to science to validate the status quo. As Canada learned to its cost, we could be betting the farm: the odds may seem good but the consequences could be catastrophic.

Fish or Cut Bait: Solutions for Our Seas

Carl Safina and Carrie Brownstein

One Man's Story

At ninety years old, Fritz Goldstein still remembers with sharp precision the details of his lifetime in the seafood business. Stationed at his kitchen table in the outskirts of Philadelphia, his ancient eyes light up as he recounts tales of a career journey he can still scarcely fathom. Who would have known, his expression conveys, that in the early 1900s the son of a Russian immigrant fishmonger could grow up to participate in the growth and globalization of the modern seafood industry?

In his early years, Fritz awoke at three o'clock each morning to haggle with local dealers at his father's wholesale fish market on Philadelphia's bustling Dock Street. He was a fifteen-year-old with a tight schedule; after work he still had to make it across town before the first school bell rang. Fritz sold freshwater carp and whitefish hauled from the Great Lakes and the relatively more pristine waters of Wisconsin and Nebraska. The saltwater fish — croakers and porgies — travelled a shorter distance; all were caught off nearby Cape May and Wildwood, New Jersey. It was the Depression in the United States and fish was cheap — five dollars for a hundred-pound box.

The gruelling and unglamorous life of a fishmonger was never Fritz's dream. So when he graduated high school in 1932, he made other plans. Packed and ready with a scholarship to launch a football career at the University of Alabama, Fritz was intercepted by his father who pleaded for him to stay and help with the business. With a commitment to family stronger than a desire for football and academics, Fritz's decision was made. He returned to the fish market. Less than a decade later, he founded Liberty Fish Company. In partnership with his four brothers, Fritz built Liberty Fish into a major player in the international seafood industry.[1]

Fishing Goes High Tech

When Fritz Goldstein first started working at the fish market in the late 1920s, human capacity to catch fish was limited by communications, transportation, and technology. Fritz recalls one harrowing journey to buy Lake Whitefish from Lac La Biche, one of Alberta, Canada's largest lakes. One way, the trip required eight airplane flights plus a twelve-mile (nineteen-kilometre) trek on a dogsled.[2]

Even when diesel engines largely replaced steam power on fishing boats after the First World War, and fishing efficiency increased markedly, some places were simply too far or too deep to fish. Most fisheries occurred relatively close to shore and consequently, there were natural refuges for fish to hide and reproduce. Deep-dwelling species were impractical targets back then, so by default some naturally vulnerable species such as orange roughy were protected from exploitation. The Second World War and its aftermath, however, not only changed the social and political landscape of the world, but dramatically transformed how and where fishing occurred.

Savvy fishers discovered that by applying naval battle technology to fishing boats, they could radically improve their capacity to catch fish. SONAR, designed to detect enemy submarines, became an effective fish finding device. RADAR allowed safe operation in dense fog. LORAN permitted pinpoint navigation to fish hide-outs with push-button ease. And with the availability of new synthetic materials like nylon, which did not rot as easily as natural fibre nets, fishers could fish longer than before. These technological improvements made it possible for seafood buyers like Fritz Goldstein to introduce new fish to the market. On his first trip to New Zealand, for example, Fritz's customers presented him with the once-elusive orange roughy.[3] Before long, few species remained undiscovered.

The Seafood Market Goes Global

While seafood markets in coastal communities still feature some locally caught species, most fish markets in the developed countries now thrive on imported seafood. At major trade centres such as New York City's Fulton Fish Market, shouting fishmongers entice chefs and other buyers with a vast assortment of fish, fresh and frozen, live and dead. The world's largest fish market, Tsukiji in Tokyo, Japan, has the most diverse selection. Tautog and summer flounder from the U.S. East Coast, and lobsters from Maine are featured among fish, shellfish, and invertebrates extracted from virtually every fishable body of water on the planet.[4]

As the world's first- and second-largest importers of seafood, Japan and the U.S.A., respectively, are highly influential in determining the global fish catch. Having overexploited many of their domestic fisheries, the United States and other major importing nations now depend on developing countries to meet their demand. China and Peru report the largest catches of wild fishes, followed by Japan, the U.S.A., Chile, Indonesia, the Russian Federation, and India. The fish trade is big business today. According to the United Nations' Food and Agriculture Organization (FAO), trade in seafood products in 2000 reached US$55.2 billion.[5] Consequently, when we discuss fisheries and aquaculture in the world today, we must retain a global perspective.

The value of seafood stretches far beyond that of a commodity bought and sold in the world market. Globally, people depend on fish for food and for work. Over one billion people in the world today depend on fish for at least 30 percent of their animal protein intake. And over half of the world's population relies on fish for at least 20 percent of their animal protein. Coastal communities tend to eat more fish than inland communities. And in some small island states, fish is the sole source of animal protein. Furthermore, the FAO estimates that 35 million people worldwide are employed full- or part-time in fisheries and aquaculture (seafood farming). The distribution of these workers (Asia, 85 percent; Africa, 7 percent; Europe, South America, and North and Central America, 2 percent each; and Oceania, 0.2 percent) reflects the general population distribution and predominance of labour-intensive economies.[6]

The Oceans Feel the Pressure

The global seafood market, as we recognize it today, grew relatively quickly after the Second World War. Global catches of wild species increased rapidly in the 1950s and 1960s as a result of the factors described previously — increased efficiency from improvements in technology, transportation, and communications. According to the FAO, the increases continued, albeit at a slower rate and with some exceptions, until peaking at 83 million tonnes in 1989. The exceptions were quite significant: in 1972 the world's largest fishery, Peruvian anchoveta, collapsed, partially due to oceanographic conditions related to El Niño. (In the mid-1990s El Niño period, the anchoveta fishery again declined substantially.) In its latest report on the status of world fisheries, the FAO suggested that catches have since recovered to levels seen in the early 1990s, prior to the latest major decline in Peruvian anchoveta: 77–78 million tonnes.

In the 1990s the FAO attributed global total fish-catch increases to production from China. China's reported catches are so high — almost 20 percent of total world production in 1998 — that they significantly affect the global total.[7] Ever since the collapse of the Peruvian anchoveta fishery in the early 1970s, scientists have warned of the upper limits to our oceans' capacity to supply fish. While the FAO has acknowledged that these claims are substantiated,[8] its portrayal of the status of the world's fisheries has been overly optimistic. Collecting statistics on the world's fisheries is clearly challenging. Relying on member countries to provide their own catch reports, the FAO has few safeguards to ensure that its statistics are accurate.

Specifically, there were some indications that China's catch reports were too high. For example, some of China's major fish populations were declared overexploited decades ago. In 2001,

Watson and Pauly published an eye-opening study in the journal *Nature* about the true status of our world's fisheries. These researchers used a statistical model to compare China's officially reported catches to those that would be expected, given oceanographic conditions and other factors. They determined that China's actual catches were likely closer to one half their reported levels. The implications of China's over-reporting are dramatic: instead of global catches increasing by 0.33 million tonnes per year since 1988, as reported by the FAO, catches have actually declined by 0.36 million tonnes per year. And when catches of Peruvian anchoveta, a species whose abundance fluctuates naturally with changing environmental conditions are excluded, the declines for all other species are even more pronounced at 0.66 million tonnes per year.[9] Watson and Pauly's findings showed that fisheries are not, in fact, keeping pace with people's demand for fish. Instead, real catches had been declining since about the early 1990s.

Furthermore, even with high-tech fish-finders, fishing is not as simple as reaching down and catching a tuna by its tail. Many of the pervasive methods for fishing today are indiscriminate: fishers not only catch targeted species, they incidentally catch other species as well. When last estimated, this non-targeted catch, known as "bycatch," added up to 18–40 million tonnes (at least one-quarter of total catches).[10] These days, instead of being discarded dead, more of the non-targeted catch is being ground up and used as fishmeal for aquaculture.[11] But the impact on the ecosystem of killing such an enormous quantity of wildlife is still the same.

Today's high bycatch stems from the transition to fishing with non-selective fishing gear that occurred a half-century ago. Traditionally, most tuna, for example, were caught with pole-and-line gear, which usually hooked the big tunas that fishers wanted. Today, however, far fewer fishers employ this method. Instead, fishers use purse seine nets to target yellowfin and skipjack tuna for the canned tuna market. In addition to the high volume of tunas caught, purse seines also catch substantial numbers of billfish, sharks, sea turtles, and marine mammals.[12] And the pelagic longline fishery, targeting the higher-value tunas and swordfish, has among the highest bycatch worldwide. Monofilament or steel longlines can stretch for miles parallel to the sea surface, with as many as 12,000 baited hooks hanging vertically per line.[13] With 100,000 miles (160,000 kilometres) of line and 5 million baited hooks set each day throughout the world's oceans, many other species are caught in the process of fishing for tunas and swordfish. Sharks are the most substantial bycatch in longline fisheries, causing population declines for many shark species. In the Northwest Atlantic, most shark species caught in pelagic longlines are declining.[14] Longline bycatch also includes many juvenile individuals of targeted species as well as billfishes, mammals, seabirds, and endangered sea turtles.[15]

Although longlining is inherently an unselective method of catching tunas and swordfish, with technological ingenuity fisheries can reduce bycatch of some species. Experiments in the U.S. Atlantic, for example, showed that using circle-shaped hooks instead of the typical J-hooks, and mackerel bait instead of squid, reduced bycatch of leatherback and loggerhead sea turtles by 67 percent and 92 percent, respectively. Fishery managers in Hawaii now require that Hawaii-based swordfish boats use this more turtle-friendly gear.[16] Adoption of these methods in longline fisheries in other regions of the world, coupled with protecting sea turtle habitat, reducing illegal hunting of sea turtles for meat, and adhering to fishery regulations that protect turtles in other fisheries, could make a tremendous difference to the world's sea turtle populations.

Shrimp fisheries, using mobile trawls to catch America's favourite seafood, have some of the highest bycatch of all, accounting for over one-third of discards globally when last assessed.[17] Bycatch in shrimp fisheries includes finfish, invertebrates, and sea turtles.[18] In some shrimp fisheries, including the U.S. South Atlantic and Gulf of Mexico, fishers are reducing overall bycatch using Bycatch Reduction Devices (BRDs) and incidental catches of sea turtles using Turtle Excluder Devices (TEDs). However, despite regulatory efforts to ensure that shrimp imported to the U.S.A. come from turtle-safe fisheries, outside the U.S.A. many shrimp fishers fail to comply with TED regulations. In Central America, for example, weak enforcement allows the majority of fishers to claim they are TED-certified without properly using the turtle escape devices.[19]

The Broader Effects of Fishing

Concerned about the broader implications of fishing, scientists increasingly monitor the impacts of fishing on marine communities and ecosystems. In a widely publicized study, Myers and Worm showed that longline catch rates of large predatory fishes today are a mere 10 percent of catch rates at the start of industrial fishing. They infer a 90-percent loss of large predatory fishes from the ocean. Their study marked the first demonstration of declines in whole communities among diverse ecosystems; other analyses have shown declines in single species. Declines occurred rapidly: fishing reduced community biomass by 80 percent in fifteen years.[20]

We do not yet know what the long-term ecosystem effects of removing 90 percent of predators might be. And under the modern fishery management paradigm, regulatory agencies are doing little to stop overexploitation of species before we can find out. Fishery management agencies and commissions usually implement regulatory measures after industrialized fishing has become widespread. Consequently, they're working to stabilize populations at low levels of abundance. This approach may continue to have grave consequences for fishers as they suffer from low economic yields, and also for marine ecosystems in both coastal and oceanic ecosystems.[21]

Scientist Daniel Pauly coined the phrase "Fishing down marine food webs" to describe fishers' shift from catching large predator fishes to smaller fishes and invertebrates.[22] Later, Pauly et al. analyzed species and their trophic levels (the level in the food web that a species occupies, with algae at a trophic level of one).[23] The research showed that as large fish have been depleted, fishing operations have been shifting their targets down the food chain at a rate of 0.5 to 1.0 trophic levels per decade. This demonstrates a worldwide trend in coastal and oceanic fisheries since the early 1950s. Where fisheries are most developed, mostly in northern temperate areas, trophic levels have steadily declined in the last few decades.

The consequences, Pauly et al. state, are significant shifts in the structure of marine food webs.[24] Contrary to some people's hopes, fishing out the largest fish doesn't necessarily release the smaller fish from predation. Nor does it offer more fish for humans to catch. Rather, removing the large fish increases the populations of previously suppressed species, such as invertebrates. While markets exist for some invertebrates like squid and jellyfish, other species are toxic. The Groundlings comedy group have produced a short film in which a couple dining in an upscale restaurant of the future orders the catch-of-the-day, only to find that the catch-of-the-day, today and everyday, is a bowl of jellyfish soup because that's all that's left.[25]

Can Aquaculture Keep Fish on Our Plates?

Globally, aquaculture, or seafood farming, is already a significant contributor to seafood supply. According to the FAO, aquaculture is the fastest growing of all animal food-producing sectors (9.2 percent per year since 1970 compared to 1.4 percent for capture fisheries and 2.8 percent for terrestrial meat production). And it continues to contribute increasing amounts of fish, crustaceans, and molluscs to total global seafood production: from 3.9 percent in 1970 to 27.3 percent in 2000. China has reported the fastest growth. However, the FAO states that China may have over-estimated production in this sector as well.[26]

Proponents of aquaculture suggest that it can lessen our overfishing burden on wild fish populations, and can enhance food supplies. (When asked in 2004 whether he ever imagined that we could catch too many fish, even ninety-year-old Fritz Goldstein replied, "Oh no, because we're farming fish now."[27]) Many people still do not know, however, that production of some species is inefficient and unsustainable. Many species farmed today are carnivores dependent on wild-caught fish for feed. Farming carnivores entails a net loss of protein and fails to conserve wild fish populations.[28] In 2001, salmon and shrimp — two of the top four groups under aquaculture worldwide — relied on fish meal and fish oil for their feed. Presently around 29 percent of world fish production goes to non-food products, most of which is for fish meal and oil.[29]

Even if non-fish-based feeds become more commercially available and viable, aquaculture's sustainability depends on production methods and the types of inputs and outputs. The general system-design is a good overall proxy for the operation's effect on the surrounding environment. For example, net pen systems used to raise farmed salmon allow excess feeds and fish faeces to be released directly into open bodies of water. In contrast, closed tank systems confine wastes, making it easier to control internal and external water quality. Other important factors in determining aquaculture's potentially harmful impacts include: 1) use of pollutants such as pesticides, paraciticides, and antibiotics; 2) the frequency with which species escape from fish farms, and whether escaped species are native or non-native to the farmed areas; 3) the environment's relative ecological sensitivity and whether it is occupied, converted, or adversely affected by aquaculture; and 4) the presence and effectiveness of regulations on water quality, pollution, and other effects of aquaculture. Still, some aquaculture operations today are already sustainably producing seafood. Native species of filter-feeding shellfish, when suspended in bags, nets, or cages — as opposed to being dredged — are a good example.[30]

Important Steps for Restoring the Oceans to Balance

CREATING A SUSTAINABLE SEAFOOD MARKET

Increasingly, the public is beginning to connect the fish on their plate with an ocean or fish farm where it once swam. Media coverage of overfishing has grown, leading more people to wonder how their favourite fish are faring. We know firsthand that consumers want to know which fish are ocean friendly and which aren't. In response to the public's question, "What's okay to eat?" we published our first guide to seafood in 1998.[31] Today, millions of guides to ocean-friendly seafood are in circulation by us at the Blue Ocean Institute and other organizations such as Environmental Defense and the Monterey Bay Aquarium.

Despite the popularity of consumer-education tools like the seafood guides, many species remain hidden from the general public eye. Most consumers are still not yet aware of what's entailed in bringing their favourite fish to the table, or if the species is healthy or in poor shape. Some of these considerations include: Does a wild-caught species have natural vulnerabilities to fishing pressure such as late maturation? Is the species abundant or depleted? Is there strong management in place? Is the species caught in ways that don't harm the environment or other creatures?[32]

The sustainable seafood movement has thus far shown that when people learn a species is in poor shape, or that catching or farming it has serious ecological consequences, they want a better option. Once they're aware of what their choices entail, it's unacceptable to eat something on the brink of endangerment. At the same time, consumers who know a fish enjoys healthy levels of abundance, and is sustainably caught or farmed, feel motivated to chose the more ocean- or environmentally friendly option.

In the food world, chefs set the trends. With the help of industry's creative marketing — like renaming Patagonian toothfish "Chilean seabass" to increase its appeal — skilful chefs can lift a fish from relative obscurity to "must-have" status on menus nationwide. A poorly managed species can suffer tremendously from a trend. The Chilean seabass craze increased illegal fishing, and caused a decline of toothfish populations to low levels. Furthermore, large numbers of endangered albatrosses and petrels are hooked and drowned as they try to steal bait from longline vessels targeting toothfish.[33]

Informed chefs, concerned about sustainability, can set new standards for how seafood is selected and promoted. Their culinary prowess can subtly if explicitly guide consumer choices. Chefs can also help provide economic incentives for improved fishery management. In 1998, around the time we published the first consumer guide to ocean-friendly seafood, over 700 top chefs on the U.S. East Coast teamed up with conservation organizations Seaweb, and the National Resources Defense Council, to launch the "Give Swordfish a Break Campaign." Nationally renowned chefs, including Nora Pouillon from Restaurant Nora (Washington, DC) and Rick Moonen, now of RM Restaurant (New York), took swordfish off their menus. This prompted the international fishery commission, responsible for managing Atlantic swordfish, to cut catch-quotas, and the U.S.A. to close important juvenile nursery grounds. When the boycott affected the price of swordfish, and the management agencies felt enough pressure to implement stronger conservation measures, the boycott was called off.[34]

The campaign was effective — the number of juvenile swordfish has increased.[35] Time, and continued conservation measures, will determine whether swordfish can truly rebound. But the campaign clearly demonstrated that consumers and chefs can powerfully affect fishery decisions and help shift public consciousness. Campaigns for species protection, improved fishery management, and aquaculture reform are currently in effect for toothfish ("Take a Pass on Chilean Seabass"), Caspian Sea Sturgeon ("Caviar Emptor"), and farmed salmon ("Farmed and Dangerous"). These campaigns are undeniably increasing awareness among seafood consumers.

Changing consumer behaviour may require publicly visible events such as boycotts to draw initial attention to an issue. Boycotts can work if they have a tangible goal. Once that goal is met, the boycott ends. Making changes that last, however, requires moving beyond trend-setting, because trends are, by their very nature, ephemeral. The backlash against the anti-fur movement is a good example. In 1989, People for the Ethical Treatment of Animals launched its campaign to dissuade consumers from wearing fur. Disturbing images of wild minks, foxes, rabbits, and other animals killed for fur, and the inhumane conditions at fur farms, persuaded many consumers to respond by boycotting fur coats and other fur garments.[36] Some top fashion models endorsed the campaign and it became unfashionable to wear fur. Industry felt the effects. Throughout the nineties, consumer rejection substantially decreased purchases of pelts and fur garments, so that many trappers and ranchers went out of business. The campaign also affected public policy. Several American states and eighty-five countries banned steel-jaw leghold traps. The United

Kingdom, Holland, and Austria have banned farming some selected animals for fur altogether.[37] The fashion industry, however, retaliated with a marketing campaign of its own. In the current fur revival, fashion magazine covers feature some of the models who only a decade ago swore they'd rather be naked than wear fur.[38] Thus, the creation of lasting shifts in consciousness, and subsequently in behaviour, entails something deeper. Lasting change comes from developing personal relationships with the world and the living things around us.

CREATING LASTING CHANGE, INSPIRING A SEA ETHIC

In his 1949 book, *A Sand County Almanac*, Aldo Leopold articulated a framework for how we might consider our relationship with our environment. His idea: that our sense of community can extend beyond humanity to encompass people as well as the living landscape. His sensibility had a moral component, which he called the Land Ethic. "A thing is right," he wrote, "when it tends to preserve the integrity, stability, and beauty of the biotic community, and wrong when it tends otherwise."[39] Right actions safeguard present and future options — not just for people but for the whole living world.

Leopold's Land Ethic includes all forms of life — human and non-human — in our concept of community. It's possible that Leopold's Land Ethic (really a Nature Ethic) excluded the oceans because his own life experience was focused on the mid-western part of the United States. A more likely reason, however, is that when he formulated his Land Ethic, he — and most of the world — was unaware that the oceans were in trouble. At that time there was little or no documentation of fishery collapses, ocean dumping, coral bleaching, or any of the other crises that have since grown acute. Now, few individuals are truly removed from impacting the oceans. One-third to one-half of the world's population now lives within fifty miles (eighty kilometres) of a coast. Even inlanders consume seafood caught or farmed in the oceans, products shipped across the oceans, or rely on energy sources, like fossil fuels, that indirectly affect the oceans through climate change. Understanding the state of the oceans today tells us that it's time we extend our sense of community below high tide — we need now a Sea Ethic.

How do we begin to see ourselves, the oceans, and the oceans' creatures as part of the same community? Mirroring the way a sense of belonging to a human community is rooted in the personal relationships that individuals have with one another, we can develop a Sea Ethic by cultivating personal connections to the ocean and ocean wildlife. Millions of people now aspire to meet the oceans' creatures on their own turf. They attach tanks to their backs, defying what once were physiological limitations to merge with the sea world. For those who find this interaction too extreme, we bring ocean life to land. We simulate the wild places. Anyone who doubts the impression that visiting an aquarium can make, hasn't seen a child pressing her face to the glass as she witnesses for her first time ever a shark passing only inches by her nose.

Beginning a relationship with the sea doesn't require that we immediately run off to get sand between our toes. Living in the modern world, we are already interacting with the ocean in our daily lives. But one way we can honour our relationship with the sea, and become more conscious of how our choices affect ocean life, is by changing our personal approach to selecting seafood. When we peruse a menu or stand before the fish counter at a grocery store, our criteria for selecting seafood can extend beyond taste and cost. We can begin thinking about and discussing which seafoods are ocean friendly and which aren't. And with reflection, we create ideas and ideals about our community in the largest sense. In essence, we formulate a Sea Ethic.

ECOSYSTEM MANAGEMENT: THINKING BIGGER

In ecological parlance, a "community" is defined by all the organisms — including entire populations of different species — that inhabit a particular area and that have a potential to interact. When we consider both a community and the abiotic (that is, non-living) factors that the community interacts with, we call the combination an "ecosystem."[40] Today we're interacting with our marine ecosystems on multiple levels — from manipulating abundance of individual species populations to altering climate, which ultimately affects the oceanographic conditions that drive production at the base of marine food webs. Thus, more than ever before, the time is right for an ecosystem-based approach to marine conservation.

Many marine conservationists in North America and the rest of the world hail Ecosystem Management as a framework for policy making. Ecosystem Management means looking beyond the pervasive single-species approach to the broader implications of fishing. Under the single-species approach, management policies usually address only the total catch of the target species and when, where, and how fishing for that species can occur. Unfortunately, the single-species approach has a poor record. In U.S. waters alone, where there is a formal management structure for fisheries, but most fisheries are managed on a species-by-species basis, the status of 75 percent of species populations is still unknown. Of those that we know enough about, managers have officially declared 36 percent over-fished.[41] An ecosystem approach goes beyond single-species management by expanding: 1) the list of stresses on a fish population beyond fishing to include habitat degradation and general environmental quality; 2) our understanding of an ecosystem's response to fishing beyond the effect of fishing mortality on a targeted species to include other components of the ecosystem; and 3) the scope of benefits beyond the economic value of fish to include the non-monetary benefits of ecosystem services and the benefits of other human activities.[42]

Considering fisheries from an ecosystem perspective can help address the challenges of managing species and populations that are inherently unpredictable. Unlike the plants in a productive garden, where you can count exactly how many seeds you've planted and estimate with reasonable confidence how many plants your seeds will yield and where they will grow, fish are intrinsically elusive. They move and they are hidden underwater. You can't count them like seeds from a packet. Fish are subject to a wide range of variables that affect their productivity, including trophic interactions, oceanographic fluctuations, and community interactions. Although fishery scientists have a range of sophisticated tools for assessing and predicting population sizes and productivity, there will always be unknowns, especially as we still don't *know* how many fish we're actually catching. In addition to the problem of over-reporting discussed earlier, illegal, unregulated, and unreported (IUU) catches are increasing.[43] In the face of all this uncertainty, "managing the ecosystem" is extremely difficult. What we have to do is manage human activity, with an ecosystem perspective.

Conservationists commonly refer to a concept, the "Precautionary Principle," whereby we use resources conservatively today to secure their availability for the future. In the developed world, people plan their financial future either by investments or through government programs like social security. In developing countries, people still plan for the future — as we used to do — by having children, as a way to help them when they can no longer work. We can apply the same philosophical principle to our future food sources. By building safety measures into our management methods, we can help ensure that we have fish to eat in the future.

OCEAN ZONING:
A NEW TOOL IN THE OCEAN CONSERVATION TOOLBOX

Ecosystem Management provides resource managers and conservationists with a framework for addressing the wide range of goals people have for using ocean resources. In an increasingly crowded and hungry world, we look to the oceans for many different reasons: aesthetics, conserving biodiversity, extracting food, relaxation and recreation, or even intensely competitive sports, like the single-handed boat-races around the world. These activities often conflict, creating territorial battles that sometimes erupt in the courtroom and within communities. One ongoing conflict involves recreational and commercial fishers competing over prime fishing grounds. And as society's desires change, new conflicts arise. In Cape Cod, Massachusetts, for example, residents wanting to maintain a particular aesthetic along the coastline are at odds with others who want to place energy-generating windmills in coastal waters. Resolving user-conflicts like these requires managing people and their resource use from an ecosystem perspective.

Tangibly, we can approach Ecosystem Management using tools and techniques we already know and understand. On land, for example, planning starts with assessing a need, surveying the land's capacity to meet the need, and creating blueprints that represent the plan. Many communities manage competing demands on space and resources by creating land-use plans that zone areas as residential, commercial, agricultural, industrial, and recreational. Moving away from our current open-access, free-for-all approach to ocean management, toward a method that utilizes zoning, is a way to handle the competition for ocean resources among the world's growing population. As architects for sustainable seas, we can create blueprints that *plan* for biological, economic, aesthetic, and spiritual needs.

Designing and implementing a zoning strategy requires that the public, marine-resource managers, and policy-makers understand that the ocean is not a blank space between continents, but instead is a diverse environment where some places are biological hotspots, and others vary in their ecological sensitivity. Accounting for this diversity, we can allocate appropriate areas for commercial fishing, aquaculture, shipping, scientific research, and pleasure activities like scuba-diving, recreational fishing, and boating. Some areas will be multiple use, some restricted use, and others places will preclude resource extraction of any kind ("no-take" zones). These protected areas can help to increase marine fish production and protect marine ecosystems, and, in turn, help generate food for the future.

Worldwide, we already have several examples of successful government-supported marine zoning initiatives. Australia's Great Barrier Reef Marine Park is the most famous. Established under the Great Barrier Reef Act of 1975, and further implemented under the Great Barrier Reef Marine Zoning Plan

2003, the Marine Park works to protect biodiversity in all habitat types and maintain and enhance cultural, tourism, and recreational values. Areas are zoned for particular types of fishing (for example, some sections restrict trawling), shipping, and recreational uses.[44]

Following Australia's lead, other countries have implemented zoning programs. They include Belize's Marine Reserves at Hol Chan and Glover's Reef, and the U.S.A.'s Florida Keys National Sanctuary. While the geographic extent of these programs is small relative to our need for a comprehensive ocean management strategy, they provide an important launching point for planning future initiatives. Additionally, the U.S.A. already has various fishing-gear restrictions (no trawling and no longlining in some areas), extraction limits (oil leases), and limits on activities such as jet skiing in certain National Marine Sanctuaries. Still, there is no comprehensive approach to regional planning and management. New technologies such as wind-generators and widespread aquaculture will only further complicate future conflicts unless a zoning discussion gets underway.

We suggest that the time is right to begin formal discussions about ocean zoning. To date, premature conflicts between the conservation and fishing communities over what specific areas would be protected — and how large these areas would be — has stymied public support for Marine Protected Areas (or "no-take" zones) in the United States. People have failed to understand that no-take zones are only one type of "zone," albeit an important one in a comprehensive zoning strategy.

Fritz Goldstein smiles softly as he concludes his stories of memorable travels around the world in search of new seafood sources and lifelong business partners and friendships. In his palm he holds a tiny, delicately carved figurine of a Vietnamese fisherman pulling his catch from a net. Fish-inspired artwork displayed throughout his apartment is the last remaining relic to his half-century in the seafood business. And so for Fritz, telling his story rekindles feelings of happiness and pride.

Imagination and ambition, enabled by developments in communication, transportation, and technology, led Fritz Goldstein and other well-meaning architects of the modern seafood industry to redefine the perception of the oceans held by the generations before them. The capacity to fish where no-one had gone before transformed their image of the oceans from a blank yet dangerous void between continents to a seemingly inexhaustible source of food and business opportunity. In their eyes, their relationship with the oceans undoubtedly was an improvement from years past.

In the last few decades, our natural curiosity prompted us to further explore our ocean world. In the process, we learned that the ocean is far more alive and intricate than we had ever imagined. From below the surface, we extracted images of multicoloured fish staking their territory among vibrant coral reefs, sharks dwelling in deep ocean caves, and migrating giant bluefin tuna chasing their bait at breakneck pace. With this imagery, we triggered human fascination. And people began to care.

We cannot heal the oceans overnight. Pollution, invasive species, habitat destruction, overfishing, aquaculture, coastal development, and climate change are all threatening our oceans today.[45] With inspired imagination, intelligence, motivation, and skill, however, we can reconfigure our current relationship with the seas. Acting from a place of hope, we can restore abundance to the seas.

DIET FOR A SMALLER PLANET: REAL SOURCES OF ABUNDANCE

Frances Moore Lappé and Anna Lappé

My daughter and I are walking down a basement hallway at UC Berkeley's Agriculture Department. I've brought her to the spot where thirty years ago I burrowed myself in the Ag Department library to write *Diet for a Small Planet*. At the ripe young age of twenty-six, I had responded to the experts' cry, daily echoed in the media, that we faced imminent global famine. Books like Paul Ehrlich's *The Population Bomb* had just exploded, along with the even more alarming title: *Famine 1975* by the brothers William and Paul Paddock.

I wanted to dig deeper, asking, *Is hunger inevitable? Why is there hunger at all?* My research returned a startling fact: there is more than enough food to feed the world. At the time, this claim was heresy. I was saying the experts were wrong. I secretly feared I'd misplaced a decimal point. But the research held. And what I discovered then is just as true today: the world produces more than enough for all of us to thrive.

Thirty years later, the two of us decided to revisit the themes of *Diet for a Small Planet* asking why hunger in a world of plenty. Beginning the research for our book *Hope's Edge*, an exploration of holistic, community-based solutions to hunger, we returned to where *Diet* had been conceived. We searched for the library where I had pored over UN documents and other data to understand the world food crisis.

But the dimly lit hallway was empty; the library long-since relocated. As we turned to leave, Anna spotted a lone article tacked to an otherwise barren bulletin board. It read: "World Demand for Food Expected to Outstrip Production." We looked at each other, stunned. Headlines exactly like this leaping off the daily papers had been my motivation to explore the root causes of hunger thirty years ago. Here we were reading a headline dated November 7, 1999, proclaiming the same scarcity scare.

Articles like this were helping fuel the campaign for genetically modified foods, or GMOs — plants bred with technology that inserts DNA from another species in ways that nature and traditional breeding never could. Corporations developing and marketing GMOs were telling us we should swallow — literally — what many argue is risky technology or face scarcity in a hungry world. By this logic, blocking GMOs is tantamount to taking food from the mouths of the starving.

There are a few critical kinks in this logic. Most glaring of all is that our food crisis is not a crisis of scarcity. We already produce enough food to feed the world. In fact, we have grain alone to provide nearly 3,000 calories per person (not even counting all the beans, potatoes, nuts, fruits, root crops, and vegetables produced). That's enough not only to feed us, but to make us all chubby![1]

Yet, hunger is still widespread. Although advances have been made in certain regions of the world, almost one in six people on the planet is undernourished today, according to the United Nations Food and Agriculture Organization.

No, the root of the tragedy is not the scarcity of food; perhaps it has never been. Rather, hunger is caused by a scarcity of democracy. By democracy we don't mean merely the institutions of democracy — multiple parties, constitutional protections, a tripartite governmental structure. We mean *living democracy* in which everyone has a say in their own futures and in which, therefore, the right to life's essentials, including food, is protected. Since no one chooses to go hungry, the very existence of hunger is proof that democracy has not yet been realized.

Without such a living democracy, what happens? Here in perhaps the richest country in the world, it means that almost 35 million people live in households experiencing food insecurity.[2] And in the Global South, India — a country with all the formal trappings of democracy — has the world's greatest number of hungry people. Half the children under the age of four suffer from malnutrition, while surplus grain pours out of over-full warehouses.[3] When we travelled to India in 2000, the government minister in charge of food distribution himself acknowledged to us, "Ours is not a problem of scarcity, it's a problem of plenty."[4]

Without a living democracy, we end up creating the very scarcity we say we fear. With income and wealth so skewed within and among countries, hungry people don't have the wherewithal to buy the food they need. So the market, responding only to wealth, ends up creating a farming system that shrinks artificial oversupply — artificial because it reflects not real demand, only market demand. Worldwide, we now feed almost half of all grain to livestock that return to us in meat only a tiny fraction of the nutrients we feed them.[5] Cattle, for example — ruminants prized for turning inedible substances into protein-rich food — consume in the U.S.A. sixteen pounds of grain and soy, plus thousands of gallons of water, to produce just one pound of steak.[6]

The world food crisis is more accurately a world *democracy* crisis. More and more people are cut out of decision-making about life's essentials as control over land for farming, seeds for planting, and the means for buying and selling moves into fewer and fewer hands. Billions are left to pick up the crumbs, forced to sit on the sidelines in the making of the most fundamental questions of our time.

The Blinders of Measurement

Understanding hunger and democracy, we see the striving to create abundance with new eyes. Typically, when we think about abundance, we turn immediately to the question of production. But once grasping the social roots of the hunger crisis, we can see that thinking of abundance simply in terms of output misses the mark.

Consider the parallel with a reliance on the ubiquitous indicator for economic well-being and wealth: the Gross Domestic Product, a measure of the total dollar value of all goods and services made and purchased within a year. We assume an increasing GDP is progress; its careening down is bad.

For decades, economists and savvy citizen organizations have been knocking at the door of government institutions, arguing that the GDP is a flawed indicator of progress. Many argue it often measures just the opposite. In 1968, Robert F. Kennedy said the GDP "measures everything . . . except that which makes life worthwhile." The San Francisco-based

non-profit Redefining Progress has articulated just this problem; car crashes are a boon, just think of those repairs or new
cars needed; divorce a windfall, think of costly lawyers, psychi-
atrist visits, separate homes. And cancer and death? Cancer
treatment is a multi-billion-dollar business and the funeral
industry is one of the strongest in the economy, with little
competition and a guaranteed clientele. Yet despite its limitations, we still rely on the GDP. In the process, the measurement
itself turns our attention away from aspects of our economy —
and our lives — that determine real wealth.

The GDP does not meaningfully measure our social health
— infant mortality, illness, morbidity, crime, depression —
nor does it even accurately measure our economic health. The
GDP can go up while unemployment, poverty, and inequality
do too. The GDP also doesn't capture the depletion of natural
resources that ultimately undermines long-term economic,
social, and physical well-being: the loss of forests, farmland,
and soil fertility. And the list goes on.

Using strategies to broaden indicators of agricultural
"productivity," economists have been developing alternative
indicators that do measure this more complex — and accurate
— picture. Redefining Progress's Genuine Progress Indicator
(GPI) is one. Developed in 1995, it uses the accounting framework of the GDP, but adds in the economic contributions of
household and unpaid work, while subtracting negatives such
as crime, pollution, and family breakdown. The GPI is updated
every year to "document a more truthful picture of economic
progress," according to its founders.[7]

Similar to the GDP's myopia, a narrow-minded focus on
agricultural production can blur a critical truth — that we can

have more food and yet more hunger. Focusing narrowly on production draws us away from the essential challenge: ensuring that people actually get to eat and that what we produce, and the ways we produce it, are healthy for us and for the Earth, now and in the future.

Today's food system bypasses this essential challenge; it not only leaves nearly a billion people hungry, it also means that many who *do* have access to food are getting sick from what they eat. In fact, more than a billion people around the world are *overfed*.[8] And many of these are mal-fed. In the United States, the mortality and health care costs of obesity-related diseases now rival those from smoking, according to the U.S. Centers for Disease Control and Prevention.[9]

In order to perceive and promote *true* abundance, we must look beyond mere measurements of gross production. We must remember that the heart of the hunger crisis is the faltering of democracy. When it comes to food and farming, people go hungry because they are denied democratic participation in decisions governing the most fundamental aspects of production: land, seeds, capital, and trade.

This Land Is My Land, This Land Is Your Land

One needn't be a farmer, agricultural economist, or a plant scientist to grasp that what is grown and who has access to it depends in large measure on who controls the land. To make this obvious point come to life, we traveled to Brazil as part of our research for *Hope's Edge*.

We were drawn to Brazil because, in part, it suffers among the world's most extreme inequalities of income and wealth (fourth, behind Sierra Leone, Central African Republic, and Swaziland). Just 3 percent of landowners control more than half of Brazil's arable land, much of it left idle.[10] In fact, while Brazil's arable land totals 964 million acres (390 million hectares), one-third of it — a land area the size of Peru — goes unused.[11]

Such staggering inequality helps explain why Brazil is a striking example of the disconnection of production from the creation of abundance that would end hunger. While Brazil has become one of the world's largest agricultural exporters, tens of thousands of its children die every year from hunger and more than 5 million rural people have no land at all.

The concentration of control over Brazil's land has gone hand-in-hand with government policies favouring export-oriented agriculture and large, industrialized operations that push small farmers off the land and provide few jobs to the rural landless. This agricultural system has fuelled massive urbanization. In the past thirty years, 30 million people have fled rural areas for the cities, causing untold pressures on Brazilian cities to feed, house, and support these new residents. By the 1990s, Brazil had changed from a largely rural country to an urban one, with 75 percent of Brazilians living in cities.[12]

Brazil is the world's second leading exporter of soy products, the largest exporter of coffee and orange juice, and a major exporter of poultry and sugar. Hunger there is obviously not caused by inadequate production.[13] So, for decades, Brazilian church leaders, farmers, and human rights and hunger activists have seen clearly that narrowly focusing on increasing agricultural output could never eradicate hunger. To reduce hunger requires asking what is keeping the poor from *feeding themselves*. The answer in Brazil, as in much of the world, is that the poor are denied fair access to land. In fact, over several centuries, it's been actively taken from them.

Many of the largest Brazilian landholdings today can be traced back centuries to when the Portuguese Crown carved up the country's vast acreage. Since then, wealthy landowners have used political favours and legal loopholes to expand control at the expense of the poor.

For centuries efforts by peasants to gain fairer access to land had been defeated, snuffed out with peasant blood. But opening for real change began toward the end of Brazil's military dictatorship, which held power between 1964 and 1985. During Brazil's transition to democracy, leaders of religious communities and social movements came together to form the Landless Workers Movement, or MST, an acronym from its Portuguese name, *Movimento dos Trabalhadores Rurals Sem Terra*, to push for just land reform.

As the fledging democracy drafted its constitution, the MST and others struggling for the rights of the landless ensured that a clause was included to allow the government to expropriate and redistribute idle land in order to fight hunger. The constitution now reads:

> It is within the power of the Union to expropriate on account of social interest, for purposes of agrarian reform, the rural property which is not performing its social function.[14]

Despite this clear constitutional mandate, the MST frequently has had to resort to civil disobedience to pressure the government to make good on the constitution's promise. Often fighting against the wishes of local, state, and national politicians more responsive to wealthy landowners than landless peasants, the

MST has helped to settle more than a quarter of a million families on 17 million acres (7 million hectares) of formerly idle land. This achievement has been at great cost. In the struggle for land, the Landless Workers Movement has lost more than 1,000 members to violence, more than all those "disappeared" during Brazil's military dictatorship.

As the MST grew, its leadership told us, the movement also evolved its understanding of where solutions lie. "We started out working on access to land," a former nun and now an MST organizer had told us at a member-training seminar deep in the rural heart of the southern Brazilian state of Parana, "but soon we realized that every aspect of life has to be included — health, gender, education, leadership, philosophy . . ."[15]

With members in almost every Brazilian state, the MST has not only settled hundreds of thousands of families in new communities; it has developed educational programs, schools, businesses, health clinics. In the process, the movement has multiplied five-fold the incomes of the formerly landless and drastically reduced infant mortality among its members.[16] With a growing consciousness about the need to ensure sustainability, the movement also created the first organic seed line in Brazil. "It's not just that farming without pesticides means less hazard and lower costs for us," one farmer told us when we asked why they were choosing organic methods. "Why would we go to all this trouble and risk to grow food that's just going to hurt people? We are concerned about the people in the cities, too."[17]

What lessons does the Landless Workers Movement hold for other countries? For countries of the Global South, the lesson is that fair access to land, generated by a strong, vocal civil society, is possible, although far from easy.

For industrialized countries, where farmland is ever-more concentrated in large farms and farmers are increasingly mere contract workers for non-farm corporations, Brazil's example calls us to ask: What would fairness look like here?

We can see the struggle for greater fairness in citizens throughout the United States challenging corporate control of farming. In nine Midwest states, farmers and their allies have initiated and passed laws prohibiting corporations from owning farmland. These states collectively produce over 30 percent of the U.S.A.'s agricultural output, according to the Community Environmental Legal Defense Fund. In Pennsylvania, ten townships passed similar ordinances outlawing corporations from owning farmland. Two have gone even further. They've passed "corporate rights elimination ordinances" which deny corporations constitutional protections of persons, including those in the commerce and contracts clauses of the constitution. Proponents of these ordinances discovered that such restrictions offered the only protection from corporations introducing huge hog-confinement operations, causing serious environmental and health hazards in their communities.[18]

Here, land fairness would also mean a critical review of the contracting system, in which farmers lose decision-making power to corporations. By 2001, these contract farmers made up 36 percent of the total value of all crop and livestock sold in the United States — and nearly *all* poultry production.[19] In these contract arrangements, it is the farmer who shoulders all the debt and all the risk from crop loss or livestock illness.

Moreover, here, fairness might not begin with land redistribution per se, but with a call for remaking a government subsidy system that disproportionately rewards large farms at the expense of small, family-owned ones.

When most people hear "farm subsidies," they imagine our government helping poor, struggling farmers survive, not enhancing the bottom line of our nation's largest corporations. But between 1995 and 2002, 10 percent of the biggest and often most profitable crop producers collected 71 percent of all subsidies, averaging $34,800 in annual payments, while the bottom 80 percent received only $846 on average per year, according to a report from the Environmental Working Group.[20]

In 2002, the U.S. government spent more than $12 billion on farm subsidies, of which nearly $2 billion went to corn producers alone. In other words, our tax dollars are going to big business, worsening the inequality in power over our nation's farming practices and land. These multi-billion-dollar subsidies also help keep the prices for raw material artificially low. This means big savings (effectively subsidies) for ConAgra, Altria (formerly Philip Morris), Cargill, and other agribusiness giants who trade and process the subsidized commodities.

Government agricultural research, moreover, disproportionately goes to industrial farming, not to innovations in sustainable methods. In fact, the Sustainable Agriculture Research and Education program represents less than one half of 1 percent of USDA research and education funding annually.[21]

Imagine the abundance possible if we were to radically redirect research dollars to sustainable practices. Imagine the abundance that could emerge from subsidies helping small farmers stay on the land, protecting natural environments with sustainable practices, and ensuring the health of communities able to consume local foods raised without chemicals, now and for future generations.

Seeding the Future

Land and resource inequality is easy to observe; but control over other vital aspects of food and farming is more challenging to perceive. I think about this when I remember my son's insights more than three decades ago. I had just taken my children, then three and five years old, on a research trip to Guatemala. One day the three of us climbed to the top of a nearby hill and looked out over the town where we were staying. With a child's wisdom, my son Anthony asked: "Why do so few people have all the land and all the other people have to live so close together?"

Land inequality was easy for even a five-year-old to see. Inequality over the control of seed supplies is harder to perceive, but equally as critical. Along with the other most basic natural elements — soil, sun, and water — seeds are essential to farming and food. Since the advent of agriculture more than 10,000 years ago, farmers have been saving and sharing seeds year-to-year. But over the past century a steady stream of laws — primarily in the United States but now going global through world trade agreements — have transferred ownership and control over seeds from farmers to corporations.

Just one hundred years ago *all* crops in the U.S.A. were grown from farmer-bred varieties, according to Hope Shand, research director of the ETC Group, a Canadian-based organization that examines the social and economic impacts of new technologies.[22] At the turn of the ninteenth century, a government program actively encouraged the sharing and saving of farmer varieties. In 1897, at the peak of its seed sharing promotion, the U.S. government gave away 22 million seed packets, Shand reports. The prevailing wisdom was that the more you encourage sharing and experimenting with seeds, the more farmers will breed diverse, high-yielding, healthy crops. In the twentieth century, that very principle was turned on its head.

Late nineteenth-century seed-sharing programs operated from the belief that the more you give, the more abundance you gain. Today's version of a market economy is based on the opposite premise: It assumes that what you give away you lose. During the twentieth century, the scarcity model won; the abundance principle lost.

Starting with the Plant Patent Act of 1930, which allowed the patenting of asexually reproduced crops but excluded food crops, and continuing with the landmark 1970 Plant Variety Protection Act and key amendments in the 1990s, corporations have gained increasing rights over crops and now food crops too, according to Shand.

In 1994 the U.S. Congress passed a critical amendment to the Plant Variety Protection Act, critical because "it amended the Act to restrict the amount of proprietary seed that farmers can save for re-planting and prohibited farmers from selling harvested seed to other farmers," Shand explains. "It was a first step in eroding the principle of farmers' rights in the U.S. legislation, which had previously recognized the farmers' exemption — the right to save and sell proprietary seed."[23] This amendment built on the power given to corporations by the 1985 ruling of the U.S. Patent and Trademark Office, which made utility patents available for plants, bioengineered ones as well as those bred naturally.

Concentration in the industry has also increased in the past several decades. Since 1970, multinational companies have bought or taken control of nearly a thousand, once independent, seed companies.[24] By 2002, Monsanto had spent more than $8 billion acquiring seed and biotech companies. Today, virtually all companies protect their plants with patents, with just one, Monsanto, accounting for virtually all genetically modified soybean seed technology grown in 2000 worldwide,[25] and the top ten seed firms now control nearly one-third of the $24.4 billion commercial seed market.[26]

Shand, and others who study corporate control over seeds, point to a number of dangerous consequences of this dynamic. One is decreasing diversity within the seed gene pool, which in turn makes our food system more vulnerable to disease.[27] Because measuring seed diversity is challenging, estimates vary about the percent of plant species that have disappeared. In one example, the authors of *Shattering: Food, Politics, and the Loss of Genetic Diversity* found that 97 percent of the varieties in a turn-of-the-nineteenth-century list of vegetables from the U.S. Department of Agriculture are now extinct.[28] Possible cross-pollination and other contamination by GMOs further threaten plant as well as wildlife diversity and ecosystem health.

In response to concern about GMOs contaminating the seed-lines of non-GMO plants, the United Nations ratified the Cartagena Protocol on Biosafety in September 2003. It establishes rules governing the introduction and import/export of GMOs, which now make up the majority of certain U.S. crops. Today, 38 percent of corn, 80 percent of soy, 70 percent of cotton, and more than 60 percent of canola in the United States are genetically modified.[29]

Globally, these four crops — soy, cotton, canola, and corn — account for most genetically modified acreage. By 2003, one-quarter of the 672 million acres (272 million hectares) of these crops planted worldwide, or roughly 167 million acres (68 million hectares), was transgenic.[30] But while GMOs continue to spread, the rate of growth has been slowed by citizen concern worldwide, with only six countries growing 99 percent of all genetically modified foods.[31]

In a drive to protect profits derived from patented seeds, some corporations use the legal system to enforce their rights against farmers. They send investigators into communities to ensure that farmers are not illegally saving seeds, suing those farmers who are perceived to be violating the law. According to Shand, Monsanto has filed more than 475 lawsuits against farmers in the U.S.A. for patent infringement and violation of technology user agreements.

Although proponents claim GMOs will help farmers to "feed the hungry world," critics argue that lawsuits such as these, plus a research focus neglecting the crops and seed qualities most used and needed by the poor — such as drought resistance — reveal the real corporate goal: increasing market share and profits, not ending world hunger. In fact, A. F. Leu, the chairman of the Organic Federation of Australia, points out that the latest direction of GMO technology is toward "BioPharm" where plants such as corn, sugarcane, and tobacco "are modified to produce new compounds such as hormones, vaccines, plastics, polymers, and other non-food compounds. All of these developments will mean that less food is grown on some of the world's most productive farmland."[32]

The debate over GMOs reflects the underlying crisis of democracy. For example: even the Food and Agriculture Organization of the United Nations, a public body whose explicit commitment is to end hunger, now spends its precious time cajoling global seed corporations to refocus at least some GMO research on the needs of the poor.[33] It responds to an agenda that's *already* been set — set by a handful of corporate giants. By contrast, an action agenda of the majority of the world's farmers — mostly small, subsistence producers — would likely be quite different. Why not instead direct the $3 billion now going annually to seed biotechnology toward improving water and soil-saving practices? Such a reallocation using local, low-cost materials, along with spreading local seed-breeding and exchange, could free farmers in the developing world from dependence on the corporate giants.

The GMO path was deliberately undertaken in a manner to avoid public deliberation, giving citizens no opportunity to weigh risks and benefits.[34] Yet in 2004, less than a decade after GMOs became widely used, the Union of Concerned Scientists reports that in the U.S.A. "seeds of traditional varieties of corn, soybeans, and canola are pervasively contaminated with low levels of DNA sequences derived from transgenic [GMO] varieties."[35] While no farmers or consumers asked for this technology, we, the public, bear the as-yet unknown health consequences of such genetic contamination, let alone the ecological risk.

What does the control over seeds have to do with hunger and with real abundance? Everything. Almost one and a half billion small farmers in the developing world depend on saved seeds as their primary seed source; these are people whose average income barely creeps above two dollars a day, often not even above one. Imagine what it would mean if these farmers were suddenly required to pay distant corporations for every seed they planted. Imagine what it would mean for these farmers to relinquish centuries-old local agricultural practices for techniques and products developed and controlled by faraway corporations over which they have no say?

We don't need to imagine. We can look to another agricultural revolution and learn from history. Today's "Gene Revolution," after all, is in many ways a reprise of the 1960s Green Revolution, which used technological innovation to increase yields across the developing world. The key to the Green Revolution was the development of high-yield hybrid seeds, or what critics of the technology call "high-responding" because they require extensive application of inputs — including water, fertilizer, and pesticides. Although hybrid seeds produce "heterosis" or hybrid vigor (crossing two genetically distant parent plants creates offspring "superior" in terms of yield), this benefit disappears after the first generation.[36]

In a recent speech, Norman Borlaug, father of the Green Revolution and the 1970 Nobel Peace Prize winner, provided statistics to prove that the Green Revolution doubled, and even trebled, cereal production in some regions of the developing world from 1961 to 2000.[37] But his accompanying PowerPoint slide also showed a *thirty-five-fold increase* in fertilizer use in those same regions and increased reliance on tractors, irrigation, and other expensive technology. Borlaug also failed to mention sinking water tables, salinization, deteriorating topsoil, and farmers displaced from the land. Nor did he mention increasing rates of suicide among farmers facing insurmountable debt and devastating crop loss.

In 2002, when we visited the Punjab, the much-heralded proving ground of this technology, we were struck by the social and ecological devastation. The Green Revolution not only depleted natural resources (soil and water), it also depleted financial ones. Farmers were encouraged to take out loans for costly inputs and to buy expensive farming equipment. Driving along the dusty Punjabi roads, we saw countless abandoned tractors, left to rust by farmers who could no longer make their payments.

In one village, we spoke with a group of more than fifty Sikh farmers. One gestured to the men around him, explaining that almost all his neighbours were deep in debt to the banks, many on the brink of losing everything. "Two years ago, the bollworm [a moth that attacks cotton] and crop failures swept through Andhra Pradesh," Afsar Jafri, a scientist promoting organic cultivation with the Indian activist farmers' network, Navdanya, told us. In one district Jafri researched, pesticide use had increased 2,000 percent in the past three years, but crops still failed. The bollworm had become resistant. The year before, in a nearby village, hundreds of farmers had committed suicide, many by drinking the very pesticides partly responsible for their indebtedness.

The cautionary tale of the Punjab is just one illustration of what can happen when a myopic focus on production blinds us to the systemic effects of a technology. A similar myopia reveals itself in the push for GMOs.

But around the world, citizen organizations are seeking to protect the diversity at the heart of abundance. They want to ensure that small farmers around the globe, dependent on seed saving and sharing, can continue to do what they have done for generations.

We travelled to India to learn about just such an organization: the farmers' network Navdanya, started by internationally

renowned environmental activist and physicist Vandana Shiva
to protect farmers' seed rights, seed diversity, and traditional
practices.

On one of our first nights in the country, we slept on a narrow cot in a bare room with only jars of seeds for company, in
the foothills of the Indian Himalayas. The room was one of
Navdanya's seed-saving hubs.

The next morning, we traveled to Uttirchha, a village of
about eighty families whose white-washed stone homes clung
to the hillsides. As far as we felt from our respective American
homes in New York and Boston, the presence of the industrialized world surprised us. Decisions in far-off boardrooms and
distant courtrooms directly affected the villagers, who were
celebrating a recent win in the European patent offices. W. R.
Grace, along with the U.S. Department of Agriculture, had
taken out a patent on the Indian neem tree. Navdanya, along
with several other international groups, had filed suit, arguing
that the patent unfairly claimed "ownership" of knowledge
that had been developed over centuries by Indian farmers and
healers. Navdanya helped bring a delegation to the hearings to
deliver a protest petition with half a million signatures. In a
rare win, the patent office overturned that patent, stating
"claims were not novel in view of prior use, which had taken
place in India."[38]

Navdanya is also encouraging villagers to be proactive in
protecting their biological heritage. The morning that we sat
with village elders in Uttirchha, they showed us their community
biodiversity registry, a creative strategy to create "community intellectual rights" that would have comparable legal standing to corporate intellectual property rights. Their registry was

an oversized hand-bound book with sample specimens of plants. Each page included details about a specimen's uses — medicinal, edible, or both. The village elder, Darshan Lal Chowary, told us: "We'll have more than one thousand plants in here before we're finished. Now, no one can come into our community and claim a patent on these plants and tell us they've discovered the plant's uses. Anyone who wants this will have to get our permission first."[39]

Navdanya and farmers' rights organizations around the world are working to ensure that community intellectual rights can stand up in international courts and be recognized by such councils as the World Trade Organization. In 1994, for instance, the Third World Network developed the Community Intellectual Rights Act, "to establish a *sui generis* system for the protection of the innovations and the intellectual knowledge of local communities."[40] Navdanya's work builds on this legal language.

Navdanya is also active on the ground, providing technical assistance to promote traditional seed sharing and saving. We visited the community seed bank at the Navdanya organic demonstration farm, housed on Dr. Shiva's family homestead near Dehra Dun, India. We drove out down narrowing dirt roads from the city whose population has exploded since Dr. Shiva was a child. It wasn't harvest season so the fields were dormant, but the farmers led us into large rooms filled with jars and bushels of seeds. The floors were covered with tarps layered with thousands of seeds, waiting to be dried, labeled, and preserved in their own containers. Along with their work on the farm, Navdanya members travel to nearby villages, teaching organic farming principles, and gathering more seed savers — and sharers — for the network.

Navdanya is actively involved in promoting organic farm-ing, not only in the region near Dehra Dun but across the coun-try. In the Punjab, we heard the painful stories of farmers who had bought the Green Revolution promise. Navdanya trainers tried to convince many to try organic practices — a hard sell for those desperate for a quick fix. Shortly after we returned from our trip, though, Afsar Jafri, wrote to tell us that more than one hundred farmers in the village we visited had begun using Navdanya's traditional wheat varieties and organic prac-tices. Though yields were roughly half to three-quarters what they had produced with Green Revolution varieties, the farmers were faring much better. Their cost of production without chemicals was *one-quarter* what it had been.[41]

Wider surveys of sustainable techniques show even more promise. In the world's largest study of sustainable agriculture, researchers from the University of Essex in England analyzed more than 200 projects in 52 countries, covering 70 million acres (28 million hectares) and involving nearly 9 million farmers. The research indicated that crop yields increased on average 73 percent under sustainable methods, and concluded that "sustainable practices can lead to substantial increases in per hectare food production."[42] In cases where yields per acre of cereals had not increased, substantial improvement still occurred in "domestic food consumption or increasing local food barters or sales through biointensive gardens, or better water management."[43]

The projects the researchers analyzed were not just iso-lated, small communities. They included 223,000 farmers in southern Brazil using "green manures and cover crop, dou-bling their yields of maize and wheat" — and, as well, 200,000 farmers in Kenya, 45,000 in Guatemala and Honduras, 100,000 in Mexico, and more than one million wetland rice farmers in Bangladesh, China, India, Indonesia, Malaysia, Philippines, Sri Lanka, Thailand, and Vietnam.

Navdanya's work is part of this growing international movement promoting sustainable practices, seed sharing, and community intellectual property rights. Their efforts remind us that supporting community rights over seeds is a critical way to ensure abundance now, and in the future. Many of these efforts are connected through Via Campesina, an international co-ordinating body, bringing together peasant organizations, small and middle-scale producers, and indigenous communities in Europe, Northeast and Southeast Asia, South Asia, North America, the Caribbean, Central America, and South America, and Africa.

Show Me the Money

Another essential ingredient for creating abundance — often ignored, if obvious — is income for producers. Not income for ADM or Novartis or Monsanto, but for small family-farmers living on the land.

Economist and Nobel laureate Amartya Sen wisely notes that falling prices to farmers depress production; yet, while we've seen precisely that trend over the past several decades, little has been done on an international level to respond. Since the 1950s, real prices for grain have shrunk by two-thirds. Some commodities, like coffee, recently fetched their lowest price in history. On average, all commodities, save fuel, now bring farmers less than half as much as they did thirty years ago.[44]

Sitting with a coffee-farmer near Nairobi, Kenya, a few years ago we learned firsthand what these abstract figures can mean. Farmer Mumo Musyoka had to work all year for her coffee harvest; yet after subtracting payments for inputs and the middlemen, coffee prices were so low that she came out with zero income. And, as she told us, if you don't make any money on your coffee yield, "you can't eat your crop."

So it would seem obvious that a critical component of increasing production — and particularly *sustainable* production — is to ensure that small farmers get a fair price for their work. Instead, unfair prices within an unfair trade system is the norm.

The coffee trade is one of the best examples. Coffee is the second most valuable commodity in the world after oil, but low world prices have left 25 million small farmers in fifty countries in dire poverty.[45]

Coffee prices hit their lowest levels in part due to political decisions that date back to the late 1980s when the U.S.A., under the Reagan administration, pulled out of the International Coffee Agreement. Without this system, which had helped to stabilize prices and production, prices plummeted and production skyrocketed as farmers struggled to make up in volume what they were losing in price. This of course pushed prices down even further.

The result was tens of thousands of displaced farm families. The tragedy triggered the birth of a movement to create a coffee trading system based on fair, not exploitative, prices.

Seventy percent of the world's coffee is grown by small family farmers, who often have no choice but to sell to middlemen who pay as little as 25 cents per pound (55 cents per kilogram). With fair trade, farmers are ensured $1.26 per pound ($2.78 per kilogram) and slightly more, $1.41 ($3.11 per kilogram), for organic (still much less than we pay here). When the world price rises above that floor, farmers get paid more.

Since 1999, TransFair USA, a California-based non-profit organization, has been certifying fair trade products to sell in the United States, and business is booming. TransFair USA–certified coffee almost doubled in 2003 compared to the previous year, jumping from 9.8 to 18.7 million pounds (from 4.4 to 8.5 million kilograms). The fair trade movement is now expanding beyond its coffee programs, certifying not only coffee but cocoa, tea, and bananas, and — starting this year — mangoes, pineapples, grapes, and bananas. Across the globe, these fair trade efforts are benefiting more than one million family farmers in forty-five countries in Latin America, Africa, Asia, and Europe.[46]

Fair trade also has positive ripple effects on the environment — and for future abundance. Small coffee-farmers are some of the best stewards of the land, many still growing coffee in traditional ways, under the shade of forest overhang and without chemicals. "Fair Trade supports some of the most biodiverse farming systems in the world," according to leading expert on agroecology, UC Berkeley Professor Miguel Altieri.

Today, the fair trade movement is a rapidly growing international network with enormous potential for continuing to transform the health and well-being of communities worldwide.

Rethinking Abundance

We were asked to contribute a chapter about solutions to hunger, about how we might best realize abundance. At first, we began trolling through studies showing that organic, biodynamic small- and medium-sized farms could compete with the production levels of large-scale industrialized North American farms. We started pulling together research that revealed the hidden costs of industrial agriculture — the polluted waterways, air, and soil — costs not accounted for in production totals. Our initial instinct was to show how, acre-by-acre, sustainable farming systems outdo industrial ones.

The evidence wasn't that hard to find. As we've noted, studies are proving that sustainable approaches can produce comparable and even higher yields than the chemical model.[47]

But while a snapshot, yields-per-acre analysis is one way to measure productivity, another is to look at the productivity of the land over time. Here, sustainable agriculture beats industrial farming hands down. One of the fundamentals of sustainable agriculture is the understanding that the soil is alive — and healthy soil is the cornerstone of productive farming — quite the opposite to industrial, extractive farming where soil fertility is something to be created with the right combination of chemical inputs.

More and more research on sustainable practices informs us that accessible, low-tech, sustainable solutions produce comparable yields to industrial agriculture. They also best meet the needs of third-world farmers. Jules Pretty, lead researcher in the University of Essex report, explains: "Above all [sustainable practices using cheap, locally available technology] most help the people who need help the most — poor farmers and their families, who make up the majority of the world's hungry people."[48]

This premise — that there is enough, that third-world farmers can feed themselves — forces us to ask the harder questions about what elements of our social, economic, and international trading systems create hunger amidst plenty? What is democracy if it is not about each person having a voice to secure lives and their share of the future?

Asking these questions, in turn, forces us to talk about power, including the power over land, seeds, income, and trade, which determines who does and does not eat on this abundant planet. It forces us to acknowledge how we ourselves create scarcity from plenty.

Turning aside from these deeper questions, GMO and extractive, industrial agriculture promoters foment the fear of famine — a fear that blinds us to the solutions at hand.

That was exactly the aim of the alarming headline from the article tacked to the bulletin board in that deserted UC Berkeley hallway. Such fear promotion, diverting us from real causes and real solutions, seems to be everywhere. Consider President George W. Bush's comments in 2003 at a biotechnology conference: "We should encourage the spread of safe effective biotechnology to win the fight against global hunger."[49]

Either risk untested technology or face famine — we must remind ourselves what we need *not* fear. There is enough food to feed the world. There is enough. Repeat it twice.

Fear is a funny thing. When we feel it, we look for quick answers, sure bets, fast fixes. Feeling fear, it's easy to get tunnel vision; it's harder to hear nuanced arguments. But we need not let the fear-mongers set up shop in our minds. Instead, we can stay open to the complexity of hunger's roots.

As important as production levels are in measuring success, other indicators might fall off our mental map if we're not careful. We can measure true abundance, for example, in whether all human beings have access to healthy food. To achieve such abundance, we can rethink and remake control over land, seeds, and trade, as the ingenious social movements we've described here — from the Landless Workers Movement to the Navdanya movement to the fair trade movement — are doing. Refusing to succumb to the scarcity scare, these movements help us to understand the relationship between democracy — in its richer, more participatory forms — and the creation of sustainable abundance.

OVERFEEDING THE FUTURE

Kelly Brownell

Consider the following:

1) In its peak year, the primary U.S. government nutrition education program (called 5 a Day) was given $3 million for promotion. The food industry spends one thousand times that much to advertise fast foods, just to children.
2) The most recognized corporate logo in China, aside from those of Chinese companies, is KFC's.
3) Ronald McDonald is the second most recognized figure in the world, next to Santa Claus.
4) Creating major news in September of 2002, McDonald's announced that by February 2003 it would change the oil used for its fried products to decrease (but not eliminate) trans fats. McDonald's President Mike Roberts spoke of a "healthier nutrition profile" in heralding the company's concern for public health, and the CEO lauded his company for being a "leader in social responsibility." In February of

2003, the company quietly announced a change in plans (there would be a "delay"). The delay is still in effect.

5) Kraft Foods announced in 2003 it would cut portion sizes of some products to "help arrest the rise in obesity." Less than a year later, Kraft announced this plan had been scrapped.

6) Promoters to the juvenile market have declared the cell phone their next horizon, noting that tens of millions of children power up a cell phone at the same time each day (after school). Satellite technology allows marketers to know a child's precise location, and enables them to beam advertisements, coupons, and directions to nearby eating establishments.

7) The Food Guide Pyramid created by the U.S. Department of Agriculture (USDA) recommends that meat, poultry, fish, and eggs comprise 14 percent of the diet, yet 52 percent of USDA food-promotion resources are allocated to these foods. The pyramid recommends 33 percent of the diet from fruits and vegetables, but they receive 5 percent of the USDA budget. The meat and dairy industries "outlobby" the fruit and vegetable sectors by orders of magnitude.

This list could include thousands more. Stampeding technology, corporate interests, authorities caught unaware, and the market stigmatization of overweight people (which emphasizes personal over corporate responsibility) have created an environment that guarantees poor diet, physical inactivity, and obesity. The world now faces a crisis of overfeeding.

Until recently, a book on feeding the future would have focused solely on the need to feed the world's population. Without a doubt, hunger is still a major issue, but it will soon be surpassed in many countries by overconsumption as the leading public health nutrition issue. In countries not traditionally considered prone to obesity, such as Mexico, Brazil, Morocco, Thailand, and China, hunger and obesity coexist. The World Health Organization (WHO) has declared obesity a global epidemic, increasing in every country throughout the world.

Words like "crisis," "epidemic," and "global emergency" used to describe a public health problem evoke a predictable backlash of blame on those affected by obesity. Such has been the case with AIDS, tobacco, drug abuse, and other problems. Business interests are commonly pitted against public health, and there are calls for change focusing either on the individual or broad social factors. Food must now be considered in a similar light.

The world faces important questions about what and how we eat. Who is responsible for increasing rates of obesity? What are the causes? What are the relative contributions of poor diet and physical inactivity? Can the food industry be trusted? Must children be protected from a "toxic" environment? What must change?

In this chapter I focus on the causes and consequences of overfeeding the world, and, most importantly, on some solutions.

Our Big Food Problem

The most visible consequence of poor diet and physical inactivity, obesity involves a cascade of other medical, social, and psychological issues. The explosion of media coverage has brought attention to this significant problem, but its downside implies that obesity is the only consequence of modern living. In fact, poor diet and sedentary lifestyle are risk factors for many major chronic diseases independent of a person's weight. For example, children in affluent countries frequently show detectable signs of heart disease, regardless of weight.[1] For the first time in North American history, experts have asked whether children will lead shorter lives than their parents.

Throughout the 1980s and 1990s, paper after paper in the scientific literature showed that obesity is increasing around the world. Rates are burgeoning in industrialized countries (the U.S.A., Canada, Britain, Australia, and so on), in particularly wealthy countries such as Saudi Arabia, but also in little-known island nations and developing counties. Clinics for the treatment of obese children opened in Beijing, where only decades ago malnutrition was the most serious problem.

In 1998, the WHO released a report declaring obesity a global epidemic. Since then, the organization has been at the forefront in raising global awareness, documenting rising weights in country after country and highlighting the associated disease burden.[2] The WHO has also proposed proactive solutions, as we will see later.[3]

Related to many of the leading causes of death, obesity is also involved in problems such as sleep disturbance, pain, and arthritis that can affect quality of life (see Table 1). The risk of coronary heart disease increases nearly 60 percent in men and 179 percent in women, and risk for diabetes increases five-fold for men and eight-fold in women as weight increases from normal to very obese. The poor diet and inactivity causing obesity contribute independently to many of the same outcomes. Rand Corporation economist Roland Sturm has shown that obesity's health effects now surpass those of smoking, and that it carries the same risk as aging two decades.[4]

Since poor diet and inactivity can affect health, they are likely to have other powerful impacts. Lost productivity, a less alert work force, and declining school grades are some. It is

well documented that poor diet affects cognitive and intellectual performance in undernourished children, and the same
could well occur in the case of overnutrition.

Researchers estimate obesity-related health care costs in
the U.S.A. alone to be $75 billion, with taxpayers financing
about half these costs through Medicare and Medicaid.[5] In a
study of 200,000 employees of General Motors, researchers
estimated that obese individuals incur up to $1,500 more in
health care costs per year compared to normal-weight peers.[6]

Table 1
Medical Conditions Associated with Obesity[7]

Birth Defects	Impaired Respiratory
Breast Cancer	Function
Cancer of Esophagus	Infections Following Wounds
and Gastric Cardia	Infertility
Colorectal Cancer	Liver Disease
Cardiovascular Disease	Low Back Pain
Carpal Tunnel Syndrome	Obstetric and Gynecologic
Chronic Venous Insufficiency	Complications
Daytime Sleepiness	Osteoarthritis
Deep Vein Thrombosis	Pain Pancreatitis
Diabetes (Type 2)	Renal Cell Cancer
End Stage Renal Disease	Rheumatoid Arthritis
Gallbladder Disease	Sleep Apnea
Gout	Stroke
Heat Disorders	Surgical Complications
Hypertension	Urinary Stress Incontinence
Impaired Immune Response	

Not So Obvious Consequences

Obese individuals incur severe social stigmas. They include a phalanx of negative characteristics such as laziness and lack of motivation, and also charges of core personality and integrity defects (being stupid, dishonest, dirty, and more). An imperfect body reflects an imperfect personality, so the thinking goes, hence bias and discrimination can be justified by the old adage that people get what they deserve and deserve what they get. These attributions result from cultural norms in which obesity is repulsive, that link social status with physical attractiveness, and construct weight as a matter of personal control. Research clearly shows that overweight people are targets of discrimination in areas central to health and happiness (employment, housing, income, and health care).[8]

Given the prevalence of obesity, it is natural to ask whether a more overweight population would lead to less bias. In a 1961 study, a group of researchers showed children line-drawings of children who were obese or had a variety of physical disfigurements.[9] The majority ranked the obese child as the one they would least like to have as a friend. Latner and Stunkard repeated the study (in 2003) and found even stronger bias against the overweight child.[10] Weight stigma is very difficult to shake.

If bias and discrimination affect the happiness and well-being of stigmatized groups, they affect health. The experience of bias may affect health directly, say, by influencing risk factors such as blood pressure, lipids, or immune function. Bias can also exert influence through psychological factors (such as vulnerability to depression), which in turn influence health or it can alter a person's experience with the health care system.

There are studies showing that overweight individuals are less likely to obtain preventive care, perhaps due to shame from interacting with providers and fear of negative comments.

Combining the more and less obvious consequences of unhealthy eating with sedentary lifestyle and obesity, we see problems that cannot be ignored. Tremendous human suffering is occurring. Young adults in their twenties and thirties now suffer from complications of Type 2 diabetes (formerly called adult onset diabetes), which begins before the age of ten. Some are blind, some have limbs amputated, and some have died.

In other words, overfeeding the world is a crisis by any standard — one that demands aggressive, innovative action. How to take action depends in great part on how nations construe the causes.

How the World Gained So Much So Fast

The world is increasingly exposed to what I have labelled a "toxic environment," in which food and agriculture companies produce too many calories, particularly in meat and highly processed foods. Food has become artificially inexpensive and is engineered to maximize taste. Reasonable at first glance, this exacts a tragic price on both health and the environment. The U.S.A., Canada, Britain, and Australia exemplify these negative conditions, but nearly every country is following suit.

Eating is influenced by a number of factors, the most powerful being accessibility, convenience, promotion, taste, and cost (see Table 2). Each has been distorted in ways that encourage unhealthy eating.

Table 2
Primary Factors That Affect Human Eating[11]

Unhealthy Foods	Healthy Foods
Highly accessible	Less accessible
Convenient	Less convenient
Promoted heavily	Barely promoted
Good-tasting	Less tasty
Cheap	More expensive

THE MULTIPLE-CAUSES DISTRACTION

It is standard to say that obesity has multiple causes — to cite biology, psychology, and the environment as contributors. This explains everything and nothing at the same time. Of course obesity has multiple causes — everything does, but not all causes are equal. Much depends on whether we look for causes in individuals or in larger groups like a country or even the world.

Conceptualizing the cause of obesity for an individual necessitates understanding a variety of factors, including biology, a person's upbringing, psychology, and socio-economic status. But when one looks to population increases in obesity, we ask, for example, why Japan has more obesity this year than last, why some nations are heavier than others, why an entire population is vulnerable to changing diets, and what might be done to reduce the problem. From this point of view, there is a clear explanation for rampant obesity — the environment has become fattening or "obesigenic."

Because so many people are overweight, we can infer that most individuals have a "willing" biological profile that fosters high energy intake and the efficient storage of energy as body fat. The environment, however, causes energy intake to rise and calorific expenditure to decline. High levels of obesity in developed countries, and low levels in poor countries, cannot be explained by population genetics, particularly considering studies documenting weight gain as a predictable consequence of moving from a country with little obesity to another with more.

In the absence of a fattening environment, few people will become overweight. Obesity occurs as the environment promotes unhealthy eating and inactivity. The cause is the environment, and the environment in a growing number of countries is an ideal recipe for fattening the population.

GLOBAL CHANGES AND THE NUTRITION TRANSITION

Barry Popkin and his colleagues have done the most careful and extensive work on the "nutrition transition" that occurs as nations modernize.[12] He and colleagues define five patterns that characterize this transition:

Pattern 1: Collecting Food. Food comes from hunting and gathering. The diet is high in carbohydrates and fibre and low in fat. Activity levels are high and there is little obesity.

Pattern 2: Famine. Diet is less varied, scarcity occurs, and malnutrition is common. Obesity is rare.

Pattern 3: Receding Famine. Consumption of fruit, vegetables, and animal protein increases, as do inactivity and leisure time.

Pattern 4: Nutrition-Related Non-Communicable Disease. The diet is high in fat, cholesterol, sugar and other refined carbohydrates, and low in polyunsaturated fat and fibre. Sedentary behaviour increases. Obesity increases as does chronic disease.

Pattern 5: Behavioural Change. The desire to prevent disease leads to changes in diet and physical activity, sometimes self-driven by consumers and other times stimulated by government action.

Popkin notes that many countries are in Patterns 3 and 4. Developing nations in particular are transitioning from receding famine to energy-dense diets and declining physical activity. A good example is China, where in the 1970s 10 percent of calories came from fat. Now one-third of families eat a diet with more than 30 percent of calories from fat, the number of televisions has risen dramatically, and the number of jobs requiring physical labour is decreasing. Popkin notes that in countries like China, with rapid advances from food shortages to a healthier diet, the line is quickly crossed where eating too much, and corresponding weight gain, become key concerns.[13]

WILLINGNESS TO DAMAGE THE ENVIRONMENT

As you might expect, supporting the growing calorie-needs of a world gaining weight requires more food. This issue is particularly acute when one considers that highly processed foods and certain meats are particularly resource intensive. To get the staggering amounts of cheap food the world consumes, the food system must be structured for mass production. To fully understand the obesity crisis, one must look at how food is produced. This is what Michael Pollan did in an important article published in 2002.[14]

Pollan, a well-known food and agriculture writer, bought a cow that was raised for beef. He followed the cow from farm to fork, in order to document exactly this part of the food chain. Pollan considered the amount of energy used to raise the cow, compared to the energy the cow would later introduce into the food supply. One analysis is that fully 283 gallons (1,071 litres) of oil are used to bring a 1,250-pound (570-kilogram) steer to your table.

Most of us are not aware of the considerable energy from fossil fuels required to create hamburger or steak. Energy is needed to produce the fertilizers and pesticides applied to feed-grain and corn; for the hormones injected into the cow to optimize its growth; to truck the meat to distant markets, and to keep it refrigerated. Also relevant is the environmental damage (such as the 12,000-square-mile (31,000-square-kilometre) "dead zone" in the Gulf of Mexico from nitrogen and pesticide runoff into the Mississippi River), pollution created from shipping, and depletion of the world's energy supplies. In Pollan's words, "We have succeeded in industrializing the beef calf, transforming what was once a solar-powered ruminant into the very last thing we need: another fossil-fuel machine."

The energy quotient of Pollan's cow can be supported by many different examples. An estimated 2,200 kcal of energy are needed to produce a 1-kcal can of Diet Coke. In parts of India, public outcry has denied water licences to Coca Cola and Pepsi, where they have significantly affected groundwater resources to the point of producing shortages for local residents.[15] Table 3 shows estimates of the environmental impact of food production.

Table 3

**Percentage of U.S. Environmental Impact Attributable
to Food Production[16]**

Climate Change: Greenhouse Gases	12%
Air Pollution: Common	17%
Air Pollution: Toxic	9%
Water Pollution: Common	38%
Water Pollution: Toxic	22%
Habitat Alteration: Water	73%
Habitat Alteration: Land	45%

One could argue that overconsumption occurs where food and agriculture industries exploit the environment to maximize production, and governments fail to intervene.

Food subsidies are another little-known factor allowing high consumption at low consumer-cost. Raising the 1,250-pound steer requires a great deal of feed, and most cattle in North America are raised on grain and then on corn. Corn can be an expensive crop, but the U.S. government subsidizes the farmers, making certain the price of corn remains artificially low, which in turn allows the fast food restaurant to sell you a "supersized" beef patty for a startlingly low price. And then what happens? Consumption of beef and similar products escalates.

The same dynamic helps sell soft drinks. Many soft drinks are sweetened with high fructose corn syrup, which again comes from subsidized corn crops. It costs companies like Coca-Cola and Pepsi little to sweeten a litre of water and sell it for a few dollars. This allows companies to increase portions at virtually no cost, again making overconsumption more likely.

THE KEY DETERMINANTS OF EATING

Table 2 shows so much the reverse of what is needed that one could say the food system is totally backward.

Unhealthy food is ubiquitous. The proliferation of vending machines, fast-food restaurants, convenience stores, and eating opportunities in gas stations, shopping malls, and drug stores, makes food everywhere available around the clock. Long gone are school days when children ate only during lunch periods, when highway rest stops were not oriented around fast food, and when snacks were not designed for automobile cup-holders. High-calorie foods are available from drive-through windows, in microwaveable containers, and carry-out packages. Hurried lifestyles increase the value of convenience, particularly for second-income families. Unhealthy foods far outnumber healthy foods.

Most troubling is the massive promotion of unhealthy foods directed at children. The typical American child sees 10,000 TV advertisements per year, mostly for soft drinks, fast foods, candy, sugared cereals, and snack foods. Children at all ages (even very young children) are affected in ways that health experts deplore — hence the repeated, and repeatedly ignored, calls for regulation.[17] Leading sports stars, cartoon characters, and music celebrities continue to promote unhealthy foods.

Product placements in movies and video games, virtual product placements in reruns of television shows, television food promotions in schools (for example, Channel One, the education channel, now runs in 12,000 U.S. schools), vending machines in schools (which lend themselves to advertising), all these — and more — add to the commercial bombardment. Children receive a great deal of nutritional "instruction," most of it delivered by a food industry that has strong incentives to maximize children's consumption of unhealthy foods.

Taste is a key determinant of human eating. In general, foods high in sugar, fat, or both, taste good. Such foods tend to thwart any regulatory system the body may have, so that weight gain occurs. Our ancestors ate as much energy-dense foods as they could. Their dietary pattern enabled them both to survive periods of scarcity and thus contribute to the gene pool. This once-adaptive tendency is now mismatched to modern conditions of abundance.

Cost is another important cause of obesity, especially for poorer individuals. Studies show that a market basket of healthy foods costs more than a basket of unhealthy foods. People in some neighbourhoods do not have access to supermarkets, and therefore pay a premium in small markets, even in the rare cases when the markets carry items like fresh fruits and vegetables.

Consider pricing incentives. Fast-food restaurants have package ("value-added") meals that offer the customer more when foods are grouped together. Larger or "supersized" drinks and fries are retailed at an apparently slighter additional cost. The concept of more product for less money isn't inherently bad, but it is applied almost exclusively to unhealthy foods. If one buys six oranges rather than three, the price per orange does not decline.

Pricing incentives for larger portion sizes create a real problem. Value can be added to the consumer by offering the same amount of food for a lower price, or by increasing the amount for smaller price increases. The latter approach maximizes producer profits. Big portions, highly desirable for the industry, redefine a reasonable serving. The current small serving of fries at fast-food restaurants was once the large size; soft drinks, once in 8-oz. (237-ml) bottles, are now in 12-oz. (355-ml) and 20-oz. (591-ml) servings; and a muffin, once the size of a baseball, is now softball size.

Paul Rozin and others have made a cultural comparison of serving sizes in the United States and France.[18] The French serve smaller portions of attractively presented and nicely prepared foods than Americans. French meals (even at fast-food restaurants) are eaten slowly, and their amount is not enough for leftovers. (The "doggie bag" is unknown in much of the world.)

Research by Barbara Rolls and others shows that people served more food eat more.[19] Consumers are drawn to large portions, and the food industry exploits this by attaching words like "super," "mega," and "extreme" to their foods. Thus the same hype plays out over and over: the consumer who buys more food, consumes more. And the companies maximize profits from selling larger portions. A fast-food patron may happily pay 39 cents to "upsize" to the largest size of fries and drink, and the bargain is struck. The incremental cost to the company is small, and it also seems minimal to the consumer. But excessive calorific intake can be the consequence.

These powerful and unrelenting factors encourage unhealthy eating. It occurs partly because of the food industry's marketing practices, which are woven into economics, technology, and the fabric of modern life. To identify the threads, to reverse the troubling situation we now face, which has already had a profound global impact, environmentally and individually, will require nothing short of aggressive action.

Can the Food Industry Be Trusted?

In *Food Politics*, Marion Nestle documents how profoundly
the food industry has influenced legislation, regulation, and
public policy related to nutrition.[20] Her examples include the
industry's undue influence in establishing the U.S. Food
Guide Pyramid, and in blocking attempts to regulate food
advertising directed at children. Food and agriculture companies demand that governments act in their interest, and that
politicians grant their wishes.[21] Nonetheless, agribusiness
claims it can be trusted, and that the obesity problem will not
be solved without industry involvement. The language of
cooperation and "involvement of stakeholders" is used to justify this stance.

The food industry is no monolith. Generalizations cannot
apply to all players. Organic tomato growers, supermarkets
now specializing in organic, natural, "whole" foods, Girl
Scouts selling cookies — these are part of its diversity. But the
industry does include massive companies like Kraft (large
enough to own Nabisco), McDonald's, PepsiCo (large enough
to own Frito-Lay), and Coca-Cola. To complicate matters,
companies that sell unhealthy products nearly always sell
healthier ones as well, so it can be difficult to separate the
good from the bad. McDonald's, for example, has yogurt and
salads on its menu. Yet, as we have seen, it has indefinitely
delayed in coming through on its promise to change cooking
oils. And it has a massive budget to promote energy-dense
foods to children.

Some food companies devote considerable resources to
publicizing healthier new products, hoping perhaps to escape
the tidal wave of unhealthy food marketing. Creating the
appearance of corporate social responsibility is now a priority,

but whether appearance is matched by substance is yet to be determined. As the food industry faces new challenges, we can revisit important lessons learned from the deadly history of another industry, tobacco.

Tobacco companies asked for the same privileges food companies now demand, namely, that their promotions be taken at face value. Tobacco companies, like the food industry, claimed concern for public health, pledged cooperation with the government and health authorities, introduced filtered cigarettes they claimed were better for consumers, and assured the public they had the best interests of children at heart. These tactics were accepted by government authorities for years, with tragic consequences. The food industry, which also asks to be trusted, makes many of the same arguments as did tobacco companies almost to the word.

In *A Question of Intent*, David Kessler, former Commissioner of the U.S. Food and Drug Administration, wrote "Devised in the 1950s and '60s, the tobacco industry's strategy was embodied in a script written by the lawyers. Every tobacco company executive in the public eye was told to learn the script backwards and forwards, no deviation was allowed. The basic premise was simple — smoking had not been proved to cause cancer. Not proven, not proven, not proven — this would be stated insistently and repeatedly. Inject a thin wedge of doubt, create controversy, never deviate from the prepared line. It was a simple plan and it worked."[22] The script was written and performed by lobbyists, public relations firms hired by the industry, scientists paid by the industry, members of Congress financed by the industry, the main industry trade association (Tobacco Institute), and of course company executives themselves.

THE FOOD INDUSTRY PLAYBOOK

How does the food business resemble tobacco? In a paper I wrote with Kenneth Warner, examining tobacco and food industry responses to health crises, we noted striking similarities in the scripts (playbook) used by the food and tobacco industries to still public concern and stall or prevent policies that would hurt business.[23] The fact the food industry has a script is indisputable. Trade associations, some of the same public relations and advertising agencies formerly used by tobacco, scientists funded by the industry, and of course company spokespersons — all have their parts in the playbook. The key features are as follows:

- Introduce products perceived to be healthier.
- Publicize corporate social responsibility.
- Fund programs focusing on physical activity.
- Claim that lack of personal responsibility is at the heart of the population's unhealthy diet.
- Plead that personal freedom is at stake, hence government should not contemplate regulation or legislation.
- Vilify critics with totalitarian language, characterizing them as the food police, leaders of a nanny state, even "food fascists," and accuse them of desires to strip people of civil liberties.
- Emphasize physical activity over diet.
- State there are no good or bad foods, hence no food or food type (soft drinks, fast foods, and so on) should be targeted for change.
- Dispute the science to plant doubt.

The first three items in the playbook may have positive consequences, but vigilance is in order. The industry often introduces products that are made to sound healthy. Examples are snacks and drinks with "fruit" in the name. Cynicism about corporate social responsibility is also natural, given the tobacco experience. In 2000, Philip Morris spent $115 million on social causes such as the arts, helping flood victims, and supporting shelters for abuse victims. The company spent $150 million publicizing these acts. The remaining six parts of the script are likely to have negative consequences.

The food industry notes that food is different from tobacco, in that people have to eat. Hence, the argument goes, big food can profit as much if people eat healthier foods. In their attempts to alleviate controversy, industry insiders argue that we are all on the same side. This argument can be challenged on several grounds. A move by the public toward healthier foods means lower sales of foods with high profit margins (highly processed convenience foods). But the stark reality is more important: the only way the population can lose weight is if food intake goes down (and activity increases), hence less food must be sold overall. This places the industry squarely at odds with public health priorities.

Given these factors, the world must assess whether food companies can be trusted. It must also decide whether the industry should be included or excluded from policy decisions. But there are other ways of establishing an industry's trustworthiness. One is to examine the use or misuse of science.

INDUSTRY (AND GOVERNMENT) DISPUTING SCIENCE

A robust literature currently exists on the impact of food advertising directed at children. In the U.S.A. alone, children under twelve spend $35 billion a year on their own, and influence another $200 billion of household spending.[24] A number of scientists and authoritative organizations have examined the available science, reaching a remarkable consensus.

For example, the World Health Organization concludes that ". . . marketing affects food choice and influences dietary habits, with subsequent implications for weight gain and obesity."[25] The American Psychological Association concurs: "Such advertising efforts, in our view, are fundamentally unfair because of young children's limited comprehension of the nature and purpose of television advertising, and therefore warrant government action to protect young children from commercial exploitation."[26]

The American Academy of Pediatrics has issued this position statement: "Advertising and promotion of energy-dense, nutrient-poor food products to children may need to be regulated or curtailed."[27] In a comprehensive report, the Kaiser Family Foundation reached a similar conclusion: ". . . it appears likely that the main mechanism by which media use contributes to childhood obesity may well be through children's exposure to billions of dollars of food advertising and cross-promotional marketing year after year, starting at the youngest ages, with children's favorite media characters often enlisted in the sales pitch."[28]

In an excellent review article, Mary Story and Simone French conclude, "The research evidence is strong showing that preschoolers' and grade school children's food preferences and food purchase requests for high sugar and high fat foods are influenced by television exposure to food advertising. . . . The heavy marketing of high fat, high sugar foods to this age group [< age 8] can be viewed as exploitative because young children do not understand that commercials are designed to sell products."[29]

These statements, based on considerable science, paint a clear picture. Contrast the industry's position, exemplified by William McLeod, representative of the Grocery Manufacturers of America (the world's largest food industry lobbying group), in response to questions about the damaging effects of advertising to children raised by the Kaiser Family Foundation report: "There is very little evidence that we have seen. As a matter of fact, I think the conclusions in the report we've heard today indicate that the jury is still out." McLeod added, "The evidence that is not in these studies and the evidence that I don't think we are ever going to see is that advertising is telling kids or encouraging kids to eat too much or exercise too little."[30]

Here is another food industry spokesperson on the issue. When asked, "What, if any, is the relationship between marketing and obesity?" Shelley Rosen, speaking for McDonald's, said, "There is no connection." And, "When you ask if obesity is a marketing and communications issue, the answer is no."[31]

The science on soft drink consumption, calorie intake, and body weight reveals a similar pattern. Here, the considerable literature ranges from laboratory studies with animals to large-scale human epidemiology studies. First, let's look at the conclusions from scientists. A research paper by David Ludwig and colleagues on soft drinks and childhood obesity concluded, "Consumption of sugar-sweetened drinks is associated with obesity in children."[32] George Bray, Samara Nielsen, and Barry Popkin, who conducted research on obesity and high fructose corn syrup (HFCS) in beverages, concluded, "It is becoming increasingly clear that soft drink consumption may be an important contributor to the epidemic of obesity, in part through the larger portion sizes of those beverages and from the increased intake of fructose from HFCS and sucrose."[33]

In yet another research paper, Samara Nielsen and Barry Popkin looked at changes in beverage consumptions: ". . . soft drink consumption is rising and is a significant contributor to total caloric intake for many individuals, especially children and adolescents." Further to the point, "This would seem to be one of the simpler ways to reduce obesity in the United States."[34]

Now for the soft drink industry position, as stated by the industry's trade association. According to the National Soft Drink Association, "Soft drink consumption by children is not linked to pediatric obesity, poor diet quality, or a lack of exercise."[35] Sean McBride, the spokesperson of the National Soft Drink Association, was asked to respond to schools' eliminating soft drinks. Employing the familiar diversion tactic of physical activity, he stated that obesity "is about the couch and not the can."[36]

The industry's disingenuous response on children's food advertising and soft drinks illustrates larger problems. There are many other cases where industry competes with public health and where its actions are the opposite of what health experts recommend (for example, snack foods in schools, fast food consumption and obesity, and agriculture subsidies). The education system is one place where this conflict is acted out.

In some countries, the sale and promotion of unhealthy food in schools has occurred for so many years that it has become part of the funding equation for education. The problem is especially acute in the United States. It is common for schools to have "pouring rights" contracts with soft drink companies, multiple snack food machines with high-calorie products, food company logos on scoreboards, abundant food advertising on "free" news channels (such as Channel One), and homework programs rewarding children with free food from companies like Dunkin' Donuts and Pizza Hut.

Schools often perceive these arrangements as consistent with their educational mission: food sales fund important programs, appear to be a "free" source of money, and allow communities to provide less funding for education. The soft drink industry exploits these relationships for both money and public relations (they boast of their caring about children and their role in education).

In fact, these connections drain money from communities. Children put money into the machines and the companies take away the profit. The band uniforms or school trips the money supports are purchased by children and their parents, but with the industry first taking its share. And beyond the direct profits from sales, the industry benefits from the massive advertising exposure on vending machines, sports spectators seeing logos on scoreboards, and more.

Business self-interest may be expected, but governmental failure to correct the situation, or worse yet, collusion in ways that damage public health, is especially troubling. On the issue of children's food advertising, does the U.S. government side with science/public health or with the industry?

The U.S. government found itself isolated from the world community in 2003–04 by its stiff opposition to a report of the World Health Organization that proposed a global strategy for confronting problems with diet, inactivity, and obesity.[37] In particular, the sugar industry exerted heavy pressure on both the U.S. government and the WHO to change recommendations that sugar intake should decrease. Part of the U.S. response to the report was a pointed letter to the WHO from an assistant to Secretary of Health and Human Services,

Tommy Thompson, saying, "The assertion that heavy market-ing of energy-dense foods increases the risk of obesity is sup-ported by almost no data."[38] The Federal Trade Commission chairman, Timothy Muris, took the same stance on food advertising directed at children: "A ban would be ineffective because there is no reason to think that the ads kids see make them obese."[39]

Example after example could be interpreted as collusion between government and the food industry. National nutrition policy in the U.S.A. is established by the USDA, whose primary task is to help the food industry sell more products. For years there has been an open "revolving door" of industry executives running the USDA and then returning to industry. A few examples occurred in 2004 when the head of the USDA appointed a deputy chief of staff who was vice president of leg-islative affairs with the International Dairy Foods Association, along with a director of communications who had worked with the National Cattleman's Beef Association.

There is abundant evidence that the food industry has not always acted in the interests of the public eating less food or better food. Which prevails when public health and profits are in conflict? Kraft's and McDonald's highly visible pronounce-ments suggest that the answer is clear. McDonald's promised to use healthier oil for its fried foods, and Kraft said it would offer its food in smaller portions. To date, both companies have failed to follow through on their announcements. Public opinion may ultimately force the industry to act differently, or courageous government officials might one day overlook busi-ness interests and be creative with legislation and regulation. Until that day, a skeptical eye must be turned to industry's pleas that it be trusted.

Necessary Shifts in Thinking

Fundamental shifts in public opinion are necessary before unhealthy eating habits can change. Public opinion did turn against the tobacco companies, permitting unprecedented policy changes: the smoking ban in public places, very high taxes, forbidding the use of an icon — Joe Camel — that allegedly encouraged children to smoke, and so on. The realization that there were victims (children being seduced to smoke, non-smokers hurt by secondhand smoke), awareness of the human toll produced by smoking, and the release of internal documents from the industry showing callous, calculating behaviour designed to maximize sales of products that can kill users — all this facilitated an enormous attitude shift. When the history of the obesity issue is finally written, key shifts in public opinion will probably be seen as preceding key advances.

Some of those changes may be occurring already. We see children as a protected group. Nations safeguard children by requiring immunizations, mandating the use of safety restraints in automobiles, and more. There is increasing recognition that great harm has occurred by not protecting children from conditions that lead to unhealthy eating and a sedentary lifestyle. Moves to ban soft drinks and snack foods from schools and to regulate children's food advertising are examples of actions based on a needed shift in thinking. There are more.

INDIVIDUAL RESPONSIBILITY VERSUS NATIONAL FAILURES

The time-worn argument against legislation is that eating is a matter of personal responsibility, and that the "nanny state" should not tell people what is good for them because it infringes on free choice. It is a powerful argument, and one that bears refuting.

As an aside, there *are* food police who tell people what to eat. That police force is the food industry with billions of dollars at its disposal to convince people, particularly children, what to eat. Even if the government were willing to fight the industry, as it finally did tobacco, the resources it could bring to the effort would be trivial in comparison.

In an article I wrote with Marion Nestle, we noted four fundamental points in response to the argument that personal responsibility is the cause and solution to the obesity problem:[40] Fundamentally wrong, the argument cannot be supported by either science or common sense. The rate of obesity increases year after year, in country after country. It is difficult to argue that the world's people were less responsible in 2002 than in 2001 or that irresponsibility is sweeping the globe.

Secondly, the argument ignores biology. Humans like foods high in sugar, fat, and calories as a survival strategy. Lab animals, responding strictly to their biology, can triple their body weights when given access to high-fat, high-sugar foods found at any convenience store. Imagine the folly of attributing the animals' normal weights to the exercise of responsibility, and the heavier weights to failures in animal character.

Thirdly, the argument fails to lead to constructive action. For years, food companies have urged that people should eat better and exercise more — in other words, should be more responsible. How much higher can obesity rates climb before such blandishments are seen for what they are?

Finally, the personal responsibility approach is a trap. It insists that the environment should remain unchanged, that the food industry will do business as usual, and that pious government officials will continue to defend the status quo while claiming credit for taking action. The picture startlingly resembles the history of the tobacco industry, which argued that damage caused by dangerous products were the fault of the people who used them.

BOTTOM-UP VERSUS TOP-DOWN PRIORITIES (CREATING SOCIAL CONTAGION)

Will change occur from the top down, with central governments taking the lead? Or will it come from the bottom up, with grassroots, local, and state changes forcing central change? It appears that the victories are occurring in a bottom-up fashion in the United States, but in Europe and Scandinavia there is more hope for constructive action from the top.

In the U.S.A. the federal government talks much about obesity. Looking beyond this rhetoric, one sees minimal allocation of resources — and the classic escape tactic, imploring people to be more responsible. Outside North America, central governments are more likely to take constructive action. The British government is considering action to limit food advertising directed at children, and politicians are debating food taxes. Sweden prohibits advertising aimed at children. Finland has undertaken impressive health promotion efforts. Such efforts must be tracked and evaluated so other countries can consider taking action.

At the local level, many impressive changes are occurring.[41] School districts are banning soft drinks and snack foods, school lunch programs are improving in some areas, communities are building bike/walking trails, there is increasing pressure on schools to add back physical education, organic gardens are being built on school grounds and are integrated with the core education, calls are being made for regulation of children's advertising, and more. Even though the support for such programs is insignificant compared to food industry promotion, these programs can become models for other communities and may ultimately have a major impact.

These programs have national or even global potential, but only if evaluated and spread around the world. Rapid evaluation of these efforts would be very helpful, as would better understanding about how positive contagion can occur (when other communities adopt successful programs).

Specific Actions

A number of actions have been suggested for reducing obesity. The key is to develop cost-effective preventative approaches that improve diet and enhance physical activity.

It is important to hold the food industry accountable. We should insist it earns the trust it seeks. Constructive actions, say, when a company introduces a healthier product, cannot excuse countless damaging practices. It would be helpful to establish specific criteria that industry must meet to be considered trustworthy. A beginning would be for the industry to develop a new playbook. That playbook would include the following criteria:[42]

- Promote only healthy foods to children and, ultimately, minimize promotion of unhealthy foods to adults.
- Cease sales and promotion of unhealthy foods in schools.
- Change marketing, pricing, and promotion strategies that encourage overeating and the consumption of unhealthy foods.

- Alter the industry focus from personal responsibility to environmental changes that encourage and enable people to make healthy decisions.
- Place approximately equal emphasis on diet and physical activity.
- Permit objective parties to interpret science and avoid manipulating science as a marketing and public relations tool.
- Acknowledge that personal freedom is enhanced as the environment becomes healthier.

One suggestion my colleagues and I have repeatedly made is to introduce a food tax. A lightning rod for controversy, the proposal has been attacked with great vehemence by the food industry, food trade associations, and conservative political groups. Once thought completely radical but now part of legitimate debate, a food tax is being considered by several national governments.

A tax could be conceptualized in several ways. The most dramatic would be to impose a tax on unhealthy foods. The tax would be large enough to decrease consumption, and to raise sufficient revenue to subsidize the sale of healthy foods. Research would be needed to determine the necessary level of tax.

Less radical would be a small tax on soft drinks, snack foods, and fast foods to generate revenue for needed programs.[43] For instance, a U.S. national tax of one penny per soft-drink can or bottle would raise $1.5 billion per year. The revenue would be much larger if the tax were just two pennies, and was applied to other classes of foods. I have recommended that the revenue be earmarked for a "nutrition superfund" that could be used to promote healthy eating to children.

Such small taxes are now in effect in a number of American states and municipalities, but in all cases have been implemented to raise general revenues rather than to improve nutrition. Such taxes are acceptable to the public. The challenge is to earmark the revenue to healthy eating.

Based on what is known, my colleagues and I have suggested a number of actions that might be considered to improve the nutrition landscape.[44] The hope is to develop approaches that offer promise in preventing obesity, change conditions in ways that improve diet and physical activity, and are cost effective.

SOCIAL ATTITUDE CHANGE

- Focus on environmental change and recognize that personal resources (responsibility) can be overwhelmed when the environment is toxic.
- Replace the "no good foods or bad foods" stance with a public health focus on what foods must be generally consumed.
- Recognize that treating obesity is very difficult and can be costly, thus making prevention and children the priorities. See obesity as a matter of social justice: As obesity is highest in low-income groups, social justice and race issues are linked with diet, inactivity, and obesity. Correcting social disparities is one means of fighting obesity. Civil rights, anti-poverty, anti-hunger, and community organizations might be allies for public health experts working on obesity.

GLOBAL PRIORITIES

- Learn from successes in countries such as Finland and Mauritius about large-scale efforts to change diet and activity.

- Support research to understand transitions in nutrition and activity.
- Emphasize disparity issues and the impact of obesity on developing countries.
- Work with the WHO as the prime organizing unit.
- Establish a world culture where promoting unhealthy food is unacceptable.

PHYSICAL ACTIVITY

- Develop national strategic plans to increase physical activity.
- Earmark transportation funding for non-motorized transport.
- Design activity-friendly communities and offer incentives for activity.
- Build and promote exercise opportunities in communities, schools, worksites, and physician practices. Promote walking and biking to school.

COMMERCIALIZATION OF CHILDHOOD

- Prevent exploitation of children as market objects.
- Protest the use of cartoon characters and celebrity endorsements to promote unhealthy foods.
- Discourage product placements in movies, TV shows, video games, and food company web sites with games for children.
- Encourage legislators to prohibit marketing of products to children, or at least to create equal time for pro-nutrition messages.
- Create a nutrition "superfund" to promote healthy eating, perhaps from fees placed on food advertisements or small taxes on the sale of unhealthy foods.

- Promote media literacy (advertising inoculation) among children.

FOOD AND SOFT DRINKS IN SCHOOLS

- Identify how eating and activity affect academic performance. Education and public health officials should be allies in this effort. Soft drinks and snack foods will be banished from schools, the instant schools officials learn that poor diet is affecting standardized test scores.
- Prohibit TV programming with food promotion, rid schools of food company logos and references to unhealthy foods in educational materials, have only non-food fundraisers, and use only healthy foods as academic incentives.
- Improve school lunch programs and use the cafeteria as a learning laboratory.
- Find alternatives to snack foods, soft drinks, and fast foods.
- Improve nutrition and activity instruction.
- Use zoning laws to prohibit food establishments from operating near schools.
- Have only healthy foods/beverages in vending machines.

PORTION SIZING

- Raise awareness that larger portions lead to more eating, encourage companies to sell and advertise reasonable portions, and educate people on serving sizes.
- Require food labelling at restaurants, and food companies to list the number of USDA servings on the front of containers.

ECONOMIC ISSUES

- Increase awareness of the fundamental imbalance of incentives to eat well versus poorly, and highlight the connections of poverty with obesity.
- Engage programs such as the U.S.A.'s National School Lunch Program, Food Stamp Program, Head Start, and WIC (the special supplemental nutrition program for women, infants, and children) to fight poor diet.
- Change the food price structure, first by lowering costs of healthy foods and perhaps by increasing the costs of unhealthy foods.
- Think of food taxes not as punitive measures but as a means to support nutrition programs.

INTERACTING WITH THE FOOD INDUSTRY AND GOVERNMENT

- Support positive industry changes, but also increase public awareness of industry tactics that influence policy and promote unhealthy eating.
- Challenge the industry for hidden funding of political and nutrition front groups.
- Encourage bold action free of industry influence among political leaders.
- Curb food commercialism in public institutions (such as ads in museums, in hospitals, on police cars).
- Promote activities known to help with body weight (for example, breast feeding, decreased television watching).
- Mobilize parents to demand a healthy environment for their children.

EXPLORE INNOVATIVE COALITIONS

- Making coalitions of concerned groups increases the power of social movements. Because improved diet should boost academic performance, explore coalitions with education groups, and also with traditional medicine. Other creative avenues could include connections with groups focused on environmental sustainability.[45] Improving dietary habits would benefit these groups as well as public health.

Summary

Poor diet, inactivity, and obesity are severe global problems. Modern conditions, which have bred the obesity pandemic, simply must change. This will require considerable attention to the food and physical activity environments, bold action on the part of national leaders (who must be separated from their food company interests), support of creativity at the grass-roots, considerable funding, and the will to persist in the face of vexing systemic problems.

Blaming individuals for obesity, table-pounding exhortations for increased personal responsibility, and protecting the food industry's status quo do not work. They have been tried for years and have failed, yet they are precisely what many in government propose as a means of moving ahead. Helping the population make responsible decisions by creating an environment that promotes rather than prevents healthy eating and activity is a worthy goal, but it will require fundamental changes in the economics of food, the activity environment, and the way the food industry does business.

Positive signs exist. Awareness of the problem is increasing, the media are publicizing obesity as a public health issue (not just how to diet), and government leaders are beginning to resist industry pressures. Grassroots victories have occurred, and are having a contagious effect. Support of these movements offers the greatest hope of progress. But it has yet to be combined with the work that legislators must do.

Bringing Ingenuity to Energy

Thomas Homer-Dixon

E nergy is our lifeblood. Without an adequate supply at the right times and places, our economy and society would grind to a halt.

Canadians are profligate users of energy; in fact, we have one of the highest per-capita rates of consumption in the world. If we were smarter about things, we would consume much less energy to support our current standard of living, and we would produce this energy with much less damage to our natural environment.

What does it mean to be smarter about things? Over the past decade I've given a lot of thought to this question. I've tried to understand why some people and societies are good at solving problems while others aren't. A key factor, I've decided, is the ability to generate and implement practical ideas. I call these practical ideas *ingenuity*, and people, organizations, and societies that can't supply enough ingenuity at the right times and places face an *ingenuity gap*.[1] This perspective helps us to understand why we're finding it so hard to change our energy habits.

Ingenuity, as I define it, consists of sets of instructions that tell us how to arrange the stuff in our world in ways that help us to achieve our goals. The sets of instructions are like cooking recipes, and these recipes allow us to manipulate, process, and reconfigure the matter around us — the materials in the ground, the gases in the atmosphere, and the organic components of our biosphere — into things that improve our lives.

Take, for example, the laptop that I'm working on at the moment. By itself, this machine probably has more power than all the computers available to the U.S. Department of Defense in the 1960s taken together. Yet this device consists of nothing more than reconfigured rock and hydrocarbons. We have extracted materials from the ground and, by following an immensely long and elaborate set of instructions, refined and manipulated those materials into the remarkable object sitting in front of me. The same is true for every human-made thing around us, including the lights above our heads, the furniture we're sitting on, and the food on our plates.

If *technical ingenuity* consists of recipes for reconfiguring matter to make technologies like laptops, cars, and furniture, then *social ingenuity* consists of recipes for arranging people to form key organizations and institutions like court systems, markets, and parliamentary democracies. Although ideas for new technologies tend to attract most of our attention, it turns out that social ingenuity is more important. In fact, social ingenuity is a prerequisite for technical ingenuity. We don't get the new technologies we want unless our economic institutions — especially our markets — reward innovators for the risks they take; and well-functioning markets take huge amounts of ingenuity to design, set up, and run.

This ingenuity model subsumes, and is ultimately far more powerful than, the conventional neoclassical economic model that dominates policy discussion surrounding critical issues like energy. Within the economic model, human beings are defined as rational maximizers of their well-being. The model's keystone concepts — concepts that we see every day in the business pages of our newspapers — are consumption, production, investment, and savings. And the model's system inputs — what economists call factors of production — are capital and labour. (For economists, capital consists mainly of the machines used to make things like cars or laptops, while labour is the work applied to running these machines.) In general, conventional economists give little thought to the independent productive role of ideas.

In contrast, within the ingenuity model, human beings are defined as pragmatic problem solvers. The model's keystone concepts are ingenuity requirement and supply. And the model's system inputs — or what we might call factors of problem solving — are ideas, energy, and matter. Human beings use their *ideas* to guide the application of their *energy* to reconfigure the *matter* around them into the things that meet their needs. Within the economic model it sometimes seems that human beings are little more than walking appetites. According to the ingenuity model, however, our most important characteristic, and the thing that truly distinguishes us from other species, is our capacity to generate and implement ideas to solve our problems.

How can we use the ingenuity model to better understand the problems of energy consumption and production in Canada? For one thing, this model disciplines us to focus on two separate issues: the factors that boost our requirement for energy-related ingenuity, and the factors that hinder our ability to supply the needed ingenuity at the right times and places. The model also encourages us to recognize that the really big obstacles we face are social, not technical.

In the remainder of this brief chapter, I'm going to focus on why it's so hard for us to make the transition to "green" energy production, including solar, wind, micro-hydro, and landfill methane power generation. The obstacles to green energy in Canada are mainly social, and the ingenuity we must supply to overcome them is also therefore mainly social.

Let's begin with the economic obstacles to green energy. I believe that there are two main ones: first, our energy prices don't reflect energy's true costs, and second, we need high consumption to sustain our economy. The first is a tough problem, but it's potentially solvable within the context of our current economic system. The second is far more intractable, because it goes to the very heart of the way modern capitalist economies function.

Green energy could compete with conventional energy — from sources such as oil, natural gas, coal, hydro, and nuclear — if the prices we paid for conventional energy accurately reflected the full costs of its production and use. At the moment, our society, the natural environment, and future generations are all providing huge subsidies to conventional energy. As Joyce McLean of Toronto Hydro notes, "The crux here is that people are not paying the true cost of their [energy] bill. Green power, with no hidden costs, is far from being more expensive. But that's confusing to the average person."[2]

Economists use the term "negative externalities" to refer to costs not included in a good's price because they are borne by people not directly involved in producing, buying, selling, or using the good. For example, the prices of gasoline and electricity in Ontario don't reflect the cost to public health of air pollution produced when people burn gasoline to run their cars or fossil fuels to produce electricity. Similarly, these prices don't remotely reflect the likely cost of the climate change caused by the carbon dioxide emitted when we burn gasoline or fossil fuels.

These external costs of energy generation are very high. Public health officials estimate that air pollution in Toronto alone causes "between 730 and 1,400 premature deaths, and between 3,300 and 7,600 hospital admissions each year." They go on:

> These premature mortality and hospitalization estimates, while significant, greatly underestimate illness associated with poor air quality in Toronto. For the last 15 years, it has been well recognized that air pollution produces a "pyramid" of health effects, with the relatively rare but more serious health outcomes (such as premature deaths and hospitalizations) at the peak of the pyramid, and the less but more numerous health outcomes such as asthma symptom days and respiratory infections (such as pneumonia) appearing in progressive layers below that peak.[3]

A major study released in July 2003 by the International Institute for Sustainable Development in Winnipeg puts numbers on some of these external costs. The results are impressive and important. The study used advanced methods of "full-cost accounting" to estimate the health and climate-change costs per kilowatt-hour of electricity generated in eastern Canada's thermal power plants. Even using a relatively limited tally of costs (since many of pollution's effects on health are almost impossible to estimate), the study showed that the full cost of producing electricity by burning coal is actually 50 percent higher than the current market cost.[4]

Much of this cost will be borne by our children and grandchildren in the form of poorer health and a damaged natural environment. This is a subsidy paid across time — paid by generations in the future to us in the present. Conventional energy is also heavily subsidized across economic sectors and geographic locations. For example, the Ontario public have been saddled with an immense debt from the construction of nuclear reactors, and will be paying that debt through their Hydro bills every month *for decades.* And throughout Canada, urban residents are subsidizing the provision and maintenance of infrastructure, including energy infrastructure, in surrounding suburbs.

Not all subsidies are bad. Sometimes they're needed to balance social fairness against economic efficiency. But the subsidies provided by hidden external costs produce all kinds of nasty results. When people don't pay the full costs of the production and use of a good, they have an incentive to waste it and a disincentive to apply ingenuity to conserve it. If conventional energy were properly priced, it would be far more expensive, and we would see a dramatic increase in the flow of ingenuity to conserve this energy and find alternatives to it. The short-term adjustment would be harsh — there would be major economic dislocations — but, in the medium to long term, Canadian society could be much wealthier, because all that new ingenuity would make our economy vastly more efficient and technically advanced. We could also sell this energy-related ingenuity around the world.

Users of conventional energy are, in a sense, the biggest welfare bums in town. The corporations that produce this energy, and the industries and consumers who burn it, which means every one of us, are all on the dole. It's time to start paying our way.

We might be able to tackle the deeply rooted vested interests that benefit from, and rely upon, these subsidies. It's just possible that, through an immense effort of political and social will, we could reform our energy markets sufficiently to do the job. Unfortunately, though, we would still have to deal with the second economic obstacle: healthy capitalist economies rely upon ferociously high rates of consumption of goods and services, and this reliance tends to discourage a transition to a green economy whose principal aim is to lower the throughput of energy in the economy.

Understanding this obstacle requires a short digression on the nature of modern capitalism. Competition among firms encourages relentless technological innovation, which in turn steadily boosts labour productivity: as companies try to win in a Darwinian marketplace, they often replace relatively expensive labour with new technologies. This means that an individual worker can produce more for a company, but it also means that redundant workers are laid off. In order to prevent this pool of technologically displaced labour from becoming too large and both a drag on the economy and a source of social unrest, new jobs must be created through economic growth. In other words, as some sectors of the economy use less and less labour, new sectors and enterprises must be created to absorb the displaced labour.

If these new sectors and enterprises are to prosper, there must be sufficient economic demand for their products. Capitalist societies are therefore constantly engaged in demand creation. They must socialize their citizens to be insatiable consumers (the "walking appetites" of the neoclassical economic model discussed above). Advanced capitalism can only survive if it generates constantly rising material expectations and, in turn, chronic material discontent within the economically active population, despite increasing material abundance.

A large body of research shows that, beyond a modest threshold of per-capita income (less than one-third of the level of per-capita income in advanced economies), the correlation between greater wealth and greater happiness breaks down.[5] If so, why are we — and our elites, policy-makers, and governments — so obsessed with sustaining economic growth and generating endlessly greater wealth per capita? It's as if we've become addicted to buying things. The act doesn't really make us happy, except for a moment after the purchase, but we keep doing it over and over again anyway.

Western societies, and increasingly our global society as a whole, have locked themselves into an economic and social system that can remain stable only through endless growth. Without such growth, and the constantly rising personal consumption that accompanies it, new jobs won't be created, economic demand will stagnate, and deflation will set in. (Note that the world economy is currently struggling with exactly this problem: enormous excess productive capacity, vast pools of surplus capital and labour, insufficient demand to absorb

these factors of production, and, as a result, incipient deflation.) Moreover, the distributional struggles between rich and
poor — struggles ever-present beneath the surface of societies
with highly unequal distributions of wealth and power —
could tear our societies apart. Without the cultivation of insatiable desires, some technologically displaced labour will
remain unemployed, which over time could produce a powerfully aggrieved and potentially revolutionary underclass.

In this macroeconomic environment, appeals for energy
conservation must climb a very steep hill. Conservation has a
pejorative "eat your peas" connotation. The not-so-subtle
implication is that it's bad for the economy — and almost un-
Canadian. We need to consume in order to grow, and we need
to grow in order to be happy. Dealing with this problem will
require advocates of green energy to revisit some fundamental
issues about economic growth and the nature of capitalist
economies that they've been reluctant to address since the
aborted "limits to growth" debate of the 1970s.

If these economic obstacles to green energy are formidable,
so are the political obstacles. Again I see two. First, the political
and bureaucratic systems that form the environment within
which advocates of green energy must press their case, and that
generate the regulations governing green energy's deployment,
are often hopelessly cumbersome and inefficient. Journalist
Gordon Laird writes, for example, about the Toronto
Renewable Energy Co-operative's attempts to get approval for a
wind turbine at Ashbridge's Bay, east of Toronto:

> There are three levels of government, technical and
> compatibility problems, city bylaws that need to be

rewritten or revised, and a host of other complications. The growing list of government jurisdictions
and departments requiring reports and approval is
considerable — City of Toronto, Navigation Canada,
Transport Canada, Toronto airport, Committee of
Adjustment — and then there is the federal environmental assessment, a process that requires its own
small mountain of paperwork and consultations.
There's also a list of unwritten "unofficial approvals . . .
wink-wink approvals you better have."[6]

Moreover, as was shown years ago by the economist Mancur
Olson, bureaucracies, political systems, and economies become
more complex and rigid — even sclerotic — over time as they
add layer upon layer of law and regulation, and as they accumu-
late competing and overlapping centres of authority. As years
go by, powerful vested interests establish themselves in the
niches of these systems and do everything they can to prevent
change that would affect their interests.

Energy supply and use affect every person, group, and seg-
ment of society, so everybody has a powerful interest in these
matters. In such an environment, it's very difficult to reach a
political consensus, and it's very easy for powerful interest
groups to derail reforms.

The second political obstacle arises, somewhat paradoxically, from green energy's greatest strength — its emphasis on
small-scale, local, and decentralized energy production. Its
advocates tend to be small, community-based, and loosely net-
worked groups, with commensurately little political clout. On
the other hand, large, centralized power projects like nuclear

stations, massive fossil fuel generating plants, and hydroelectric dams depend on huge corporations and government bureaucracies to build, run, and maintain them. These corporations and bureaucracies become concentrations of political and economic power in Canadian society, and too often they become immense and focused vested interests opposed to real reform of our energy practices. Green energy's advocates, in contrast, are often underfinanced, poorly co-ordinated, and ideologically diffuse. In the fierce political struggle over energy policy, they can't hope to win against very powerful, very rich, and very entrenched vested interests.

The four obstacles to green energy that I've identified here — two economic and two political — are formidable barriers to change. Most fundamentally, they are serious obstacles to the supply of the ingenuity we need to solve the energy problems we face. There are things, however, that we can do. Canadians can lobby their governments to adjust energy markets so that prices better reflect energy's true costs. They can work to streamline the political and bureaucratic decision-making processes that affect new energy policies. And green-energy advocates can make their political action more co-ordinated and coherent, in order to counterbalance the dead weight of vested interests behind conventional energy.

But as Canadians we also need to reflect much more on our broader context of institutions, incentives, and values — a context that leads us, too often, to choose a mode of living that requires huge amounts of energy over one that treads more lightly on Earth.

At the Frontier of Energy

Gordon Laird

S ome thirty years after they were banished from Canada's
Western Arctic, pipeline workers are back again. Pushed
out by intense Aboriginal lobbying and the Berger Royal
Commission of 1977, which concluded that the Mackenzie
Valley wasn't ready for a massive energy boom, drillers, seismic
crews, and company officials are now returning to this huge
span of river, tundra, and boreal forest. At the very top of the
Mackenzie — the very edge of Canada's northwestern frontier
— lie more than 1.7 trillion cubic metres of recoverable natural
gas reserves, with untold trillions more possibly hidden along
the pipeline route, part of a rich sedimentary basin that runs
all the way from Alberta to the Arctic Ocean.[1]

From the Alberta border north, the Mackenzie River
snakes through mountains, boreal forests, and modest
Aboriginal communities. As it approaches the Arctic Ocean,
the Mackenzie sprawls sideways and becomes the world's
tenth-largest river delta — a flat expanse surrounded by endless

tundra and scrub. Beneath this land at the top of the Mackenzie, some of the richest gas plays on the continent lie under caribou wintering grounds.

It is for this prize that the pipeline workers return, driven by continental markets anxious about looming natural gas shortages. And, incredibly, the region known for one of the biggest industrial flops in living memory — the stillborn pipeline of the 1970s was just one aspect of Pierre Trudeau's failed Arctic energy plan — could be shipping natural gas by 2015.

How did this happen? Through some 180-degree turn of history, you are now just as likely to see Inuvialuit, Gwitch'in, or Sahtu running business meetings, cutting deals, and working the drillfloor. Indeed, the First Nations of the Mackenzie are one-third owners of what will become Canada's first Arctic megaproject, right alongside corporate majors like Imperial, Shell, Conoco, and ExxonMobil, all of whom hold substantial reserves from the Arctic's first wave of gas exploration. The result will be the continent's single longest pipeline and the first megaproject of the twenty-first century: a 1,350-kilometre-long string of steel that would carry a twenty-year supply of natural gas to hungry North American markets.[2]

It's a long way from the days when Aboriginal leaders accused companies of genocide and colonization. "We're business-oriented people around here now," explains Roy "Bunker" Wilson, an Inuvialuit community liaison for Imperial Oil. "People [are] not just asking about jobs, but about ownership of those jobs. It's not just, can I go work? — it's more like, can I send my truck to work?"

We're on the land south of Inuvik, a rough Arctic boomtown that serves as control centre for all things pipeline. But out here at the treeline, overlooking the barrens to the north, a small piece of history unfolds. Two weeks before the winter ice roads close, a mobile drill unit plods along the proposed pipeline route. On the edge of the Mackenzie Delta's alluvial plain, I watch as a geotechnical team drills nine-metre core samples in the permafrost. Theirs is the mundane work of extracting soil for regulatory applications and pipeline engineering plans, all part of a $270-million project definition program launched by the Aboriginal Pipeline Group and its corporate partners.

Even to locals, the shift in perspective is nothing short of astounding, although social changes were happening well before the first Arctic energy boom of the 1970s. "It's the elders who are the most connected to the land. It wasn't until the 1950s and 1960s that we got into a cash economy," explains Bunker as we traverse the border of the Arctic barrens in a giant snowcat, not more than forty kilometres from the Mackenzie Delta. Dwarf trees scatter the land out to the south, and rolling hills, the wintering ground for caribou, run to the north. "My generation and the generation before me now live a different life." It's a common story in Canada's North: many Aboriginals want jobs, partly because traditional pursuits like hunting and trapping can't pay for groceries and rent.

The sheer scale of this project, all privately financed, underlines the importance placed on energy frontiers in the twenty-first century. The $16.2-billion pipeline, and the political momentum behind it, shows the trajectory of power in the new century. Considerable wealth and effort will be mobilized in order to sustain the energy norms of the previous century, even if this means laying pipe across some of the world's most forsaken terrain.

The global push to control and develop frontier resources is one of the great dynamics of the twenty-first century. Nations and multinationals are delving deeper and deeper into remote territory to locate marketable fossil fuels, a trend that's reflected in efforts to create "secure supplies" through energy megaprojects — everything from Canada's oil sands to China's Three Gorges Dam to a global wave of nuclear reactor construction — as we attempt to forestall the inevitable and final depletion of non-renewable energy.

A surge in new megaprojects is accelerated by a series of tectonic economic shifts that are transforming previously cheap commodities like natural gas into one of Earth's most strategic resources. A fuel like natural gas, valued for its versatility and relatively clean burn, is the energy source that could bridge a global shift to more diversified, sustainable forms of power — energy efficiency, renewables, hydrogen cells, and beyond. Visionaries have proclaimed natural gas as the missing link between a fossil fuel economy and a sustainable energy economy, one that not only runs cleaner burning gas turbines that replace coal power, but also for next-generation sources, such as fuel-cell technologies that might one day convert natural gas directly to electricity.

Yet the reality is a lot more complicated. As old coal plants convert to high-efficiency gas turbines, electricity prices are increasingly tied to natural gas; petrochemical production is highly gas intensive. And continental power demand has not been effectively managed, so that mass inefficiencies and waste will boost commodity prices. Moreover, new and unconventional sources of crude oil, such as the booming oil sands of northern Alberta, are being developed to feed our outsized energy hunger. It is one of the largest industrial developments in the world, with an estimated $120 billion in existing and new projects. Crude oil output in Canada is predicted to nearly double by 2020, and of this, the oil sands will account for more than 80 percent of production, tapping a bitumen pool that is claimed to be almost as large as the proven reserves of Saudi Arabia.

The energy requirements for unconventional crude production are profound. For example: at Shell's Athabasca Oil Sands Project, energy usage per tonne of production in 2006 was approximately 6 gigajoules per tonne produced.[3] Even with cutting-edge operating technologies, Shell's reported oil sands intensities ranged roughly six times more than conventional oil; other companies claim intensities as little as four times. Some critics have actually described oil-sands crude production as an energy upgrading process, not a new resource.

Given the scale of development — oil-sands crude surpassed conventional output in Alberta by 231 percent in 2006 — it is widely expected that Canada's production of synthetic crude will profoundly erode natural gas reserves.[4] "There does not seem to be enough natural gas in sight to supply both the oil and the gas desired by the U.S. above Canada's internal needs," noted a 2002 study from the Colorado School of Mines.[5] By 2010, it predicts that oil-sands operations will consume more than 25 percent of Alberta's existing gas production. "Within a few years Canada may have to choose between selling part of their natural gas versus synthetic oil to the United States."

The compound effect of spiraling demand and fossil fuel scarcity, combined with the vulnerability of an economy that often rewards wasted energy, suggests that we could see power shortages and an energy-driven economic crisis in our century's second decade, possibly on the heels of the credit collapse and recession that began in 2008. On average, North American natural gas demand continues to increase, with American consumption increasing more than 6 percent in 2007 alone, while conventional supplies continue to deplete.[6] Even with new efforts to drill into unconventional sources like coal bed methane and deep water wells in the Gulf of Mexico, there remains a relentless push to open up costly Arctic reserves, including a competing $26 billion pipeline to tap the rich gas reserves of Alaska's North Slope, a 3,200-kilometre megaproject championed by former vice presidential candidate Sarah Palin.[7] In 2008, reports surfaced estimating that the construction cost of the Alaska pipeline had increased 50 percent between 2002 and 2008, reflecting a similar trend in the much-delayed Mackenzie pipeline, where estimated cost has more than tripled since the early 2000s.[8]

Pipelines play a central role in our effort to sustain the kind of growth and prosperity enjoyed by previous generations. But it is a strategy of diminishing returns and increasing complexity. Along with the profound climactic and environmental liabilities that massive reinvestment in hydrocarbon energy sources threaten, price volatility and erratic supply have already afflicted markets — most notably demonstrated by crude oil in 2008 with a four-month swing between $147 and $44 USD per barrel — and this will be followed by more fundamental challenges such as energy nationalism and long-term short supply of crude, electricity, and natural gas. Once one of the cheapest of resource commodities, the value of natural gas itself has already changed profoundly: between 1995 and 2005, for example, the US average wellhead price of natural gas increased 250 percent amid supply fears, speculation, and pipeline bottlenecks.[9]

Consequently, many oil and gas multinationals are still making long-term bets on conventional fossil sources extracted from unlikely sources and exotic locales: as Exxon's CEO predicted in December 2008, world energy demand will increase 35 percent between 2005 and 2030, with hydrocarbon energy sources still comprising 80 percent of global demand by 2030.[10]

In other words, there is no escape from the contingencies of demand and the uncertainties of non-renewable supply. In short, North America's huge, energy-guzzling fleet of SUVs and minivans, single-handedly responsible for the worst auto-efficiency rates since the 1970s, has much to do with why Inuvialuit drillers are punching exploration gas wells across Canada's Western Arctic. And why, if current oil sands trends hold true, there might not be much new natural gas left over to fuel more sustainable alternatives.

Out on the ice of the Mackenzie River, I happen upon a debate over renewable energy, of all things. It's the Muskrat Jamboree in Inuvik, and as locals prepare for annual dogsled races, there's a fierce discussion about the merits of wind power. "Well, we tried it, and it fell flat," says one manager from the local power utility. "And the micro-turbines on the gas pipeline don't perform to spec, either."

Up in the Arctic, energy is a constant focus. Hunters need fuel for snowmobile forays onto pack ice and tundra, animals need vast quantities of land to get enough food energy, and everyone worries about the sheer cost of conventional energy, since few people live out on the land anymore and many communities rely upon toxin-laden diesel turbines. The fierce economics of fossil fuel consumption are clear above the sixtieth parallel. Imported diesel consumes money that would be better spent on providing local health care, supporting the indigenous hunting economy, and addressing the chronic housing shortage that can be found in almost all of Canada's Northern communities.

Inuvik has been an energy centre for years. With its own natural gas sources, it has more economic resources to put toward economic development. And as I talk to more people on the ice of the Mackenzie, I find that there are alternative energy projects across the North, from faulty gas micro-turbines in Inuvik to wind power on Holman Island. Through sheer economic necessity — and meagre government grants — people are trying to launch alternative energy projects and ambitious conservation efforts on a scale that, per capita, is unheard of in the rest of Canada. Consequently, many Northerners know the advantages and disadvantages of renewables and various energy technologies because they are already using them. It turns out that there is often a steep learning curve for any renewable application, and the North is an important testing ground for real-time energy alternatives, not just fussy little demonstration projects that we often see here in the south.

Many Northern communities are already attempting ambitious efficiency and energy projects. The community of WhaTi, near Yellowknife, has embarked on a multi-year plan, something that began with the realization that fossil fuel usage was not only poisoning residents but also dooming the local traditional economy through high energy costs. An energy audit spelled it out: ". . . with a population of about 485 people, [WhaTi] required 887,000 litres of diesel for power and space heating in 2001. At about one dollar per litre, and with transportation expenses, total cost for these two services was well over one million dollars."[11] At just over $2,000 per resident annually, it's an expense that's double or even quadruple that of most Canadians.

In 2002, WhaTi embarked on an ambitious plan to achieve greater energy efficiency and renewable power sources. Progress was made, and by 2008 plans and financing were being arranged for micro-hydro production. The local hydro-electricity using the abundant water resources of the region could replace much of the diesel generation, as well as contribute additional space heating. Solar hot water heaters will add additional capacity. By 2010, WhaTi may be one of Canada's first genuinely self-sustaining communities.

With inevitable long-term scarcity across North America, there could be high times indeed for anyone with new supplies. Rather, the trick is parsing a tightly woven web of interests, agencies, and stakeholders. Like the Inuvialuit to the north and the Sahtu to the south, the Gwitch'in people of the Mackenzie have settled their land claims and now enjoy an increasing degree of self-government. If you want to do business on their land — say, drill an exploration well or lay 1,200 kilometres of pipe — a certain degree of partnership, not to mention respect for the land itself, is now expected. Incredibly, Imperial Oil, the lead partner in the consortium with the Aboriginal Pipeline Group, actually refuses to build a pipeline without First Nations partnership. In other words, Imperial, Shell, and their partners would not build even if the Canadian federal government bulldozed local process and handed them an open ticket. "We will not proceed in the absence of the Aboriginal Pipeline Group," says Dee Brandes, Imperial's Consultation and Community Affairs manager. "If the region is opposed to the project, we're not going there."

This too is a change in perspective. Imperial, like many other companies, once took a dim view of local partnerships and control, leaving behind a surprising amount of bad feeling and mistrust along the Mackenzie. Back in the 1970s, there probably wouldn't have been Gwitch'in environmental monitors or sub-contractors. Their labour might have been menial, possibly token. And today, as we survey the geotech crew who are drilling back down into another section of permafrost, Brandes concedes that it's been a challenge forging a twenty-first-century energy alliance.

On the day that I arrive on the pipeline route, just south of Inuvik, Imperial's geotech crew is about four months late for work, simply because someone botched a land-use permit application. Environmental regulators associated with Aboriginal self-government appear to be more stringent than conventional government regulatory process. An Aboriginal official at the Gwitch'in environmental authority concurs. "Anything associated with the word 'pipeline' in the NWT everybody puts under a microscope," says Darren Campbell of the Gwitch'in Land and Water Board. "And because of that, every regulatory agency is taking the proper steps." He continues, "There is a big difference in how things work here and how they work back in Alberta. There is some head-butting involved. The best thing they did was to come in and meet face-to-face."

The local and regional regulatory process — a precondition to federal National Energy Board approval — is stringent largely because of the growing scope of self-government. "A lot of organizations here are not top-down process," Campbell says. "The chief of any given community takes direction from the population. So you need meetings, and that's not always so easy." Paradoxically, self-government in the Mackenzie also underpins the new business spirit of the region. It's precisely because Aboriginals have control that development is permitted and promoted. What this all means for the first megaproject of the twenty-first century is that the task of forging partnerships is potentially a bigger job than building the pipeline itself. The megaproject is the relationship, and that mantra shapes everything that happens along the Mackenzie.

It's been a long economic struggle to gain land claims and set up local self-government. People like former Premier Stephen Kakfwi, who was a radical opponent of the pipeline in the 1970s, now understand the future to be in compressor stations, high-tech Arctic drill rigs, and Aboriginal entrepreneurs. He explains that everything from the last thirty years has pointed toward this moment when Aboriginals can bargain as equals, and it all stems from the valid recognition of Aboriginal title, self-government, and local control. "You're on the side of the angels when you say, this is my land," he says. "Anybody would die for an opportunity to be able to say those things. I've spent my whole life trying to make it happen. It's wonderful, because you know it's possible."

This pipeline is more than another large piece of infrastructure; it is the manifestation of a new political and economic zone with its own rules and clout, something quite unlike the bloodied energy plays of the developing world. Up here, locals often call the shots. Consequently, the regulatory process has taken on a life of its own, much to the extreme frustration of Imperial and other multinationals, who have seen public hearings and consultations stretch on for years — no less than 115 days of hearings with 5,000 submissions by 2008, with no guarantee of regional approval until 2010.[12] So if it's oil and gas you want, you must first reckon with the Mackenzie.

But as locals engage with a megaproject, talk of renewables and energy alternatives seems to fade. In the Northwest Territories, for example, almost 50 percent of all funding for resource development in the early 2000s subsidized the oil and gas industry through road construction, whereas only 10 percent was devoted to economic diversification, social impacts, and environmental management.[13] With an estimated 22 percent of the world's undiscovered oil and gas reserves inside the circumpolar Arctic, there is relentless pressure to open up the tundra and Arctic Ocean to drillers and shippers.[14]

In other words, the Mackenzie pipeline is a massive social, economic, and environmental experiment: Can a megaproject serve everyone? Despite the promise of a new Aboriginal–corporate partnership, the long-term consequences are still unclear. One 2001 pilot study by the United Nations Environmental Programme (UNEP) concluded that up to 80 percent of the Arctic will be affected by mining, oil and gas exploration, ports, roads, and other developments by 2050 if development continues at its current rate.[15] "At the turn of this new millennium less than 15 percent of the Arctic's land was heavily impacted by human activity and infrastructure," says

Klaus Töpfer, Executive Director of UNEP. "However, if exploration for oil, gas, and minerals [and] developments such as
hydro-electric schemes and timber extraction continue at current rates, more than half of the Arctic will be seriously threatened in less than fifty years."

Thanks to climate change, energy alternatives, and megaprojects, Canada's North is on the cutting edge of our energy
future. But in many ways, all North Americans are caught
between the seductive lure of energy megaprojects, the dire
need for energy conservation and alternative generation, and
the economic and environmental consequences that loom in
the decades to come.

It is at the edge of our energy kingdom that we attempt to
reconcile the inevitable decline of fossil fuels with our deep
dependence on fossil-fired economies. How deep will we drill?
How far will we travel? How much will we pay to maintain the
past? Fantastic and sometimes horrible things happen out on
the world's borderlands — everything from torture in Central
Asia to pipeline sabotage in Nigeria — just so that we can
maintain the normalcy of our energy networks. But lasting
solutions based on a model of non-renewable resource extraction are, by definition, virtually impossible, so the ends of our
engineered world continue to be transitory places, prone to
extremes. These are places that manifest new innovations —
such as cutting-edge energy efficiency technology already
deployed in the oil sands — as well as instability, lawlessness,
and poverty.

At the centre of it all, again, is pipelines. In 2004, China
completed a $6 billion pipeline to export the hydrocarbon

riches of its extreme western frontier, the troubled province of Xinjiang. This massive line runs 4,000 kilometres from Urumqi to Shanghai to supply natural gas into the polluted epicentre of the Yangtze economic boom. Construction on an even larger 6,500-kilometre pipeline worth $10 billion began in 2008, and will run from Xinjiang to the south manufacturing centre of Guangzhou.[16] When they reach full operational status, both pipelines will carry as much as 50 billion cubic metres of natural gas a year. Only the Three Gorges Dam project, which cost China's government about $25 billion, is larger in economic scale.

The Central Asian frontier is crucial to China's economic survival plans, notwithstanding sporadic efforts by Uighur rebels to push colonists back across the Great Wall. Xinjiang has more than 10 trillion cubic metres of recoverable natural gas buried deep beneath the sands of the Taklamakan Desert, plus the largest single source of crude oil in China.[17] By virtue of geology, globalization, and just plain bad luck, Uighur nationalism — and its energy-rich homeland — stands in the way of the planet's most voracious consumers of power.

Consequently, surreal and sometimes brutal scenes play out here daily, a distant link in an ever-globalizing cycle of resource extraction, manufacture, and consumption.

There are many mysteries in Xinjiang, but perhaps the most unlikely one is this: Why does its capital, Urumqi, one of the most landlocked cities in the world, have so many seafood restaurants? Fresh off the plane from Beijing, this was the first question that vexed me. Not Xinjiang's simmering religious wars, nor China's western gulag with its political prisoners, nor the vast Taklamakan Desert directly to the south, cluttered with drilling rigs that plumb the vast oil and gas deposits. No, I was puzzled by the squirming eels from Guangzhou.

Wandering down Xinhua Street, past Urumqi's Holiday Inn, I'm 2,400 kilometres from the nearest ocean and all around me are seafood eateries, whose billboards and owners excitedly proffer overpriced meals from the deep. This former Silk Road outpost has, over the last decade, been transformed into a major Chinese city under a state-sponsored energy boom and mass resettlement program. Under the shadow of a giant Ferris wheel in nearby Hongshan Park, live lobsters peek out from dingy little tanks, and buckets of iced mussels sit beside halibut and squid. I've literally stumbled across a little slice of south China at the edge of Central Asia: cursing drivers, blaring pop music, and the quick promise of good eating.

Of course, the eels and lobsters are foot soldiers in a slow-burning battle between Chinese newcomers and resident Uighurs, Xinjiang's Islamic majority. Urumqi itself is a city so divided by money, power, and religion that even food has become political. Out here on the edge of Central Asia, imported seafood is a compelling sign of Chinese dominance, tacit proof of residency in a region that can hardly agree on a time zone, let alone mend fences in a struggle that's been simmering since the first century A.D. Here, Chinese entrepreneurs serve up seafood in air-conditioned splendour while Uighur vendors peddle kebabs and nan flatbread from carts and makeshift market stalls.

The seafood is a victory sign. The Chinese have largely won this war, and their conquest has much to do with the scarcity of cheap, accessible fossil fuel around the world, something

that's begun to affect the economic powerhouse that consti-
tutes China's southerly provinces and eastern coastline.
Indeed, China has achieved unprecedented growth, averaging
7 percent annually for the last twenty years, thanks to the sheer
abundance of two main factors: cheap labour and cheap
energy. This is how China has come to supply stores like Wal-
Mart with most of their product. Shenzhen, a rough economic
zone that runs along Hong Kong's northern border, alone
manufactures an estimated 70 percent of the world's toys.[18]

The inevitable and predictable consequence of building a
modern-day manufacturing empire is a deep hunger for
resources. Because if China cannot feed its factories, refineries,
and booming cities, then its growth stalls and the delicate
political balance of China's post-communist system is potentially outpaced by rural poverty, regional upheaval, and the
debilitating cost of imported crude and natural gas. In other
words, if China's Communist Party cannot engineer affordable, plentiful energy for 1.3 billion people, then chronic political instability and even civil war is possible.

In the midst of this state-sponsored energy crusade,
Uighurs have become a minority in their own capital city. The
flood of Han settlers, businesses, industrial development, and
police into Urumqi has, in turn, fueled an anti-Chinese campaign that has given Beijing serious cause for concern. Political
bombings, assassinations, and weapons smuggling continue
unabated. I've arrived in Urumqi — or Urumüqi, as the
Chinese call it — only a few months after the last major clash
between police and Uighur nationalists.

It's always been a complicated place. Xinjiang is the site
of one of Asia's longest-running intra-national conflicts, a

two thousand-year battle over a desert kingdom. It rarely captures international headlines, but open warfare, summary executions, and assassinations are commonplace. It was in Xinjiang where several fatal incidents took place during the 2008 Beijing Olympics with an estimated twenty Chinese police officers and thirty-three civilians killed in clashes and attacks during the month of August alone.[19] Consequently, the region is a major concern for international human rights groups like Amnesty International, who decry "gross and systematic" abuses here.[20]

Tightly controlled by the Chinese government, Xinjiang is all but invisible to the rest of the world, off-limits to foreign journalists — I'm here on a tourist visa — but not to major multinational oil companies like BP and Shell, who fly their flags up and down Urumqi's Beijing Avenue. Tremendous wealth is being taken from the ground beneath these old Silk Road outposts in the Taklamakan Desert, a region formerly valued for its cotton and strategic proximity to Russia, yet little affluence has reached the Islamic majority. Most Uighurs, Kazakhs, and other indigenous Central Asians still subsist on less than $270 annually. China has nevertheless pledged to modernize Xinjiang for its own good with a multi-billion-dollar plan that involves importing vast quantities of bureaucrats, soldiers, gas pipeline, and squid.

Local Chinese have been, predictably, the first to enjoy Xinjiang's boom, something that only fuels the longstanding feud. "The Chinese get all the favours and preferential treatment," complains my newfound host, Rebiya. "There are few jobs for we Uighurs." For emphasis, she points her finger like a gun and fires at a Chinese couple strolling by.

As we stroll along, Urumqi presents itself as two
hastily built Chinese metropolis of concrete, glass, a
and a Uighur stronghold full of ancient mosques and
We walk toward the Sanxihangzi Market in the centre
passing the famous White Mosque, a 200-year-old in
that, she says, is a frequent haunt of the secret police.
Sanxihangzi is the oldest market in Urumqi, G
developers recently gained permission to tear down
ern corner for a gleaming high-rise. Fourteen stori
footprint has pushed aside fruit vendors and bread p
much to the indignation of locals, who consider th
treasure of Uighur culture.

On the surface, the market is chaotic. Pakist
wave bolts of imported silk, while cartloads of na
salted and savoury — are pushed through the cr
walk through the narrow maze of stalls, Rebiya p
most choice dried apricots as a gift, along with
melons from a tall pile on a cart fresh from the
This is a place that still considers firewood as a
fuel; the earthen ovens that cook the nan bread
work with anything else.

By contrast, China operates on the Western r
increasing consumption; energy conservation i
ondary concern to adding new megawatts and
almost any price. In recent years, China's per-
energy consumption was the equivalent of less t
of standard coal, less than a half of the world's a
International Energy Agency (IEA) predicts
energy demand will grow by 2.7 percent a ye
when annual demand will reach 3.19 billion ton

coal, almost three times current rates.[21] Once a net exporter
during the 1980s, China is now the world's third-largest net
importer of oil, and accounted for nearly 40 percent of new oil
demand during the mid-2000s. Based on these estimates,
China will become the world's biggest energy consumer by
2010. Ironically, Xinjiang's natural gas reserves offer global
environmental benefit if other fossil fuels are replaced in the
process, such as coal, because even a small offset in China will
amount to a massive reduction in greenhouse gas emissions.

One foreboding consequence is that Xinjiang's racially
divided development and sustained political crackdown have
pushed the traditionally moderate local population toward
fundamentalism, now actively exported by radicals in
Pakistan, Afghanistan, and the former Soviet republics of
Central Asia. Between thirty and 300 Uighur Taliban fighters
were reported captured by American forces during the 2002
Afghanistan war.[22] Xinjiang's long, porous border ensures that
radical elements, as well as guns and ammunition, continue to
trade, despite Chinese efforts.

Ever since the attacks of September 11, 2001, Beijing has
aggressively pursued crackdowns as part of its own trumped-
up war on terrorism. Official sources claimed that Xinjiang
separatists committed more than 200 acts of terrorism in
China between 1990 and 2002, killing 162 people and injuring
more than 440.[23] Xinjiang police claim that there were 800
"separatist incidents" in the first eight months of 2001 alone.[24]
In 2002, following the war in Afghanistan, the Chinese government gained the cautious support of the Bush administration
in adding an outlawed Uighur political party, the East
Turkestan Islamic Movement, to its list of known terrorist

groups. Later in 2002, China's Foreign Ministry reported that U.S. President George W. Bush and Chinese President Jiang Zemin had agreed, "Chechnya terrorist forces and East Turkestan terrorist forces are part of the international terrorist forces, which must be firmly stopped and rebuffed."

Nevertheless, the real threat of terrorism in Xinjiang remains indeterminate.[25] Expatriate political networks have been subdued, transborder traffic in dissidents has been slowed, clerics are forced into political re-education, birth control is heavily enforced, and even the Uighur language, a distant relative of Turkish, has been banned from universities and schools for communist cadres. "With construction on the vital West-East gas pipeline just beginning and energy invest-ment into Xinjiang on the rise, the last thing Beijing wants to see is a resurgence of the separatist-linked violence that hit the region from 1996 to 1998," noted U.S. strategic analysts StratFor in a 2002 report. "Ironically, the same event that may force Uighur militants abroad to return to Xinjiang — the U.S. war against terrorism — at first appeared to offer the perfect opportunity for Beijing to intensify its crackdown in the region without endangering its international image."[26]

Indeed, anger against China is increasingly being redi-rected at the United States and its allies. "There's real disillu-sionment and growing anger, not so much against China, but against the United States. Mosques are now raising warriors to go and fight," said Dru C. Gladney, a Xinjiang expert at the University of Hawaii. Speaking to a Beijing audience in 2003, he reported that American policy in the Middle East is radical-izing the political underground in Xinjiang, which in turn may disable China's long-term ability to export cheap consumer items to the West. "There is no love or sympathy for Saddam Hussein [in Xinjiang] but there's certainly a lot more awareness of international politics and they're certainly in touch with Muslims around the world."[27]

While China helps manufacture and amplify Central Asian terrorism, western corporations have moved in. Even though China's state oil company competes with Shell in Nigeria, it is one of the largest foreign investors in China with investments totaling US$1.6 billion and had increased its investment to US$4 billion by 2006.[28] This includes a share in the $ 4.2 billion Nanhai petrochemicals plant in Guangdong, China's largest single refinery. As one Shell executive explained in 2005, China will likely become the second largest chemical market in the world by 2020 and by 2010, Shell intends to have over a third of its petrochemical production in Asia and the Middle East.[29]

Beijing has dubbed Xinjiang its "sea of hope" because of the region's rich energy deposits — but for many foreign multinationals, it is simply a foothold within the fastest-growing energy market in the world. As analysts have noted, Shell's aggressive entry into China is at least partially about cultivating relationships with Chinese government, in addition to gaining a strategic position at the confluence of Russia, China, and Central Asia. During the early 2000s, Shell was a full partner in the first Xinjiang pipeline project. "The West-East pipeline is a pathfinder for future pipelines and gas from farther afield," explained Shell Exploration (China) managing director Martin Bradshaw in 2002. "[The pipeline] will be in line with international standards and . . . will benefit all ethnic groups."[30] The beginning of a huge trans-Asian pipeline network, one as complete as those seen in Europe and North

America, begins in Xinjiang. Yet not long after, China's national oil company dumped its foreign partners and built the pipeline by itself. (Shell Canada still owns 11.4 percent of the Mackenzie pipeline project and modest gas reserves in the Mackenzie Delta.)

With the formula for Central Asian strife now solidly in place, China has begun to express the kind of explicit energy nationalism long predicted for the twenty-first century. "On the street and in the boardroom, there is a growing sense in China that we are now strong enough to do it all alone, which I think is wrong," said European Union trade commissioner Peter Mandelson in 2008, regarding ongoing trade obstacles and "an unspoken economic nationalism that implies that foreign investment is no longer wanted or needed."[31] In the West, imported crude oil is still accepted as a necessary evil, even if it indirectly funds terrorism; in China, the prospect of escalating energy costs and excessive imports are seen as the end of China's miracle boom — and the onset of chaos and collapse.

Off on the other side of the Taklamakan, within a few days' drive of the Pakistani and Afghani borders, the desert outposts of Kashgar, Yarkant, and Hotan form the nominal front lines in the fight for Xinjiang. Here, Uighurs still form the majority, and the strife is even closer to the surface: photos of bloodshed are posted to buildings, if only to warn locals of police reprisals; large banners urge Uighurs to follow China's strict family-control policy, something that has seen the assassination of several Chinese enforcement officers; and used pharmaceuticals can be purchased in the local bazaar — a reminder that annual income in the Uighur heartland remains even lower than much of the rest of China. One gets the feeling that the price of natural gas and crude oil could be more than monetary. This forsaken corner of Central Asia, largely forgotten by the rest of the world, harbours an advanced and incomplete police state, one increasingly dedicated to the mobilization of natural resources on behalf of China and a select group of foreign multinationals.

The heart of Xinjiang, a polyglot of Uighurs, Mongols, and Kazakhs, can still be found in the family home of Rebiya, who serves up a traditional welcoming feast of rice polo, tomato and cucumber salad, savoury noodles, and mint tea. We lounge around the low table in their living room and sample the food, trading words for apricot, plum, peach, and melon. As desert winds blow through Urumqi, Rebiya's sister pulls out her dutar, a long, two-stringed guitar. After performing an old Turkic folk song, she plays a Ricky Martin tune that blazed across China during the country's first televised soccer World Cup. Over the drone of the dutar, we sing: "Go, go, go, *allez, allez, allez.*" For all we know, Ricky and the dutar might be the only things holding this region together.

The one thing that everyone in the energy business can agree upon is that the world needs natural gas right now, lots of gas. Canada's proven natural gas reserves have been shrinking 12 percent every year since 1999,[32] and decreased a total of 53 percent between 1999 and 2005.[33] Europe's natural gas supplies dwindled to 5.8 trillion cubic metres (tcm) in 2007, second-lowest only to Australia (2.7 tcm), with North America and South America only slightly more (8 tcm and 7 tcm, respectively). Russia and Iran conversely account for nearly half of global conventional gas reserves, 57 tcm and 73 tcm.[34] Evidenced by Russia's attempts to hold Europe hostage over natural gas supplies, gas is already proving to be one of the most strategic commodities of the twenty-first century.[35]

What this means is that fossil fuel pipelines — and the people who control them — could soon be on a par with the railway barons of the nineteenth century. Energy suppliers hold the key to our economy, and those with transport and product will prosper. The convergence between China and the West is striking: baseline demand for gas is growing; new demand is emerging from gas turbine and retrofitting of coal-fired power plants; and economic stagnation faces any nation that cannot provide affordable supplies of power. And the contrast between Canada's North and Xinjiang is striking, as only those who control their own lands have a chance at building power and dealing as equals when governments and corporations come to collect frontier resources.

Notwithstanding the negative impact of oil sands development on gas supplies, there is a credible environmental argument in favour of Arctic gas development — and, objectionable as it may seem, even the gas of Central Asia. It has been said that a world that starves for lack of natural gas cannot, practically speaking, combat climate change or air pollution, nor could it likely develop a feasible hydrogen economy. This is, perhaps, the ultimate measure of our deep and problematic connection to global networks of resource exploration and consumption. Our energy empire is large but stretched dangerously thin.

The story isn't merely about linear depletion and the bell-curve graphs of oil and gas decline favoured by peak oil advocates: it's about how the quest for unconventional and marginal supplies of energy is progressively sabotaging the economy and efforts to transition to greener outcomes.

It's as though the world's energy system, left unchecked, engineers its own crisis; new solutions are often transitory, effectively mere stopgap measures within a limited economic horizon. This fault is increasingly evident outside of North America, where economic pressures and lack of wealth show systemic flaws more clearly. For example, China's incredible thirst for energy feeds not only a booming export market accelerated by North America's big-box stores but also the hungry appetites of an emergent middle class across Asia, one that rivals 1950s America for its growth in rates of car owner-ship and consumer accumulation. Faced with today's esti-mated 170 million itinerant workers and continued labour uprisings, Mao Zedong would have been hard-pressed to dis-cern parts of modern China from the industrial England of Karl Marx.

Now, more than ever, our industrial borderlands are places where we plumb the future and track new history — whether it is a high-tech regime of repression and resource extraction, largely condoned by China's trading partners, or, closer to home, the efforts of Northern Aboriginals to build and own part of the pipeline that ships their resource birthright south-ward. Understanding the full cost of power is perhaps one of the biggest but least-appreciated problems of the twenty-first century. If the world's energy frontiers are any indication, our collective weakness is an inability to anticipate long-term sce-narios. At some point — and we may not fully realize when this happens — North Americans could end up investing more effort and energy into shoring up dysfunction than enjoying the rich quality of life that cheap energy has provided. So the simple question still stands: What happens when the power runs out?

IS NUCLEAR ENERGY THE ANSWER?

Allison Macfarlane

I magine your neighbourhood with a nuclear power plant a short drive away. You can see the tips of the cooling towers from your upstairs window. You know the plant is a source of clean, greenhouse-gas-free (or almost-free) energy production. It is a new, "inherently safe" designed plant, built with subsidies from the federal government, your taxpayer dollars. The waste from the plant is kept on site in a reinforced bunker — that and the armed-guard force protect it from sabotage. The waste will eventually go to a repository located within 800 kilometres of your home. In fact, most communities have similar nuclear power reactors; yours is not unique. They are helping to defer the deleterious effects of greenhouse gases on the climate. But are you comfortable with it there?

Worldwide electricity demand is expected to increase in the years to come, not only from familiar residential and industrial uses but also potentially from new demands such as the formation of hydrogen fuel. Given a business-as-usual scenario of the future, where the world's population increases to about ten billion by 2100, electricity generation is expected to almost double by 2020, quadruple by 2060, and quintuple by 2100. In concert with the growing evidence of a link between fossil fuels and climate change, a decrease in reliance on fossil fuels for electricity supply is needed. Estimates suggest that by 2020, carbon emissions from electricity generation alone will contribute double that of the current rate. If these levels are not reduced, the associated climate warming may produce disastrous results. How can we meet the electricity needs of an evolving world but reduce carbon emissions? Nuclear power may provide the answer.

The Past, Present, and Future of Nuclear Power

Currently, 16 percent of the world's electricity is supplied by nuclear power. Certainly the current nuclear capacity reduces the atmospheric load of greenhouse gases that would otherwise be generated by coal-, oil-, or gas-burning plants. The question is, can nuclear step into the void and actually expand enough to take a bigger bite out of the carbon load?

First, it is important to understand where nuclear power is in relation to other sources of electricity. As of March 2003, there were 437 commercial nuclear power reactors in thirty-one countries, with a total of about 360 gigawatts capacity, enough to power 400 million California homes. In comparison, fossil fuel plants had a worldwide capacity of about 2,400 gigawatts at this time, enough for almost 3 billion California homes. Though the United States gets only 19 percent of its electricity from nuclear power, it still has the largest nuclear energy fleet in the world. As of 2003, the United States had 103 licensed operating reactors in thirty-one states.

Much has been made of the potential for expanding nuclear power, but this would only occur over the long term. Nuclear capacity has hardly grown in the last fifteen years and will not likely grow much over the next fifteen years. The United States, for instance, last ordered a new nuclear power plant in 1978, and no plant ordered after 1973 was built (in large part, this was due to the accident at Three Mile Island). Thirty-three new nuclear plants are being constructed in eleven countries, predominantly India, China, Ukraine, Russia, and Japan. Little expansion is occurring in Europe and none in the United States or Canada.

In the United States and some European countries such as France, the trend is to extend the lifetime of existing reactors. The U.S. Nuclear Regulatory Commission (NRC) has begun granting twenty-year licence extensions for power plants. Germany, Sweden, and Belgium, on the other hand, have voted to phase out nuclear power before all plants have completed their licensed lifetimes. Furthermore, Austria, Denmark, Greece, Ireland, Italy, and Norway have prohibited the use of nuclear power. At the same time, many nuclear power plants in the United States and Europe have had power uprates, which have allowed the plants to increase their electricity-generating capacity. These power uprates enable the plants to produce electricity more competitively.

Deregulation of energy markets in the United States and elsewhere has allowed the restructuring of electric utility companies. For nuclear power, that has meant consolidation. In the U.S., for example, in 1991, 101 utility companies owned 110 reactors, but by 1999, the number of owners had decreased to 87, of which 12 owned more than 50 percent of the total generating capacity. Restructuring of nuclear utilities allowed larger companies to take advantage of economies of scale in maintaining and operating their plants. Previously, a company that owned a single nuclear power station may have decided to shut down instead of investing to replace aged, expensive equipment, whereas larger power plant owners can absorb these costs more easily.

The short-term future of nuclear power in countries like the United States looks somewhat brighter than it has in years. The regulatory climate is more favourable than before, and existing plants are more economical and therefore more competitive with fossil fuels, because the capital costs of building the nuclear power plants have been paid or the costs shifted to ratepayers. Finally, there are new reactor designs on the horizon.

But the future is not clear. Currently, all major expansion is occurring in developing countries, and even that is limited. Nuclear power is stagnating or shrinking in most developed countries. But nuclear power is the only currently existing, large-scale, geographically unlimited source of greenhouse-gas-free (or at least reduced) electricity. And for those countries that do not have cheap access to fossil fuel resources, nuclear power may be one of the only sure sources of reliable electricity. What would it take to expand nuclear power on a large scale, and what scale of expansion would reduce climate-change effects?

Can Nuclear Power Reduce Greenhouse Gas Emissions?

Nuclear power will not be the only answer to our energy needs in the future. First, nuclear power can only reduce greenhouse gas emissions from electricity production — not from fossil fuel use in transportation, for example. Second, the claim that nuclear power produces no greenhouse gas emissions is not actually correct. Greenhouse gases are emitted during the extraction of uranium for fuel, as well as during uranium processing and enrichment. Greenhouse gases are also emitted in the production of construction materials for nuclear power plants, such as concrete and steel. In addition, there are some minor emissions of greenhouse gases during reactor operations by secondary generators that are required in case of accidents. These generators must be tested on a regular basis, and during the testing they emit carbon dioxide and other gases.

Most nuclear power reactors in operation in the world today — those termed light water reactors — require uranium to be enriched in one of its naturally occurring isotopes, uranium-235, for use in fuel. The enrichment process can be very energy intensive, depending on the exact method used. The most energy-intensive enrichment process is gaseous diffusion, where uranium hexafluoride gas is passed through membranes that retard the movement of the heavier uranium-238 isotope. These plants tend to be huge as well as energy intensive. The Paducah, Kentucky, gaseous diffusion plant gets most of its electricity from coal-burning power plants. Thus, its annual operation creates the emission of about as much greenhouse gases as that from three 1,100-megawatt coal plants.

Other enrichment technologies, such as centrifuge plants, are less energy intensive than gaseous diffusion; nonetheless, they still use electricity. Unless a system can be made in which all the electricity used in uranium mining, milling, and enrichment comes form nuclear power itself, nuclear-produced electricity will result in the emission of some greenhouse gases.

The larger question that we are trying to address is, what is a reasonable expectation for greenhouse-gas-emission reductions from nuclear power? Today's nuclear power plants save 600 million tonnes of carbon per year from going into the atmosphere from equivalent power-producing coal-fired plants. But this is just 10 percent of the total amount of carbon released into the atmosphere each year. Nuclear power saves even less, about 250 million tonnes of carbon per year, for gas-fired power plants. For nuclear power to make a substantial dent in carbon emissions, it would have to reduce emissions by at least a third. By 2100, given that electricity usage may have increased five-fold, nuclear power would have to increase its share of production from one-sixth (what it is today) to one-third multiplied by five, or about ten times.

What Does Expanding Nuclear Power Mean?

What does a ten-fold increase in nuclear power generation translate into?

This would entail building in the order of 3,200 new mid-sized nuclear plants worldwide, 900 of them in the United States alone. The implications of such an expansion are impressive in terms of the waste and nuclear weapons materials produced. If these 3,200 new plants were of the same variety as those that now exist in the United States, namely, light water reactors, then the amount of used nuclear fuel produced on an annual basis would be 72,000 tonnes. That amount is equivalent to that planned to fill the entire U.S. repository at Yucca Mountain, Nevada. One percent of that fuel, 720,000 kg, would be plutonium, of which only 4 kg is needed to make a nuclear weapon.

What does this mean overall? First, it is important to note that I am only considering long-term scenarios here, where the ten-fold increase takes place between 2050 and 2100. It would not be possible to increase capacity so greatly over the short term, within the next ten or twenty years. It would simply take too long to build all the nuclear plants and supply all the equipment and personnel.

Over the long run, however, it would be possible to complete such an expansion. In doing so, a number of significant issues would require resolution before the world turned to nuclear power as a (partial) solution to greenhouse gas emissions. These include the cost of building new power plants, safety issues posed by the existence of over 3,000 plants, huge volumes of nuclear wastes, nuclear weapons proliferation, and the potential for terrorist strikes on nuclear power plants. Other issues include public acceptance of nuclear power and the low-level doses of radiation it imparts, and infrastructure issues, especially those of an aging workforce with few replacements and a decreased manufacturing capability.

Obstacles to Nuclear Power Expansion: Cost

Whether nuclear power is an attractive alternative to governments and investors depends partly on the comparative costs per kilowatt-hour of electricity generated. In some countries, nuclear power is currently competitive or even cheaper than fossil fuel alternatives. This is true for countries like Japan, France, Finland, and Canada, which have few fossil fuel resources. In all countries, nuclear power is characterized by high initial capital investments in comparison to coal- and gas-fired power plants. Note that although the current per-kilowatt-hour cost of nuclear-produced electricity in France, Japan, and Canada is low, these countries are not adding new nuclear plants at the moment. That may be largely due to the high cost of capital investment needed to build a nuclear plant.

Initial capital costs for nuclear power plants tend to run about 60–70 percent of per-kilowatt-hour electricity generating costs. In contrast, nuclear power has relatively low production costs, which include fuel, operations, and maintenance. The average cost to build a new nuclear reactor in the United States is estimated to be between US$1.5 billion and US$3 billion. In comparison, the cost of building an equivalent-size natural gas power plant is around US$450 million. In the past, nuclear electricity sales have not recovered capital costs, and in the United States these costs have consistently been underestimated by about three times the original estimate.

Another variable in nuclear power economics is construction time. For a country like the United States where no nuclear power plants have been built for decades, the construction time is a great unknown. It could take as little as five years or longer than ten years. It is difficult for an investor to commit to such uncertainty on the return on investment. Construction times tend to be much longer than for an equivalent natural gas plant. In deregulated energy markets, projects with long construction times are possible only with favourable interest rates and payback periods.

In addition to the capital and production costs, there are external costs such as those for managing and disposing of nuclear waste. The U.S. Nuclear Waste Policy Act required utility companies to charge ratepayers US0.1¢ per kilowatt-hour for a Nuclear Waste Fund, which would cover the costs of disposing of spent fuel in a geologic repository. From 1983 to 2002, U.S. ratepayers paid over US$16 billion into the Nuclear Waste Fund, but only US$8 billion has been spent on the characterization of Yucca Mountain in Nevada, because the U.S. Congress has used the rest to defer budget deficits.

Other external costs are those for decommissioning nuclear power plants and those to cover insurance funds in case of catastrophic accident. Decommissioning costs may, in fact, be underestimated. In the United States, two studies showed that estimates of decommissioning costs had risen from about US$300 million per reactor to US$500 million per reactor in one year. Because evidence suggests that these costs may continue to rise, and because no light water reactor has been completely decommissioned (including spent-fuel removal), there is reason to believe that utility companies may not be collecting enough money to cover these costs in the future.

An additional source of economic uncertainty with nuclear power is the potential for high external costs from plant aging. As a plant ages, large and expensive pieces of equipment may need to be replaced. Moreover, even if the plant owner sees no need for part replacement, the regulators may require it. An example is the experiences of the Davis-Besse plant in the United States. It was a surprise to both the plant owners and the NRC that holes developed in the reactor head, which, if they had gone completely through the head, would have resulted in a large accident. The reactor owner has been trying to fix the problem, but the reactor has been off-line for over a year now and the NRC has yet to allow it to resume operations.

A ten-fold expansion in nuclear power would occur only if initial capital costs were somehow controlled. This could be done via investment guarantees and government subsidies, as some in the U.S. Senate are trying to provide. To be successful, nuclear power has to compete with other energy sources, and some renewable technologies may be less costly and more competitive in the future than they are now.

Types of Nuclear Power Plant Designs

Nuclear reactors harness the energy produced by the splitting of atoms (fission), usually uranium, though sometimes plutonium. In doing so, a reactor requires two processes: moderation of the energy of the neutrons that split the atoms to the energy needed to maximize fission, and cooling of the reactor components — to safely run the reactor. The coolant also performs the important job of transferring heat energy produced by the reactor to the turbines that produce electricity.

Reactors are generally distinguished by the types of fuel, moderator, and coolant that they use. In the United States, reactors were developed from those used in nuclear submarines. The most successful of these was the light water reactor, which used fuel slightly enriched in uranium-235. Light water reactors use regular water as both coolant and moderator. Two types of light water reactors are in use in the world today: pressurized water reactors, in which the core of the reactor and its water are kept under high pressure so that the water does not boil, and boiling water reactors, in which the water is allowed to boil, generating steam to run the turbines.

Britain and Canada decided to base their initial reactor designs on uranium fuel that didn't require enrichment. Britain developed gas-cooled reactors, which used carbon dioxide gas as a coolant and graphite as a moderator. These are known as Magnox reactors after the magnesium-rich alloy used to clad the uranium metal fuel. Later models of Britain's gas-cooled reactors used slightly enriched uranium dioxide fuel. Canada developed the CANDU (short for CANadian Deuterium Uranium) reactor, which uses natural uranium as a fuel and heavy (deuterium-based instead of hydrogen-based) water as both coolant and moderator.

Two other reactor designs merit mention. The Soviets designed a light water–cooled, graphite-moderated reactor known as the RMBK, the most infamous example of which is the Chernobyl reactor. Many of these reactor types are still in operation in Russia and Eastern Europe. The other important design is the liquid-metal fast-breeder reactor. This reactor uses fast neutrons and does not need to slow them down with a moderator. The coolant used is either sodium or lead-bismuth. Although a number of countries had fast-breeder reactor programs, many of them shut down due to cost and technical difficulties. Only three of these reactor types are in operation in the world now.

Obstacles to Nuclear Power Expansion: Safety

For those who remember them, the experiences of living through the Chernobyl and Three Mile Island nuclear power plant accidents were nail-biting moments. The 1979 Three Mile Island plant accident did not result in large releases of radiation, but the seeds of uncertainty planted in the public's mind spelled the end of expansion for the nuclear industry in the United States. The 1986 Chernobyl accident, unfortunately, was a different story; it resulted in forty-two immediate deaths (from exposed workers) and has caused a twenty-five-fold increase in childhood thyroid cancers in nearby Belarus. It will also likely result in an additional 6,500 cancer deaths in nearby residents and "liquidators" who worked to contain the radiation. A third reactor accident — involving a nuclear-weapons-production reactor, not a civilian power reactor — at the Windscale plant in Sellafield, England, in 1957 released radioactivity in amounts between that of Three Mile Island and Chernobyl.

The problem with safety issues for nuclear power is the public's well-founded fear of radiation — which can injure or kill but cannot be sensed — based on the destruction wrought by the United States' use of nuclear weapons in Japan at the end of World War II. Nonetheless, many years have passed since the nuclear industry experienced an accident. The emphasis now is on safety issues from aging nuclear power plants and the enhanced safety of new plant designs.

The existing fleet of nuclear power plants is aging fast. For example, the average age of the world's operational nuclear power reactors is twenty-one years. As mentioned earlier, the United States is already beginning to extend the licensed lifetimes of nuclear power plants from forty years to sixty years.

One example of an aging problem that could affect safety is the corroded lid on the reactor at the Davis-Besse plant.

A tenfold increase in the number of reactors would greatly increase the potential for safety issues. It would certainly over-burden existing regulatory agencies, which would have to adjust accordingly, including increases in government appro-priations. With so many reactors, would all equipment, opera-tors, and regulators be of top quality?

There are a number of new reactor designs that claim to be safer to operate than the more ubiquitous light water reactor designs of the 1970s. Some of these new reactor designs have not fallen far from the original "tree" and are based on the light water reactor workhorse in use in the United States and much of Europe and Asia. One advantage of these systems is that there will be a standardized plan for the reactors. U.S. nuclear reactors have unique designs, which has not allowed the U.S. nuclear industry to take advantage of economies of scale. The new design will be simpler and the plants will have a longer life, about sixty years. The simpler design will reduce the prob-ability of a reactor accident. Finally, the reactors will be designed to burn fuel longer, to reduce waste volumes. These designs are mostly for large-scale plants, but some are mid-size (600-megawatt) designs.

Nuclear engineers have not limited themselves to simply modifying existing reactor designs; some have designed advanced reactors. One is the high-temperature gas reactor (HTGR), the first of the new generation of which is planned for construction in South Africa. Though the design is not new, it takes advantage of a modular plan (so that additional modules can be added to a single site to increase capacity) and a more accident-resistant fuel. These reactors are expected to be much more efficient than existing nuclear power plants. The HTGR uses helium as a coolant and operates at high temperatures, about 950°C. The fuel is designed either as "pebbles" of uranium coated with carbon and silicon carbide or as uranium embedded in graphite and arranged in hexagonal prisms. The pebble type of fuel is planned for the South African reactor, thus it is termed the "Pebble Bed Reactor."

Although HTGRs are described as "inherently safe" in design, they do have some potential safety issues. One is the fact that they are designed without containments — large, reinforced structures built around the reactor vessel itself. A containment is what the Chernobyl reactor lacked, and so when it melted down, there was no structure available to contain the radioactivity. High-temperature gas reactors can be designed without containments because the probability of a meltdown is very low, due to the fuel's ability to slow the fission process (splitting of uranium atoms) as the temperature increases. On the other hand, the reactors are susceptible to fire if air or water comes into contact with the fuel, and these reactors produce more spent fuel than do comparable-size light water reactors.

The other advanced design under discussion also is not new, but entails numerous obstacles which relegate it to the far future, if it is to be used at all. This is the fast neutron reactor, which typically takes advantage of the fast neutrons emitted by plutonium and therefore requires plutonium fuel. The idea behind these reactors is that they not only produce electricity but also replace or breed their fuel through nuclear reactions with a uranium "blanket," thus they are often referred to as fast-breeder reactors. For coolant these reactors require some type of liquid metal such as sodium or lead-bismuth; others require a gas. Current designs of these plants are exorbitantly expensive. In addition, the use of plutonium fuel can lead to diversion for and proliferation of nuclear weapons.

Obstacles to Nuclear Power Expansion: Nuclear Waste

Nuclear waste remains an unresolved problem in all countries that use nuclear power for electricity production. Considering that 20 to 30 tonnes of used nuclear fuel are produced per gigawatt per year, the current capacity of the world's nuclear power plants produces between 7,000 and 11,000 tonnes of spent fuel annually. In many countries, this spent fuel continues to reside at reactor facilities, awaiting final disposal. In some countries, such as France, the United Kingdom, Russia, Germany, and Japan, this fuel has been transported to reprocessing facilities, where its unused uranium and newly produced plutonium are extracted. Only one of these reprocessing countries so far has succeeded in using a large portion of the plutonium as fuel in existing reactors; the rest simply stockpile the separated plutonium.

The reprocessors are not off the hook in dealing with nuclear waste, however. They have reduced the overall volume of high-level waste, but they have vastly increased the volumes of low-level and intermediate-level wastes. And the high-level waste contains all the thermally and radioactively hot materials that the original spent fuel contained. When disposing of waste, the volume is not as important as the heat production.

The international consensus for solving the problem of high-level waste is to dispose of it in geologic repositories,

whether in the form of spent fuel or vitrified high-level reprocessing waste. Most countries with nuclear power are developing a geologic repository, though the task has proved more
difficult than previously thought. The United States, Finland,
and Sweden have perhaps the most "advanced" waste disposal
programs, though none have come close to actually opening a
repository.

The issues facing successful disposal of nuclear waste fall
into two main categories: political and technical. Though many
in the nuclear industry claim that the nuclear waste problem is
technically solvable, there are still many uncertainties attached
to the science and engineering of nuclear waste disposal. First
of all, it is one endeavour for which we will never know the
results. If the waste leaks 1,000 years from now and affects
humans living near the repository site, a result that is judged a
failure by most repository regulations, we won't know it.

Second and perhaps more important is the fact that disposal is using the barriers provided by the local geology in
addition to the engineered ones of the waste canisters, the tunnel, backfill, and others. Because one of the main barriers to
the release of radionuclides to the environment is the geology,
predictions of geologic conditions and behaviours of radionuclides and engineered materials in the geologic system over
geologic time periods are essential to ensuring a successful
repository location. These predictions rely on geology, a retro-
dictive (explaining the past), not predictive, science. Therefore,
geologic disposal of nuclear waste will entail some amount of
uncertainty. And this is the link to the political issues.

It is not clear that, given the inherent uncertainty in ensuring safety when disposing of nuclear wastes, it will ever be
politically feasible to open a repository. There are a number of

models for attempting to do so, ranging from the democratic methods of France, Finland, and now Germany, where the public in the site location is given ultimate veto power over potential sites, to the more top-down approach favoured by the United States. U.S. site selection was essentially done by Congress in the Nuclear Waste Policy Act Amendments of 1987, in which it forewent the plan to characterize and select from three sites to one, the Yucca Mountain site in Nevada.

The problem for a future with a ten-fold increase in nuclear power production is the huge amounts of waste produced. To manage and dispose of an annual production of 70,000 to 110,000 tonnes of spent fuel will require a new way of dealing with the waste. For comparison, the Yucca Mountain site in the United States is currently designed to hold 70,000 tonnes of waste. The ten-fold increase would require tens to hundreds of Yucca Mountain–type sites. It's not clear that this will be either technically or politically feasible.

The decision may be to wait for a better alternative to geologic repositories to come around. But this would mean that an industry is allowed to continue to produce highly toxic wastes without an implemented and proven plan to deal with them. One technology on the horizon is transmutation of nuclear waste, which allows the alteration of many long-lived radionuclides into shorter-lived ones. This technology will still require some type of geologic repository for the disposal of the shorter-lived radionuclides, though. It will also require the construction of new and expensive reactors or accelerators.

Obstacles to Nuclear Power Expansion: Nuclear Weapons Proliferation

The hardest part of making a nuclear weapon is obtaining the nuclear materials to power it. Therefore, perhaps the most serious problem with a large expansion of nuclear power is the threat to international security from the proliferation of nuclear weapons. There has always been a direct connection between nuclear power and nuclear weapons because the materials used to power the weapons are the same as those used to power reactors, the fissile materials plutonium and highly enriched uranium. England obtained some of the plutonium for its nuclear weapons from power reactors. India got its first significant quantities of plutonium, used for a "peaceful nuclear explosion" in 1974, from a research reactor of Canadian power reactor design.

Our international system to detect the diversion of fissile material has already been challenged by Iraqi and North Korean diversions. How would the system handle ten times more reactors? Clearly, proliferation-resistant nuclear energy technologies are required.

One potential proliferation-resistant power reactor technology is the Radkowsky concept, which uses thorium instead of uranium fuel in existing light water reactors. The advantage here is that less plutonium is produced when the fuel is irradiated or "burned" in the reactor than in typical light water reactor designs. Thorium fuel is not a complete solution, though, as it produces the isotope uranium-233, which can be used to make nuclear weapons. The idea is to dilute this with uranium-238 to levels impossible to make usable nuclear explosions.

Another suggestion is to use high-temperature gas reactors. With this type of reactor, proliferation resistance is obtained through the high burnup (long fuel irradiation time) of the fuel, which creates plutonium isotopes that make the manufacture of nuclear weapons difficult. Of course, the reactor need not be operated in that manner. Furthermore, HTGRs use fuel that is more enriched in uranium-235 compared with that used in light water reactors. Thus, countries using HTGRs may need enrichment technologies. Once uranium is enriched to 20-percent uranium-235 (the level needed for many HTGR designs), it is relatively easy to enrich further to 90 percent, posing proliferation risk.

Finally, some have suggested fast-breeder reactor technologies in which plutonium is not separated from the fission products in the fuel. The fission products make the use of this material as a nuclear weapon impossible. Of course, a country with the right resources can still separate the plutonium from the fission products. Moreover, the use of breeder reactors creates more plutonium, increasing the diversion/theft problem.

Used nuclear fuel from light water reactors cannot be used in nuclear weapons, though the plutonium in it, which makes up about 1 percent of the mass of the fuel, can be. Perhaps the main problem with nuclear power is that some of the associated technologies — reprocessing of spent fuel to separate plutonium and uranium enrichment technologies — pose the highest proliferation threats. Separated plutonium can easily be fashioned into nuclear weapons by knowledgeable people. Highly enriched uranium is arguably even easier to make into nuclear weapons. Thus, for years the world has safeguarded these technologies in non–nuclear weapons states.

The problem with a ten-fold expansion in nuclear power is the resulting growth and spread of these technologies. Clearly, they would have to be controlled. Perhaps the best way to do so would be through the use of international uranium enrichment, reprocessing, and reactor production facilities. An additional step to ensure proliferation resistance would be internationalizing nuclear waste disposal, so that all nuclear material was controlled and accounted for from cradle to grave. The question is, how to internationalize these technologies? Who would host these facilities — and who would be dependent upon the good will of the hosts?

The problem with internationalizing these facilities is that it would create two classes of country: those deemed responsible and stable enough to host these facilities, and the rest. Furthermore, many countries find nuclear energy attractive because it allows them to become independent of others for their energy resources. Internationalizing the nuclear fuel production facilities would continue the energy dependence of many countries.

Finally, there is a problem with the large existing stocks of separated plutonium in the civilian energy sector. Over 200 tonnes of separated plutonium remains in storage in the United Kingdom, France, Russia, and other countries, with no immediate plans for its use. Though the material is (for the most part) well-guarded and accounted for, there remains the possibility of diversion or theft. These stockpiles would need to be responsibly dealt with before the step was taken of making a large expansion in nuclear power. This would increase the security of all nations by showing that there were no intentions to use this material in nuclear weapons.

Obstacles to Nuclear Power Expansion:
Security Against Theft and Sabotage

Concerns about security and terrorism at nuclear power plants are not new, but they were certainly highlighted by the September 11, 2001, terrorist attacks in the United States. Nuclear power plants have two main vulnerabilities: the core of the reactor and its spent fuel pool storage. Depending on the reactor design, both can be vulnerable. Some reactors are designed with the spent fuel pools inside the containment; in other designs they are outside, with less protection against attack and more potential for radiation release. Some reactors are designed with spent fuel pools on floors above ground level. If the pool in such a reactor was damaged, it could potentially drain the cooling water, leading to a fire and fuel meltdown. The reason spent fuel pools are of concern is that they often contain many times the amount of fuel in the reactor core, and thus the potential for fire is higher in the event of sabotage.

Most nuclear reactors are facilities that restrict the persons allowed to enter. Nonetheless, the security threat exists. The threat could be from an outside attack from the air, water (many nuclear power plants are located on bodies of water), or ground and could be assisted by one or more insiders, helping from within the facility itself. The problem of security at nuclear plants is exemplified by the over 50-percent failure rate of security tests done at U.S. reactors. With a ten-fold increase in nuclear power plants, the risk from terrorist attack also increases.

Perhaps the solution to the risk is inherently safe reactors and inherently safe fuel. There are very few new reactor designs that have these qualities, though the Swedish-designed Process Inherent Ultimate Safe (PIUS) reactor may come close. There are no obvious solutions to the security problem at this time, short of guarding the facilities as nuclear weapons facilities are guarded, a proposition far too costly for the nuclear industry.

The Bottom Line

An expansion to more than 3,500 nuclear reactors worldwide implies first tackling the major issues of cost, safety, waste, proliferation, and security. The cost of nuclear power must be competitive not only with fossil fuels but also with renewable energy technologies, such as wind, that will become mature in the twenty-first century. Safety and cost are linked, and the new, safer reactor designs must prove to be cost competitive as well, in both the industrialized and developing worlds. The nuclear waste problem must be proven solvable, given the large amounts of waste expected to be produced with a tenfold increase in generating capacity. And perhaps most importantly, there must be enough international infrastructure and organization to deal with the proliferation and security issues.

One other problem will need to be solved before expanding nuclear power. Currently, there are no plans for phasing out nuclear power — decommissioning all the reactors, ensuring that no material is diverted to nuclear weapons or terrorists, and disposing of the wastes. Given that one day nuclear power will no longer be needed, how will phase-out occur with ten times as many reactors? Is it ethical to embark on such an increase without definite plans to deal with any of these issues? In comparison to coal-fired plants, where there is no worry about diversion of fuel to nuclear weapons, the problem of nuclear power phase-out is much more complicated.

Because of all the potential problems, many of them very serious, that a ten-fold increase in nuclear power will bring, a world with increased nuclear power will not be modelled on the current situation of nuclear power use. There will have to be a way to deal with the waste problem, because it will not be solved with geologic repositories — the public simply would not allow that (seeing how they have yet to allow it). If that is the case, then some type of reprocessing and/or transmutation will be required to deal with the spent fuel. And in that case, there will have to be tight controls to avoid the proliferation of nuclear weapons. Because the amount of plutonium produced in such a scenario is on the order of 150,000 bombs' worth per year, reprocessing will need to be done in a single international centre. I suggest a single centre because the non-proliferation advantage would be lost to competition among fuel suppliers if there was more than one centre. And one centre would be the most equitable, if it were truly international.

In the end, such a large expansion in nuclear energy may only be possible if the connection between nuclear energy and nuclear weapons is fully broken. For this to be done, nuclear weapons would likely have to be abolished and sworn off by all countries. In today's world, it is difficult to imagine such a scenario.

At this time, it is not at all clear that these issues will be resolved in the long term. If they are not, the potential for harm from reactor accidents, nuclear weapons use, or terrorist attacks will make a large expansion of this energy form undesirable, even given its beneficial effects on the climate. In the end, with nuclear power we must weigh the risks and their potentials: could there be a nuclear bomb from diverted nuclear materials, and is the explosion of one of these weapons worth the money saved from renewable energy technologies and the advantages for the climate? I'm not sure we are able to answer that question right now.

Boom, Bust, and Efficiency

L. Hunter Lovins and Wyatt King

Promoters of clean energy often feel like Sisyphus, perpetually pushing a boulder up a mountainside. Just when solar, wind, and other clean technologies[1] seem poised to gain a foothold in the market, the ground collapses and the effort must begin again. This is not a new phenomenon. In the 1930s solar panels graced 30 percent of houses in Southern California and Florida. Several decades later few remained.[2]

Is the quest for clean energy doomed, or is an economy fueled by clean energy possible? What will it take to get over Sisyphus's hump?

It will require, first of all, an understanding of the role of energy efficiency, not merely a devotion to the various forms of renewable supply. The best way to understand energy efficiency is to take an end-use-least-cost approach and ask such questions as, What tasks need energy? and How can we perform those tasks in the cheapest and best ways? This approach will demonstrate that any form of clean energy supply likely will be the second-best option, and will be part of a durable answer only if integrated with the *best* choice: using less of the energy we already have.[3] Efficient use of energy should be considered before any supply technology, whether the supply is renewable, nuclear, or fossil. Unless the relationship between energy efficiency and supply is understood, any effort to convert to secure, affordable, abundant supplies of energy is likely to fail. Efficiency will then play the role of spoiler: dampening any supply strategy. It will defeat renewable energy, as surely as it has laid waste to most traditional supply technologies.

How Not to Make Energy Policy

Official government energy strategies have tended not to work. This is, in large part, because they have tried to dictate to the market technologies that cannot survive without government support. In consequence, the policies have been more honoured in the breach than in the observance. In the 1950s the Paley Commission (the first U.S. government commission to study energy and recommend policies to ensure secure, affordable supplies of future energy) called for a massive conversion to renewable energy, but its sensible and timely recommendations were completely ignored. The world seemed awash in oil at the time.

The 1973 oil embargo changed that perception. It also gave President Nixon the dubious honour of having to put forth an official energy policy. His proposed Project Independence would have had Americans spend three-quarters of all discretionary investment money in the economy on new forms of energy supply, disproportionately coal and nuclear. The market, however, took a dim view of this plan, and few of these investments ever happened. Nixon's response was to deal with the inflation caused by the run up in energy costs by capping energy prices. This move, however, denied institutional and individual decision makers the market mechanism of a price signal.

In due course, the oil markets settled down and few people beside the usual suspects of electric utility companies, oil executives, and a few beady-eyed policy wonks spent much time worrying about how the country would meet its needs for energy. A growing number of citizens, though, started to concern themselves with the consequences of the Western world's energy use. The environmental movement, in particular, launched protests against the conventional supply technologies and called for a conversion to a solar economy.

Some people thought that all that was needed was a change of administration, but when President Carter had to respond to his own energy crisis in 1979, not surprisingly his solution also featured governmental directives and a disproportionate emphasis on conventional supply. To overcome the market's continued reluctance to pay for such a prescription, Carter proposed the Energy Security Corporation and the Energy Mobilization Board. These agencies could override market mechanisms and supplant democratic institutions if either worked to impede supply expansions. In an effort to pacify environmentalists, Carter put solar panels on the White House, and his Department of Energy took a liking to every sort of centralized solar technology imaginable, from solar space satellites to solar power towers in the desert to wind machines with blades the length of a jumbo jet wing.

Once again, though, the effort to "solve" the energy problem with central mandates failed. Even the declaration that the country's energy shortages were the moral equivalent of war did not help Carter's energy program, which was so capital intensive that it failed a test of market rationality.

On the positive side, Carter was the first president to recognize the advantages of energy efficiency. His administration implemented such measures as CAFE (Corporate Average Fuel Economy) standards for vehicles. These were regulatory programs, but they did focus on eliciting the cheapest solutions to the energy problem. They also dramatically increased American security by enabling the country to buy less oil more quickly and on a larger scale than the Organization of Petroleum Exporting Countries (OPEC) could adjust to. New U.S.-built cars increased their efficiency by 7 miles per gallon (mpg; 33.6 litres per 100 kilometres [L/100 km]) in six years. Europe achieved similar oil consumption savings, but did so primarily through higher fuel taxes rather than through better efficiency standards.

Together, these changes tipped the world oil market in buyers' favour. Between 1977 and 1985, U.S. oil imports fell 42 percent, depriving OPEC of one-eighth of its market. The entire world oil market shrank by one-tenth; the United States alone accounted for one-fourth of that reduction. OPEC's share fell from 52 percent to 30 percent, forcing it to cut its output by 48 percent, which drove down world oil prices. On average, new cars each drove 1 percent fewer miles, but used 20 percent fewer gallons. Only 4 percent of those savings came from making the cars smaller.[4]

Carter's plans also put in place two measures that enabled the market to work better: they lifted the market caps on price and they initiated a variety of programs that provided information on what sorts of energy technologies were available and what citizens could do to use energy more wisely.

Carter's efficiency initiatives worked far better than his supply plans, and their beneficial effects lingered for half a decade after his term. Between 1979 and 1986, Americans cut total energy use by 5 percent — a drop in energy intensity (the amount of energy needed to produce a unit of GDP) that was five times bigger than the expanded coal and nuclear output subsequently promoted by President Reagan's policy.

Upon entering office in 1981, Reagan sought to stimulate fossil fuel and nuclear energy production, not realizing that the efforts of the previous administration had allowed the United States to cut energy intensity at the record pace of 3.5 percent per year. Five years later, energy efficiency — disdained as an intrusive sacrifice and a distraction from America's supply prowess — had pre-empted the markets that were supposed to pay for costly supply expansions. In the mid-1980s, many of the producers Reagan meant to help were ruined, as efficiency's speed and availability made energy prices crash. Despite Reagan's concerted campaign to undo the previous administration's efficiency and information programs,5 by the middle of the decade the market had had time to work. Entrepreneurs were introducing myriad technologies that were producing huge efficiency benefits. Even advocates of renewable supply were caught off guard, as well as being hampered by the inept way that government programs sought to subsidize renewables. It turned out that efficiency was simply much cheaper than any form of supply. Despite its imperfections, the market, given half a chance to work, turned out to be smarter than the supposed energy experts.

Energy efficiency came online far faster than anyone had predicted, and far faster than any expansion of supply. From

1983 to 1985, the nation's third-largest investor-owned utility was cutting its decade-ahead forecast of peak demand by about 8.5 percent *each year,* at roughly 1 percent of the cost of new supply. The nation's largest investor-owned utility signed up 25 percent of new commercial construction projects for design improvements in just three months. As a result, it raised its target for the following year — and hit it in the first nine days. Well-designed efficiency programs have captured up to 99 percent of target markets. A huge literature confirms the size of the savings and shows that the costs of achieving them can be accurately predicted and measured.[6]

This history repeated itself in 2001 as President George W. Bush, with ardour similar to Reagan's, sought to stimulate energy supplies, even though in 1996 the United States had quietly resumed saving energy by 3.2 percent a year. Bush called for opening the Arctic National Wildlife Refuge to oil exploration, and proposed massive fossil and nuclear subsidies. Meanwhile, subsidies and other policies that promoted vehicle inefficiency led to a situation where the average fuel efficiency of U.S. cars and trucks hit a twenty-two-year low in 2002: 20.4 mpg (11.5 L/100 km).[7] In June 2003, environmentalists pointed out that the average fuel efficiency of Ford cars and trucks was worse than when the company started one hundred years ago with the Model T.[8] This represents a tremendous lost opportunity. The U.S. National Academy of Sciences reported in 2001 that although light-vehicle improvements have already cut gasoline consumption by 14 percent — equivalent to the amount of oil imported from the Persian Gulf — further efficiency gains, which would be cost-effective to the driver to make, can roughly double U.S. fleet efficiency without compromising safety or performance.[9] Typical potential fuel savings range from about one-fifth for small cars to one-third for midsize SUVs and nearly one-half for big pickup trucks. Achieving such savings would be good for more than driver's pocketbooks: such vehicles are responsible for 20 percent of U.S. carbon dioxide emissions.

Such savings projections are quite conservative and assume that smarter car companies will not introduce novel designs that will disrupt the industry and put inattentive car companies at risk. While American car companies resist making their products more fuel efficient, the Japanese and Europeans are again designing the future. The Toyota Prius hybrid-electric five-seater gets 48 mpg (4.9 L/100 km); Honda's Insight gets 64 mpg (3.7 L/100 km). An entire American car fleet that efficient would save thirty-two times the amount of oil that proponents of drilling in the Arctic hope to find there.[10] DaimlerChrysler and General Motors are now testing family sedans at 72–80 mpg (3.3 L/100 km–2.9 L/100 km). Volkswagen already sells Europeans a 78-mpg (3.0-L/100-km) four-seat non-hybrid subcompact. Almost every automaker at the 2003 Tokyo Auto Show displayed good hybrid-electric prototypes, some getting more than 100 mpg (2.35 L/100 km). Volkswagen has just premiered a supersafe but ultralight diesel car that gets 285 mpg (0.83 L/100 km).[11]

Markets are, of course, imperfect. As prices fall, people easily fall back into apathy. Advertising campaigns (and tax subsidies) that encourage Americans to buy a 10-mpg (23.5-L/100-km) Hummer H2 so that they can paste an American flag on it and feel like they are patriotically supporting the troops in the Middle East ensure that those young men and women will continue to be in harm's way, driving 0.5-mpg (470-L/100-km) tanks and 17-feet-per-gallon (73,000-L/100-km) aircraft carriers. Such behaviour also ensures that we will all get to enjoy yet another energy crisis.

In 2000, California created such a crisis with its ham-handed program to "deregulate" electricity markets in such a way as to allow the incumbent "big dogs to eat first."[12] Once the world leader in energy efficiency, with financially healthy utilities and sensible resource policies, California nearly plunged the whole of the United States into the next energy crisis. Panicked by so-called power shortages and exhorted by Vice President Dick Cheney's call to build at least one power plant a week,[13] developers planned to add electricity-generating capacity equivalent to 83 percent of the state's current total demand, 96 percent of the western region's, and at least one-third of the nation's. But meanwhile, California citizens, companies, and communities woke up and implemented exactly the same solution that had worked before: reliance on efficiency, which enabled them to save their way out of the hole. Californians cut peak electricity demand per dollar of gross domestic product (GDP), adjusted for weather, by 14 percent in six months, and a third of customers cut their usage by over 20 percent. In just the first six months of 2001, customers wiped out California's previous five to ten years of demand growth, taking away proposed new power plants' markets before their plans could even be finished. This abruptly ended the crisis that the White House claimed would require 1,300 to 1,900 more power plants nationwide. By August 2001, a *Barron's* cover story noted a coming glut of electricity. Scores of plants have been cancelled for lack of demand,[14] and their irrationally exuberant builders are reeling as Wall Street, stung by Enron's collapse, downgrades their bonds.

Efficiency keeps quietly making gains. A 2002 report by the American Council for an Energy-Efficient Economy (ACEEE), "State Scorecard on Utility and Public Benefits Energy Efficiency Programs: An Update," states that there has been a halt to the decade-long trend to eliminate or reduce efficiency programs in the United States. Spending on utility and related state energy programs has rebounded modestly from the late 1990s. Annual spending on energy efficiency programs reached a high point of about US$1.6 billion in 1993 and dropped dramatically to about US$900 million in 1997. This resulted from the spread of utility deregulation in the mid-1990s. Revived interest in energy efficiency by the states has begun to reverse that trend, with total spending by states and utilities on energy efficiency programs back to about US$1.1 billion in 2000. "Our analysis clearly illustrates that there remains a vast resource of energy efficiency opportunities in the United States that is being largely ignored and untapped," stated Dan York, ACEEE's Utilities Research Associate and co-author of the report. "Most states still offer no significant support for efficiency programs, and federal energy legislation has so far ignored the need for a national matching funding mechanism for state efficiency programs. This leaves the main burden of support for efficiency programs to a few states."[15] Since that report, however, at least three states have voted to implement efficiency programs as a way to cut emissions of carbon dioxide.

Efficiency Is the Real Energy Supply Technology

In each energy crisis that has beset the world, efforts to promote one or more forms of energy supply have ignored the role of efficiency in creating a successful energy strategy. As if to spite all the brainpower and paper thrown at the energy problem (some wags suggest that the solution to the energy problem is to burn energy studies), the manifestly imperfect market has quietly bought more efficiency than it has new forms of supply. Markets are motivated by price, information, and consumer values. After 1979 there was a real perception of crisis. Prices spiked. People sought information. And when the government, utilities, and various non-profits supplied it, the market mechanisms worked rapidly to "solve" the energy crisis. Efficiency swamped supply and prices crashed.

This persistent oscillation, driven by what could be called "the overhang of profitable efficiency," has repeated itself at least four times since the 1973 Arab oil embargo, and will do so again. Every time price hikes, apparent shortages, or political instability create the perception that the time is right to convert to a different form of energy supply, efficiency, the cheaper and quicker alternative, eliminates the perception of a need for change and allows the energy status quo to resume. This fuel bazaar continues to result in bankrupt supply companies, a climate that grows less stable by the year, energy vulnerability, and war in the Middle East.

Few people other than those whose careers depend on energy analysis really want to focus on how they get their energy. If prices remain relatively low (and the world price of oil is still below that of bottled water) few people will overcome the "hassle factor" to make a change in their energy system. Every time the price for the prevailing energy source (usually oil) gets high enough to make people interested in overcoming that hurdle, the myriad ways of using energy more efficiently become more attractive. Given that it is usually faster to implement efficiency than to bring in new forms of energy supply, efficiency outpaces all supply options. This reduces demand for energy, drives prices down, and dissolves any sense of vulnerability. Proponents of supply are back at square one, the falling price of oil having diminished the relative attractiveness of their pet technologies.

Avoiding this boom-and-bust cycle requires understanding its three root causes. First, improved efficiency costs far less than new energy supplies, so most people, given the choice, opt for efficiency. Second, when policies promote *both* efficiency and supply, customers typically use only one, usually the cheaper one. Third, efficiency is far *faster* than new supply. Ordinary people are able to implement efficiency long before big, slow, centralized plants can be built, let alone paid for.

Since Western economies ceased to think that oil was infinite and reliably available, more efficient use has been the biggest "source" of new energy — not oil, gas, coal, or nuclear power. After the 1979 oil shock, efficient use of energy enabled Americans to cut oil consumption by 15 percent in six years while the economy grew 16 percent. There are many ways to measure progress in saving energy but even by the broadest and crudest measure — lower primary energy consumption per dollar of real GDP — progress has been dramatic. If the energy use of 1975 is taken as a base measure, by 2000, reduced "energy intensity" was providing 40 percent of all U.S. energy services. It was 73 percent greater than total U.S. oil consumption, five times greater than domestic oil production, three times greater than all oil imports, and thirteen times greater than Persian Gulf oil imports. The lower intensity was mostly achieved by more productive use of energy (such as better-insulated houses, better-designed lights and electric motors, and cars that were safer, cleaner, more powerful, and got more miles per gallon). The savings were only partly caused by shifts in the economic mix, and only slightly by behavioural change. Since 1996, saved energy has been the nation's fastest-growing major "source."[16]

In nearly every case, energy efficiency costs less, usually far less, than the fuel or electricity that it saves. It is cost effective to save at least half the energy now used in developed countries at prices averaging around 2¢ per kilowatt-hour (kWh).[17] Almost no form of new supply, and few historic ones, can compete with this.

The 40 percent drop in U.S. energy intensity since 1975 has barely dented efficiency's potential. The United States has cut annual energy bills by about US$200 billion since 1973, yet is still wasting at least US$300 billion a year. That number keeps rising as smarter technologies deliver more and better service from less energy. And the side benefits can be even more valuable; for example, studies show 6 to 16 percent higher labour productivity in energy-efficient buildings.[18]

The huge potential of efficiency can contribute to a transition to a clean energy economy, but this is unlikely to happen unless national energy policies integrate strategies to implement efficiency as a conscious part of implementing other clean technologies.

Renewable Power Technologies

We are witnessing a renewed boom in renewable energy, as advocates of clean energy call ever more loudly for a transition to clean energy. The following table illustrates this point:

Trends in Energy Use, By Source, 1995–2001	
Energy Source	Annual Rate of Growth (percent)
Wind power	+32.0
Solar photovoltaic	+21.0
Geothermal power*	+4.0
Hydroelectric power	+0.7
Oil	+1.4
Natural gas	+2.6
Nuclear power	+0.3
Coal	-0.3

*Data available through 1999

Europe is perhaps the best known of the regions pursuing renewable supply. Europeans have a much clearer understanding than North Americans that climate change is real and that effective policy measures are needed to counter it. In 2001, the European Union decreed that 22 percent of electricity, and 12 percent of all energy, should come from renewable sources such as wind within ten years. This target is part of the way the E.U. intends to meet its obligations under the Kyoto Protocol.[20]

According to a study released in 2002 by the European Wind Energy Association (EWEA), Europe's wind energy industry grew by 40 percent over the last year. In the twenty-one countries included in the study, installed wind capacity rose from 14,652 megawatts to 20,447 megawatts (MW) between October 2001 and October 2002. According to the same study, capacity on the continent could rise to 100,000 MW by the end of the decade. The European wind power industry estimates that, given the right legal and financial support, wind projects could provide energy for 50 million people in Europe in less than ten years' time.[21]

Following on the German government's decision in the late 1990s to phase out nuclear power completely, Germany has begun to pursue the most dramatic expansion of renewable energy in the world. In recent years Germany has accounted for roughly half of all wind turbines built worldwide. Bundesverband WindEnergie, the German wind energy association, recently announced that 2002 was another record-breaking year for installation of wind energy systems in that country. A total of 3,247 MW of generating capacity were installed last year, bringing German wind supplies to more than 12,000 MW, produced by nearly 14,000 wind turbines. Four and a half percent of German electricity is now generated from wind, surpassing the contribution from hydroelectric power. The wind sector in Germany now employs 45,000 people, one-fifth of whom were hired last year.[22] This rapid growth in wind power is central to reaching Germany's goal of reducing carbon emissions by 40 percent by 2020.

Authorities in Germany are now considering plans to build up to 5,000 turbines off the country's north coast. Giant turbines, double the size of conventional ones, are being developed for this use. Some of the turbines would be located in the open sea up to 45 kilometres from land — a feat never before attempted. Since wind is stronger at sea, the energy potential is highly attractive. Already the world's leading country in the development of onshore wind energy, Germany has plans to add 25,000 MW to offshore capacity by 2030, up from the current level of zero.[23]

Close behind Germany in installed wind power is Spain, which currently ranks number two in Europe with 4,079 MW installed capacity.[24]

The press in the United States is beginning to take notice of such developments. According to an article published in *USA Today* on February 7, 2002,

> Throughout Europe, wind power has turned into a serious source of energy, leaving the USA — the country that pioneered it as a modern technology — in the dust. Amid growing concern about climate change and other environmental problems blamed on the burning of fossil fuels, European governments are encouraging utility companies to harness the wind, especially at sea where it blows hardest.
>
> In 2001, EU countries produced more than four times as much energy through wind as the USA, and experts predict that within 10 years at least 10 percent of Europe's electricity will be supplied by giant wind turbines hooked up to main power grids. Even the technology used to produce power from wind, originally a US development, has moved to Europe. GE is the only company that still makes wind turbines in the US — 90 percent are now produced in Europe. According to Randall Swisher, executive director of the American Wind Energy Association, "We have frittered away our dominant role in this technology . . . We had the strategic advantage, and we lost it."

While the United States is not leading the wind revolution, it is also not ignoring it. U.S. wind-generating capacity expanded by nearly 10 percent in 2002, to a total of 4,685 MW. However, development depends largely on the existence of a federal wind tax credit, which must be renewed every two years. Growth in 2002 was slower than in previous years due to the fact that the tax credit had expired at the end of 2001 and an extension was not signed until mid-March. During those first months of 2002, many wind development projects were placed on hold.[25]

Environmental researcher and author Lester Brown of the Earth Policy Institute writes,

> Over the last decade wind has been the world's fastest-growing energy source. Rising from 4,800 megawatts of generating capacity in 1995 to 31,100 megawatts in 2002, it increased a staggering six-fold worldwide. Wind is popular because it is abundant, cheap, inexhaustible, widely distributed, climate-benign, and clean — attributes that no other energy source can match. The cost of wind-generated electricity has dropped from 38¢ a kilowatt-hour in the early 1980s to roughly 4¢ a kilowatt-hour today on prime wind sites. Some recently signed U.S. and U.K. long-term supply contracts are providing electricity at 3¢ a kilowatt-hour. Wind Force 12 projected that the average cost per kilowatt-hour of wind-generated electricity will drop to 2.6¢ by 2010 and to 2.1¢ by 2020. U.S. energy consultant Harry Braun says that if wind turbines are mass-produced on assembly lines like automobiles, the cost of wind-generated electricity could drop to 1–2¢ per kilowatt-hour. In contrast with oil, there is no OPEC to set prices for wind. And in contrast to natural gas prices, which are highly volatile and can double in

a matter of months, wind prices are declining. Another great appeal of wind is its wide distribution. In the United States, for example, some 28 states now have utility-scale wind farms feeding electricity into the local grid. While a small handful of countries controls the world's oil, nearly all countries can tap wind energy.[26]

Worldwide, wind grew by a robust 36 percent in 2001 alone.

Renewables are making headway in developing countries as well. The People's Republic of China is undertaking a rapid switch from coal to gas and investing in efficiency measures and renewable energy sources, pushed by the need to boost economic development and reverse the public-health emergency caused by air pollution. In 1996, China mined 1.4 giga-tonnes (GT) of coal. Most experts thought that would double early in the new century. But in 2002 China's coal mining was back to its 1986 level — 0.9 GT — and heading for 0.7 GT. A modern natural gas infrastructure is being built with wartime urgency in five key cities. Modern Danish wind turbines are being installed in Mongolia. China, which cut its energy intensity of economic growth in half in the 1980s, has nearly done so again, and can do more. Its transition is driven not only by the fact that coal is unacceptably dirty, but also by the realization that if coal remains the primary fuel for the country's development, there would be no rail capacity to carry anything but coal. In addition, the Chinese are taking note of hybrid-electric cars, fuel cells, and hydrogen, and they are becoming very interested in the entire concept of sustainability. The first run of the book *Natural Capitalism* sold out in two days, and they have recently created a Department of Sustainability at Peking University. The Chinese have also been active participants with Royal Dutch Shell in developing energy planning scenarios.[27]

Similarly, India is one of the world leaders in wind energy, adding 240 MW of wind capacity in 2001. As of 2002 it had 1,627 MW of installed wind turbines.

According to Lester Brown,

> Projecting future growth in such a dynamic industry is complicated, but once a country has developed 100 megawatts of wind-generating capacity, it tends to move quickly to develop its wind resources. The United States crossed this threshold in 1983. In Denmark, this occurred in 1987. In Germany, it was 1991, followed by India in 1994 and Spain in 1995.
>
> By the end of 1999, Canada, China, Italy, the Netherlands, Sweden, and the United Kingdom had crossed this threshold. During 2000, Greece, Ireland, and Portugal joined the list. And in 2001, it was France and Japan. As of early 2002, some 16 countries, containing half the world's people, have entered the fast-growth phase.[28]

Projections of worldwide use of renewables follow what is happening at the country level. In 1998 the Royal Dutch Shell external relations newsletter, "Shell Venster," stated that "in 2050 a ratio of 50/50 for fossil/renewables is a probable scenario, so we have to enter this market now!" Shell's "Dynamics as Usual" scenario finds it plausible that renewables will supply 20 percent of world energy by 2020, and a third by 2050. Their more aggressive scenario, "Spirit of the Coming Age," finds a transition to a hydrogen economy plausible by 2050, driven in part by a Chinese conversion to hydrogen.[29] In 1995 London's Delphi Group began advising its institutional investment clients that alternative energy industries offer "greater growth prospects than the carbon fuel industry."[30]

The U.S.-based Solar Energy Industries Association said that solar research has cut prices to a point where the world could expect to see photovoltaic panels competing with natural gas–fired generation within the next five to eight years. Statistics from the Global Environment Facility show that the market for photovoltaic solar energy is growing by 15 percent a year. The United Nations' World Energy Assessment said solar thermal power plants covering just 1 percent of the world's deserts could meet the entire planet's current demands for energy.[31]

Japan leads the world in installed solar-generating capacity with approximately 400 MW. Installed solar power in Germany stood at 200 MW in 2001, while the United States ranks third with approximately 179 MW in installed solar capacity.[32]

How Many Economists Does It Take to Change a Light Bulb?[33]

Efficiency is well-established and has favourable economics. Renewables are on a rapid-growth path. Shouldn't the market simply sort all this out?

Perhaps — if we had a true market, free of distorting subsidies. Unfortunately, nowhere does such a market exist in energy or any other commodity. Energy choices around the world are beset by subsidies and market distortions of all sorts, which have, in large measure, dictated the energy mix that we have today. Worldwide, it is estimated that subsidies to the energy sector, overwhelmingly to fossil fuels, top US$240 billion each year.[34] Any strategy that seeks to foster a transition to clean energy has to reckon with these distortions. Unfortunately, few government officials even acknowledge they exist.[35] This is especially true in Europe, where only recently have any competent estimates been made of subsidies to the energy sector.

In the United States, historic subsidies to nuclear power, for example, have exceeded the money spent on the Vietnam War and the space program combined. This to deliver less energy than the burning of wood. According to one estimate, U.S. government subsidies to the energy sector as a whole are at least US$30 billion per year, a disproportionate amount of which goes to support the nuclear and fossil fuel industries.[36] Because of this, "The American economy is, after Canada's, the most energy-dependent in the advanced industrialized world, requiring the equivalent of a quarter ton of oil to produce [US]$1,000 of gross domestic product. Americans require twice as much energy as Germany — and three times as much as Japan — to produce the same amount of GDP."[37]

One reason renewables have had such a hard time gaining a foothold in the United States is that they compete not only with subsidized conventional energy, but also with efficiency. Recently, the U.S. Department of Energy (DOE) reported that the use of renewable energy fell in 2001 to its lowest level in twelve years. Much of that was due to low hydroelectric output from reduced snow pack in the western states, but the DOE noted that solar-generating equipment was also being retired faster than it was being replaced.[38]

This is all clearly daft. It is also a recipe for uncompetitiveness. But in light of the 2001 Cheney energy proposals (which remain largely a gleam in the administration's eye), it is perhaps unreasonable to look to the Bush administration to provide a level playing field on which efficiency and all forms of supply might compete fairly. The administration even took money from the Energy Department's solar and renewable energy and energy conservation budgets to pay for the cost of printing its national energy plan, which called for reducing such programs and increasing subsidies to fossil and nuclear technologies. Reuters reported that "documents released under court order by the Energy Department this week revealed that [US]$135,615 was spent from the DOE's solar, renewables, and energy conservation budget to produce 10,000 copies of the White House energy plan released in May 2001."[39]

Despite public opinion polls showing support for renewable energy, there is also growing resistance to particular applications. The citizens of Cape Cod are fighting a proposed wind farm for Nantucket Sound, the first offshore facility in the United States. The *New York Times* reported, "But like residents of dozens of communities where other wind-farm projects have been proposed, many Cape Codders have put aside their larger environmental sensitivities and are demanding that their home be exempt from such projects. As (Walter) Cronkite puts it, 'Our national treasures should be off limits to industrialization.'"[40] The proposed wind farm is on hold.

There is also some question about how the electricity from the wind farms would get to market. While farmers and ranchers throughout the Heartland typically welcome wind farms as great neighbours to their cows and corn fields, the communities through whom the transmission lines would have to pass to carry the wind energy to distant power-hungry cities are considerably less enthusiastic. And it is not entirely clear where the money for the transmission lines will come from. Such capital costs will raise the cost of the *delivered* power. Once again, efficiency may come to look increasingly attractive.

The Beginnings of an Integrated Policy

While American energy policy is drafted by promoters of technologies beloved in the oil patch, the Europeans are beginning to realize that an integrated strategy of efficiency and renewables might just enable them not only to get beyond the historic boom-and-bust oscillations, but also give them a competitive edge.

In 1999, then British environment minister Michael Meacher said, "I cannot over-emphasise that improved energy efficiency, and growth in renewable energy, are not alternatives — we need to pursue both issues vigorously, and we are doing so." And the deputy prime minister, John Prescott, announced the Climate Change Programme in March of 2000 by saying, "We need a radical shake up in the way we use energy and we need to generate energy in new sustainable ways."[41]

An integrated policy is vital not only because ignoring efficiency will endanger a renewable (or conventional) supply strategy, but also because focusing first on efficiency makes any supply strategy much more attractive. In the absence of energy efficiency, supply strategies become prohibitively expensive. With efficiency, renewables can provide far less supply, and do so more cost-effectively than conventional power.[42] A dollar can only be spent once. If it buys efficiency, the best buy, more of our budget is left to buy the increasingly attractive renewable supply options. If that dollar is spent on centralized, capital-intensive conventional supply, it cannot then be spent to save the energy that will make much of that supply unnecessary —

until the higher prices that will be necessary to pay back the investments in conventional supply elicit defensive investments in efficiency. But it is exactly this sort of cycle that has ensured energy insecurity. The only answer, as the Europeans are starting to realize, is to invest first in efficiency, then in renewables, and to do so as part of a conscious, integrated plan.

A 2000 European Commission Green Paper, "Towards a European Strategy for Energy Supply Security," highlighted a central role for energy efficiency in increasing the security of supply and reducing greenhouse gas emissions. It stated that improving the efficiency with which energy is consumed by end users is central to European energy policy, since improved efficiency meets all three goals of energy policy, namely, security of supply, competitiveness, and protection of the environment. This is further developed in the European Climate Change Programme, which highlights the large potential for cost savings from improving the energy efficiency of end-use equipment.[43]

Recent pronouncements go even further. The Energy-Intelligent Europe Initiative is a cross-party, cross-nation movement within the European Parliament that calls for making Europe's economy the most energy intelligent in the world. By February 15, 2002, forty-one parliamentarians from all fifteen members states had signed the call to promote energy efficiency in Europe as the number one energy "source." Linking energy intelligence to the knowledge-based economy "will help Europe to become the most competitive economy worldwide while achieving its ultimate goal, a sustainable development." The initiative concludes that energy efficiency is not perceived as an important policy tool at the moment, but points out that a more energy-intelligent economy is what will enable Europe to remain competitive and promote a high quality of life.[44]

But critics are skeptical of such initiatives, claiming that funds for the promotion of energy efficiency remain inadequate: "The entire budget will amount to just over 1 million Euros per member state per year . . . a minor percentage increase upon budgets originally set well over a decade ago, when not even lip-service was being paid to the need to prioritize sustainable energy." They argue that "it is appropriate for the Union to concentrate on guiding and steering demand, unlike the United States, which seeks to meet demand by constantly boosting supply."[45]

The Economic Benefits of an Integrated Strategy of Efficiency and Renewables

What would an intelligent combination of efficiency and renewable supply look like? It turns out that it has been done, and the combination offers a winning way to strengthen local economies and create new jobs. The example also shows that even if national governments continue to be unable to grasp this concept, there still remains hope at the local level.

Sacramento is California's capital city, with a population of 400,000 (in a metro area of 1.8 million). The Sacramento Municipal Utility District (SMUD) demonstrated how investments in efficiency *and* locally generated power can enhance the bottom line of the utility and improve the health of the regional economy.

SMUD is the sixth-largest municipal utility in the United States, serving 1.2 million customers.[46] In 1989 its customers/owners voted to close the Rancho Seco nuclear facility. According to Jan Schori, who became general manager of the utility in 1993 and who remains at the helm today, "When we closed the Rancho Seco nuclear plant we lost 913 megawatts on a 2,100-megawatt system. It became an opportunity for us to start over."[47]

By 1995, SMUD was spending 8 percent of its gross revenue on energy efficiency and was being described "as a symbol of what's possible . . . the national poster child of green utilities."[48] This investment reduced the peak load by 12 percent and enabled SMUD to hold rates constant for ten years. Had Rancho Seco operated, rates would have increased 80 percent.

SMUD also installed:

- the nation's largest photovoltaic power plant, providing 2 MW of solar power to 500 homes, located next to the closed Rancho Seco nuclear facility;
- one of the largest utility-owned commercial wind turbine projects in the United States, producing 5 MW;
- the largest solar home project in the nation — supporting one hundred customers a year with the installation of 4-kilowatt photovoltaic panel systems on their rooftops;
- one of only two photovoltaic recharging stations for electric vehicles in the United States;
- two geothermal projects with a total generating capacity of 134 MW.[49]

SMUD partnered with the Sacramento Tree Foundation to plant 300,000 shade trees from 1990–2000, and it continues to offer customers free trees (with advice, fertilizer, and free delivery) for planting on the east, west, or south side of buildings. Full-grown trees can reduce indoor cooling requirements by up to 40 percent.[50] The district has also helped customers to purchase over 42,000 superefficient refrigerators.[51]

Continuing its focus on cost-effectively reducing energy demand, SMUD instituted a Cool Roof program. Building owners, through contractors, can earn a SMUD rebate of 20¢ per square foot for installing Energy Star sun-reflecting coating on flat roofs. The highly reflective coating helps block heat from the sun from being absorbed through a flat roof and into a building. This means less energy is consumed by air-conditioning systems.[52]

An economist calculated the present value of SMUD's 1997–2001 energy efficiency programs for the Sacramento region's economy to be US$130 million over the life of the efficiency investments. Most businesses are expected to save 10–19 percent on their energy bills, which translates into more jobs and profits, and increased wages and competitiveness. The impacts include the creation of over 150 additional job-years for a dozen years.[53] One company, which had anticipated higher rates that would force it to close, was able to stay in business, saving 2,000 jobs. Sacramento's competitive rates attracted such new factories as Apple, Intel, and a solar equipment manufacturer. The program lowered the utility's debt, upgraded its credit, and made it the most competitive utility in California.

By 2000, under SMUD's photovoltaic installation program, more than 450 residential and 30 commercial photovoltaic systems had been installed. These systems are grid-connected and feature net metering, which, by earning revenue from providing power to the electrical grid, allows SMUD to recuperate more than half of the cost of the systems.[54] The current program offers the systems to homeowners at a lower cost than private marketers do. The SMUD web site says the systems provide "virtually free energy after an

8–15 year payback period." They are expected to have a thirty-year lifespan. Though they increase home values, no additional property taxes are levied on the value of the systems. As of September 2001, the California energy shortage has caused a tremendous surge in interest in rooftop solar systems, leaving SMUD with a large backlog of orders.[55]

About half of SMUD's current power supply comes from its own hydro, wind, and photovoltaic power plants (at 8 MW, SMUD uses more solar power than any other utility in the United States) and from four highly efficient natural gas cogeneration plants built in the 1980s and 1990s. The other half of its power supply is purchased through long-term contracts, and SMUD searches for the best market prices. Despite Sacramento's continued growth, SMUD helped shave annual peak power requirements by nearly 3 percent from 1999 to 2000.[56]

In 1999 the U.S. Environmental Protection Agency (EPA) office in Richmond, California (a Bay Area suburb), became the first federal facility entirely powered by green power through a contract with SMUD. During the first year of the contract between the EPA and SMUD, 60 percent of the building's power was sourced from geothermal energy, with the remaining 40 percent coming from a landfill's gas generation. In the future, all of the building's energy will come from the landfill.[57] Other such projects were implemented in 2000 and 2001.

In October 2001, SMUD's board of directors voted for a ten-year strategic plan developed by General Manager Schori. The proposed plan calls for:

- saving enough electricity through energy efficiency to power more than 40,000 homes;

- maintaining competitive rates that are now 30 percent lower than those of the neighbouring utility, PG&E;
- adding new wind power to meet the needs of 12,000 homes and new solar power to serve up to 8,000 homes;
- building a new 500 MW combined-cycle gas-powered plant adjacent to the closed Rancho Seco plant. The new plant will meet a large portion of Sacramento's round-the-clock electricity demand and bolster SMUD's system reliability.
- The plan diversifies SMUD's fuel mix, reducing the financial risks of relying on one fuel or generating source. "As we've seen in the past 18 months, no one can predict uncertainties such as prolonged dry water years and major shifts in market conditions," Schori said. "This is a progressive yet prudent plan for meeting Sacramento's long-term energy needs with one of the cleanest, most reliable and affordable energy mixes in the state."[58]

Conclusion

Albert Camus argued that Sisyphus was free because, though condemned by the gods forever to roll his rock, he could use his trip back down the hill for personal reflection. But for promoters of renewable energy supplies, this freedom comes at a terrible cost.

In North America, we are not learning from our steps backward. We do not bother to implement a smart energy policy or a timetable for moving away from conventional fuels. Energy efficiency should be the cornerstone of any energy policy that hopes to survive the rigours of the market. It is the cheapest way to meet the demand for the benefits that energy can deliver: hot showers and cold beer, the movement of goods and people, and the development of emerging economies. Coupled with renewable energy technologies, it can meet the needs of the world for energy services while supporting local community economic development. It is cheaper than any form of supply, and in a genuinely competitive market, it will render most proposals for new supply unattractive.

Unfortunately, efficiency remains largely ignored as an energy source in North America. At least until the next energy crisis.

Reverse Engineering: Soft Energy Paths

Susan Holtz and David B. Brooks

Introduction: Why This Chapter Goes Against the Whole Concept of This Book

Let's think back to the early 1970s, when this story begins.

The modern environmental movement had by then become a political force, albeit one that was far from having broad acceptance in the mainstream. The developing concern for environmental quality had already spawned new legislation and government agencies and, most significantly in this context, a multitude of local, national, and international citizen-based environmental groups.

The 1970s saw an ever-growing number of proposals for new energy megaprojects coming under consideration, and many people — mostly environmentalists, but others as well — in Canada, the United States, and around the world began turning their attention to issues raised by such unprecedentedly large projects. These issues were as diverse as the projects, which ranged from hydro dams in wilderness areas to oil and gas production in the Arctic and the offshore, to tar-sands plants, to oil tanker and liquefied natural gas terminals, to nuclear generating stations and the new uranium mines and refineries that supply them. Given the potentially huge impacts of these projects, social and economic as well as biophysical, environmentalists began to raise questions about the actual need for so much energy. Could there really be a demand for some thirty nuclear reactor units in the Canadian Maritime provinces by 2000, as some Atomic Energy of Canada Ltd. projections suggested?

For the two preceding decades energy demand had indeed been growing rapidly, fueled by low oil prices and the post-war economic expansion. For many of the megaproject proponents, the link between growth in energy use and growth in the GDP seemed not only strong historically but inflexible and essential. Of course new supply projects would be needed!

Then in 1973 came the first oil shock. With little warning the Arab oil producers embargoed the United States for some months, and the Organization of Petroleum Exporting Countries (OPEC) declared they would no longer negotiate but would instead adopt a take-it-or-leave-it approach to oil pricing. By the end of 1974 the price of a barrel of oil was eight times higher than it had been five years earlier.[1]

The resulting impacts shocked the Western world, both economically and politically. Higher home heating bills, long lineups at the gas pump, and higher costs for transportation-dependent goods and services (even for electricity, where utilities used oil-fired thermal plants) brought the situation directly home to consumers. Politicians and business leaders overnight became concerned about the security of the energy supply, and many called on governments to accelerate plans for new domestic energy sources. And then, toward the end of 1978 and into 1979, tight oil supplies and political events in the Middle East brought a second series of major oil-price hikes, which added to the political and economic consternation.

The stage was thus set after 1973 for the fierce battles that erupted between environmentalists opposed to new megaprojects and mainstream interests who insisted on the crucial need to increase domestic energy supplies. The intensity of some of these conflicts was not lessened because both sides had valid points to make. Not only did these massive projects entail many immediate social and environmental costs, an ecological perspective shone a hard new scientific light on other impacts that were subtle and distant in time and space. Discoveries such as the fact that trees were being damaged by acid rain hundreds of kilometres distant from the fossil fuel sources of the emissions, and that lead in gasoline might affect the behaviour and IQ of children heavily exposed to automobile exhaust, were reported in the media almost weekly. At the same time, it was clearer than ever before that the very fabric of society was dependent on energy, and that problems with energy supply and sudden price jumps did pose real threats to society's stability and well-being.

Out of this intellectual impasse the concept of soft energy paths was born. The term is taken from analyst Amory B. Lovins's first major essay on the subject, "Energy Strategy: The Road Not Taken?" which was published in the prestigious journal *Foreign Affairs* in the fall of 1976. Analytically, Lovins drew two different, and opposing, pictures of energy policy, one relying on centralized, large-scale, capital-intensive technologies to meet rapidly rising demand (the "hard path"), and the other, the "soft path," emphasizing energy conservation[2] as the primary focus, with mainly smaller-scale renewable energy supply options selected to be more environmentally and socially benign.

We will discuss the content, the analytics, and some results of the soft path approach later in this chapter; for now, however, the key point is that Lovins (and subsequent soft path analysts) took both sides of the energy security vs. environment debate absolutely seriously.

Environmentalists taking a soft path approach to energy policy accepted that decision makers must consider and plan for energy security, and that economics did matter. Moreover, they met head-on one of the main criticisms of their opposition to various megaprojects. Instead of merely pointing generally to more efficient technologies and renewable energy sources when challenged as to how, exactly, the demand for energy was going to be met, analysts doing soft path studies provided the comprehensive overview, including the hard numbers detailing energy supply-and-demand balances with alternative technologies, that was required for a serious response.

Never before — and rarely since — had environmentalists developed a hard-headed vision for an entire sector of the economy. Analytically, it meant designing rigorous scenarios that took into account real-world constraints, and making choices for those scenarios that were not always ideal, yet kept sight of overriding environmental and socio-economic goals. Psychologically, it meant behaving like a decision maker rather than a critic; some might say it meant behaving like a grown-up. For social critics, this is not the most comfortable stance, nor is it necessarily the most effective way to stop some specific project that you oppose. But it provides a model for public policy debate that is especially valuable in the more recent context of sustainable development, and almost essential for environment-related issues where there are a multitude of problem sources and varying consequences of dealing with them, and where there is no one best route to achieving economic, social, and environmental goals.

So how does a soft energy path approach differ from the concept of this book? In three main ways:

First, how to "fuel the future" — that is, focusing on the supply side of the energy equation — is *not* the soft path's primary question. Rather, the soft path asks first what kinds of energy services are needed for a given society at some future point. We will elaborate the point about "services" later. For the moment, it is only necessary to emphasize that energy demand reduction through different kinds of efficiency improvements and alternative choices is *always* the first priority.

Second, and even more fundamental, soft energy paths are not primarily about technologies, or even about human ingenuity in inventing technologies. They are first and foremost about *values*. A soft energy strategy is driven by a set of choices that explicitly take into account key environmental, economic, and social considerations. The choices about which considerations to incorporate are profoundly normative; a different set or weighting of these values-based choices would mean a different outcome for the strategy. Of course, no approach to energy policy is value-free. However, most policy analysts treat values implicitly by burying them in the analysis. Soft path analysts, in contrast, not only make the values explicit but also insist that they, along with the values-related implications that are de facto results of all energy decisions, should be the starting point for analysis.

Third, a soft path approach relies on a soft path *strategy* — choices based on an analytically rigorous *overview* of a specific society's energy demand and supply in the future. This approach contrasts with the way energy policy is most often presented in the media — as a patchwork constructed by various enthusiasts, each with a vision of a grand future for some particular technology, whether solar energy, hydrogen, nuclear fission, nuclear fusion, or whatever. True, it's good to understand as much as possible about what various technologies might achieve, and there is a valuable role for single-minded innovators and promoters of technology. But looking at energy futures through their eyes alone tends to give a perspective that is compelling but oversimplified and incomplete.

The soft path approach stands back from particular technologies billed as "the answer" and evaluates their usefulness in terms of the overall picture of the entire energy sector. Among other things, this approach includes looking at what, when, and where specific energy services are needed. It also means reviewing cost, timing, and political, social, and environmental implications as comprehensively as possible. It includes using some "less bad" fossil fuels, notably natural gas, that are needed as transitional sources on the way to less damaging alternatives. The ecological dictum that "you can never do only one thing" is its touchstone. All technologies, and, indeed, all purposive human activities, have not only their intended results, like providing electricity or personal transportation, but also a host of unintended effects, such as air pollution, traffic congestion, and vulnerability to ice storms and terrorist attacks. Energy efficiency itself can have some negative implications, for example, if tighter houses don't have adequate ventilation. Thus a soft path strategy, even while making difficult choices, keeps as comprehensive a view as possible of context, constraints, and a full range of implications, recognizing that there are no simple, all-encompassing solutions.

A Closer Look at the Soft Path

To start with, it's worth making distinctions among a *soft path approach*, *soft technologies*, and a *soft path strategy* or *study*. To take the latter term first, a soft path strategy or study refers to a comprehensive demand/supply analysis using a soft path approach and employing, as much as possible, soft technologies. We will review its distinctive analytical steps in a later section.

At its basic level, a soft path approach, the most general term, is concerned with values. A soft path approach to energy policy focuses on reducing the risks of environmental and social harms that can result from energy sources and energy-using technologies, but it also accepts the importance of social and economic stability, full employment, and democratic institutions and norms. In the latter set of values the soft path approach does not differ markedly from most conventional energy planning in the Western world. (Energy planners of all stripes do tend to take economics and security seriously, even when their specific projections turn out to be dead wrong.) But the willingness to rule out altogether certain energy options on social and environmental grounds, and, for those same reasons, to emphasize the essential need for demand reduction and various mainly renewable technologies marked the soft path approach as a dramatic and controversial break with conventional policy twenty-five years ago.

Over the years, different soft path analysts have formulated the key characteristics of soft technologies — technologies appropriate to a soft path approach — in various ways. The key points behind the different formulations, however, are the same:

- Minimizing energy demand is far and away the most effective strategy for the environment;
- Renewable energy sources address sustainability and thus security over the long term; and
- Scale and diversity criteria are concerned with society's social and economic adaptability and resilience.

Some analysts add such terms as *relatively environmentally benign* and *safe-fail* to underline the safety and environmental concerns driving the analysis, or *decentralized* to make that element more explicit. But the classic description is the following one, taken from Lovins, who cites five characteristics of soft technologies:

- They rely on renewable energy flows that are always there whether we use them or not, such as sun and wind and vegetation: on energy income, not on depletable energy capital.
- They are diverse, so that as a national treasury runs on many small tax contributions, so national energy supply is an aggregate of very many individually modest contributions, each designed for maximum effectiveness in particular circumstances.

- They are flexible and relatively low technology — which does not mean unsophisticated, but rather, easy to understand and use without esoteric skills. . . .
- They are matched in scale and in geographic distribution to end use needs, taking advantage of the free distribution of most natural energy flows.
- They are matched in energy quality to end use needs. . . .[3]

The first three characteristics are easy enough to understand, but the last two, and especially the terms *end-use needs* and *energy quality,* require some explanation.

Much planning around energy is concerned with the availability and price of primary energy supplies such as coal, crude oil, and natural gas. However, what we really want is not energy for its own sake — having a barrel of crude on the front porch, or a pile of coal in the backyard — but for the *energy services* it provides. We don't want natural gas for our furnace, we want a warm house; we don't want gasoline for the car, we want to be able to haul things and get around. For analytical purposes, all these *end-use energy needs* can be grouped into the categories of lower-temperature heat, such as for warming homes or water; higher-temperature heat needed for industrial purposes; electricity-specific needs, such as for electric motors, lighting, and electronics; and motive power needed for transportation. (Transportation requirements have usually been referred to in terms of fluid fuels, since transportation requires carrying the source of motive power around with you and the high energy density of fluids makes that convenient. Nevertheless, technological advances in batteries and hydrogen allow for some other possibilities.)

Differences in energy quality were known to physicists for many years, but they were introduced into energy policy by soft path analysts. Our energy accounting system measures energy (the ability to do work) in common quantitative units like the kilowatt-hour, the joule in the International System of Units (SI), or the British thermal unit (Btu). In this sense, a joule is always a joule in that it always performs the same quantity of work. However, from a user's point of view, the kind of work (energy service) that you need is what matters. Different forms of energy, like electricity or solar radiation or natural gas, have different capabilities for delivering these different categories of energy services. The major Canadian soft energy path study conducted by Brooks et al. describes this concept this way:

> The quality of an energy form is a measure of the amount of "useful work" that can be extracted from the total energy, or enthalpy, contained in that form. For example, one joule of electricity can be used for many more things than a joule of low temperature heat, although the quantity of energy is the same in both cases. [That is, electricity can be used for low-temperature heat through baseboard coils, for the high-temperature heat of kilns, for motive power, and for lighting and electronics.] The joule of electricity is a higher quality form of energy because it can provide more useful work than the joule of low temperature heat.[4]

Using technologies that match energy quality to end-use needs has relevance to a soft path approach and the development of soft path strategies for several reasons. A large portion of society's energy needs are for lower-quality energy in the form of low-temperature heat. (Think about raising ambient room temperatures to comfortable levels, a matter of tens of degrees at most.) Using a high-quality form of energy, such as electricity, to provide these services reduces efficiency in terms of its thermodynamic potential. It represents a loss in "second law" efficiency, so-called because it is based on the second law of thermodynamics. (As phrased to many students of physics to help them remember, the first law of thermodynamics states, "You can't win: energy can't be created or destroyed, only changed in form." The second law states, "You can't even break even: any transformation of energy degrades it, making it less organized and less able to do useful work.") Traditional or "first law" efficiency is about improving the ratio of the energy input to the useful work output of some device like a furnace or a motor. Second law efficiency is about using low-grade energy for low-grade needs, avoiding the use of high-quality forms such as electricity for those same low-temperature requirements. It also requires that the vast quantities of energy that are commonly treated as waste heat be used. (Increasingly now, the two-thirds of energy that is lost when fossil fuels are burned to generate electricity is being recaptured and used for industrial purposes or space heating.)

First law efficiency has always been recognized as important because it is obvious that it can conserve resources and save dollars. Soft path analysts, however, were among the first to see that an analysis of energy demand that categorized the quality of energy needed could further increase the potential for energy conservation. They recognized that conventional planning for future energy needs was based on past trends that relied heavily on high-quality conventional supply sources for low-grade end uses and included these large losses of useful energy through conversion. This loss, in turn, pushed up the projected demand for electricity generation and primary energy sources like crude oil.

Paying attention to this qualitative dimension of energy use also provided a better understanding of how renewable energy resources could be used more efficiently, adding scope and direction to their potential. And a focus on energy quality and on the tasks for which energy is used permitted detailed bottom-up analysis of a wide range of alternatives, including lifestyle choices and different sets of economic activities. This kind of analysis is the essence of the scenario-based soft energy path studies that were developed around the world.

So How Do You Do a Soft Energy Path Study?

We assume that readers don't actually want to do a soft energy path study themselves, and so we will not present a detailed discussion of methodology here. However, it is useful to understand something about how to undertake a soft path analysis in order to better grasp what it can tell us — and what it cannot.

The analysis has five basic steps. Before describing them, though, it's important to note that the purpose of a soft energy path strategy is *not* to forecast the future. Rather, it's to explore the viability of some particular future scenario that reflects an emphasis on certain environmental, social, and economic considerations.

STEP ONE — BUILDING SCENARIOS

The first step is to determine the study's time frame and to create scenarios for what the society could look like at that future point. Major changes in the energy sector take a long time to happen. A saying in the utility business is, "Ten years down the road is yesterday," meaning that a large new generation facility typically takes at least ten years from the decision to build through financing and regulatory approval to completion. Cars and major appliances such as furnaces and hot water heaters take a decade or longer until they need replacement, and housing stock, if they are well maintained, can go on almost indefinitely. Thus, to allow for major changes in direction to have an effect, analysts must choose a date some decades in the future. For example, the large Canadian study by Brooks et al., published in 1983, set 2025 as its end point, with an interim analysis for 2000. (Of course, the further in the future, the more scope for change, but the fuzzier the details.) The researchers must then build up a picture of the whole society, determining a myriad of factors that affect energy use, such as population, household size, economic growth rates, and the industrial mix. The scenario must be tied together so that, for instance, enough shingles and steel and lumber are produced to build the projected housing required (something that can be done using an input-output model of that society's economy). Usually, more than one scenario is developed, showing a range of possible futures incorporating smaller and larger degrees of lifestyle change, economic growth, and so forth.

STEP TWO — END-USE DEMAND

Next the researchers must figure out the minimum quantity of energy required to run that society. This involves categorizing all the energy-using tasks and activities in this future society by end use, that is, by the quality of energy needed, and quantifying those categories. This step is organized by major sector;

typically, households, commercial/institutional, industrial, and transportation. Each sector is usually subdivided and analyzed according to its particulars; for example, in the household sector, types of housing stock, housing stock turnover, household size, hot water use, appliance turnover, and new appliance penetration rates must all be determined. New energy-saving technologies and practices are incorporated in the study, but only as they become reasonably economical and practical, which also must be assessed.

STEP THREE — SUPPLY MIX

This step involves matching end-use demand with supply options, again employing soft technologies based on renewable sources as they become reasonably competitive and available, and using fossil fuels and other conventional sources as transition technologies. Some existing or potential options, notably new nuclear energy units and offshore Arctic oil (though not natural gas, which poses far less threat to the environment), are excluded in virtually all studies. However, analysts may also exclude specific local options for environmental and social reasons, such as dams on wild rivers or wind-farm sites that affect scenic views. The idea is to test the degree to which soft supply technologies can, in fact, meet demand in the future, taking into account availability, technical considerations, and cost. Availability refers not only to obvious factors like whether any hydro sites are left to dam, but also to competing demands for the resource, such as sawlogs and fibre for wood, or soil amendment for crop waste. Technical considerations involve such things as the fact that the infrastructure to support major changes in transportation fuels must be co-ordinated and widely available, or that ensuring the stability of an electrical grid limits the percentage of intermittent sources (such as solar and wind) to about 25 percent.

STEP FOUR — BACKCASTING

Backcasting tests the feasibility of "getting there from here." (The term was deliberately chosen to distinguish the step from forecasting, or predicting the future.) It involves a careful review of the technical and economic path that is needed to get from the present to the future scenario(s), a process that usually involves several iterations. In each iteration, various technical and other possibilities are identified, and the demand and supply analyses are revisited to consider alternative choices.

STEP FIVE — IMPLEMENTATION

Because the purpose of a soft path strategy is to describe an alternative energy future, it is not surprising that the final step is to identify the conditions and interventions that are needed to bring about that scenario. High conventional energy prices were an important driver for the results obtained in most soft path studies; the stability of prices in recent years explains, in part, the failure to move farther along the soft energy path than we have. We will return to implementation in the last section of this essay. Here, it is only important to remember that the goal is not just to produce a scenario but to identify the policies and programs needed if it is to be achieved.

Typical Soft Path Results and Further Developments

The Canadian soft energy path study, which appeared in book form at the height of soft path interest (Bott et al., 1983), was one of the largest and most detailed ever done, but it was by no means the only one. By the time it was completed, some thirty-five other soft path studies had been published, for countries ranging from Denmark to India.[5]

The more conservative of the two scenarios of the Canadian study concluded the following:

> Under conditions of strong economic growth (an increase of more than 200% in GDP) and moderate population growth (an increase of over 50%), it would be technically feasible and cost-effective to operate the Canadian economy in 2025 with 12% less energy than it requires today, and over the same 47-year period, to shift from 16% reliance on renewable sources to 77%.[6]

It is worth noting that the study results for the same scenario at the interim point of 2000 showed an *increase* in energy use of about 4 percent. This simply demonstrates how long it takes for major improvements in energy efficiency to take hold as a result of the slow turnover of old capital stock.

The dramatic Canadian results were not atypical for soft path studies. For example, a Harvard Business School report on energy futures cited a study done in 1978 by a panel of experts from the National Academy of Science in the United States. One scenario for 2010 demonstrated that "very similar conditions of habitat, transportation, and other amenities could be provided in the United States using almost 20% less energy than used today."[7]

Compared with conventional forecasts, the early soft path studies were often so startling in the potential they identified for reductions in energy demand that they were dismissed out of hand. However, as the effects of energy conservation began to take hold in the 1980s, these results seemed less ridiculous. Some of the analytical features that were innovative in the first soft path strategies done in the 1970s, notably the bottom-up demand analyses, began to be incorporated into mainstream energy planning. More generally, the kind of thinking that started with environmental and socio-economic concerns and used a systems approach and tools like backcasting, scenario development, and analysis of end use began to be applied to more limited areas related to energy issues such as greenhouse gas emissions and to other fields like solid waste management and, especially, water management.[8]

The Energy World Post-1985: Are We There Yet?

Energy prices stopped climbing after the mid-1980s, and, in the case of crude oil, even dropped back nearly to 1973 levels (a drop caused largely by the energy glut brought about by reduced demand). Prices then remained relatively stable until after 2000, when electricity and natural gas prices started to rise. Efficiency improvements continued to gain some momentum, based on the fact that their scope was enormous and many made excellent economic sense even without further energy price hikes. Better information and government programs, as well as wider awareness of the multiple benefits of energy efficiency, also played strong roles. However, in light of lower-than-anticipated conventional energy prices, the analysts who did the Canadian soft path study had to revisit their earlier scenarios. In a shorter, revised study released in 1988,[9] Torrie et al. incorporated oil prices that were roughly half those used earlier.[10] Their conclusions about the viability of a much more efficient, conservation-oriented future remained nearly the same, with the scope for energy savings only somewhat more modest. However, the competitiveness and, given the immaturity of the technology and other barriers, the practicality of most renewable options were significantly reduced. Their percentage of the hypothesized energy mix was much smaller, with wood and hydroelectricity the only economically attractive renewable sources. The other renewables had been replaced mainly by natural gas.

As had been the case in the earlier study, the most problematic area of the supply side was transportation fuels. The 1988 analysis dropped methanol as the proposed longer-term transportation option because of more information and concerns about herbicides and soil nutrient depletion in dedicated plantations for energy using fast-growing poplar, but allowed a greater role for ethanol. Nevertheless, all the transportation options raised some concerns.

During the 1990s, the return to a "normal" world energy situation lessened the political and public interest in energy issues, especially security of supply. (That particular topic, of course, has drawn more notice since the September 11, 2001, terror attacks.) As well, moderated demand weakened the viability of many proposed megaprojects and the Chernobyl accident specifically decreased acceptance of nuclear energy. Environmental attention related to energy began to centre on greenhouse gas emissions and air quality.

How does today's world compare with that envisioned in the original soft path studies? Each country is different, of course, and the differences between the challenges faced by developing countries and those of the developed world are great. Canada, as a typical developed country but with its own unique circumstances (e.g., cold temperatures, small human population in a gigantic land mass, abundant resources), is a reasonable example. Since the major soft path study done for Canada has 2025 as its end point, perhaps the right question is not "Are we there yet?" but rather "Are we going in the right direction?"

ENERGY CONSERVATION
(DEMAND REDUCTION, EFFICIENCY IMPROVEMENTS)

Compared with conventional forecasts from the 1970s, we are much closer to a soft path than to business as usual as it was then envisioned. For example, in the more conservative scenario of the 1983 Canadian soft path study, primary energy consumption in Canada for the year 2000 was backcast to be 10,115 petajoules; in actuality it was about 10,500 petajoules — 40 percent lower than the level projected in a 1978 study done in the Long-Term Energy Assessment Program of Energy, Mines and Resources Canada. There is now an immense range of new and improved technologies and methods to conserve energy. Some of them, like the use of waste heat for co-generation in industry, are nearly invisible to most people but valued by the businesses who save money by using them. Others, such as high-efficiency windows, furnaces, and building techniques, are equally unobtrusive as they slowly become part of society's capital stock. Virtually none of the efficiency gains comes from anything approaching self-denial and a hair-shirt lifestyle, as demand reduction was widely characterized in the 1970s. One worrisome trend, however, is that fuel efficiency gains in automobiles are being undermined by increased driving and the popularity of the new gas gluttons, the SUVs. Another striking difference between the 1970s and the present is that in the 1970s, exported energy was about one-fifth of domestic demand, whereas now it is around four-fifths and moving toward equality. Much of this energy production goes to the United States, where there has been little political commitment to energy conservation. Consequently, even if Canada were wholeheartedly to adopt a domestic soft energy approach, at this level of exports there would still be important adverse social and environmental impacts from the high rates of energy production in Canada and the high rates of energy use in the United States, where Canada, obviously, has no ability to influence energy demand or to address other aspects of energy and environmental policies.

USE OF RENEWABLE SOURCES

Except for hydroelectricity, most of today's sources which were planned for or in place by the 1980s, the adoption of renewables has been very slow in Canada. The only exception is wood, the use of which grew in some regions and in 1997 contributed twice as much energy as nuclear sources (6 percent vs. 3 percent).

This is not the case elsewhere in the world. Worldwatch Institute's 2003 edition of *State of the World* reports that installed wind capacity worldwide is nearly 25 gigawatts, about 70 percent of which is in Europe, and the European Union has adopted a goal of having 22 percent of its electricity generated from small-scale renewable sources by 2010. Wind and solar are now the world's fastest-growing energy sources.[11]

HARD PATH TECHNOLOGIES

Other than those that were in planning or under construction at the time of the 1983 soft energy study for Canada, few new megaprojects have gone forward. To the contrary, several existing nuclear units in Ontario have been shut down, and although some are supposed to be restarted, it is not clear when, or even if, this will happen. Offshore natural gas production has gone forward off Nova Scotia, but this was foreseen and accepted as a transition fuel in the soft path. On the other hand, hydrocarbon exploration on the biologically productive Georges Bank was suspended under a ten-year moratorium, which was extended beyond its original 2000 end point for environmental and socio-economic reasons.

Overall, while Canada may not be exactly on the path mapped out, increased energy conservation and the curtailment of hard path projects indicate that it is not going in the opposite direction, either.

Re-visioning the Soft Path Perspective

Not surprisingly, soft path analysts think that their approach is, if anything, more appropriate now than it was twenty-five years ago. Since then, concerns about health and environmental problems related to energy have continued to grow, including avoidable respiratory illnesses and childhood asthma linked to air quality, and greenhouse gas emissions linked to fossil fuel use. It should be mentioned that soft path researchers were among the first to pay attention to climate change; Amory Lovins et al. published a book about soft path approaches in 1981 entitled *Least Cost Energy: Solving the CO_2 Problem.* Though not designed with greenhouse gas emissions in mind, even the higher energy use scenarios in the 1988 revision of the soft path study for Canada would meet our Kyoto commitments.

The strength of these early studies was recently confirmed by a study entitled *Kyoto and Beyond* that Ralph Torrie and colleagues prepared for the David Suzuki Foundation and the Climate Action Network Canada. Their sector-by-sector scenarios showed how readily available, cost-effective demand-side technologies could cut energy use by so much that Canada would not only exceed its Kyoto commitments, but consumers would save tens of billions of dollars per year.[12] The same is true elsewhere, as examples of "Factor 4" improvements — that is, reductions of 75 percent in resource use per unit of output in industrial and commercial activities — demonstrate.[13]

If nothing else, these scenarios show how much can be achieved, and without much pain — the latest scenarios have even allowed for a 50 percent increase in per-capita GDP — by following soft path prescriptions. However, they also show that pervasive energy-related problems inhere so much in the fabric of society that they cannot be addressed, let alone solved, without rigorous analytical work.

The soft path analysis is also especially relevant today in its emphasis on the relationship between a society's essential technologies and its resilience and adaptability. Again, Amory Lovins and his colleagues were far-seeing in their 1982 book *Brittle Power: Energy Strategy for National Security*, in which they identified some of the ramifications of highly centralized energy systems. Today's globally interlaced economic systems, personal connections, and political interactions make for a world of many surprises, ranging from SARS and the West Nile

virus to terrorist attacks. And concerns about the role of
nuclear power plants as sources of fissionable material for
nuclear weapons and their potential as targets of military or
terror attacks are, sadly, more credible today than they were in
previous years.

Finally, the continuing need for prioritizing energy conservation cannot be overstated. The environmental and social
implications of unchecked demand growth are enormous,
whether we are talking about livable cities, habitat loss, security of supply, or any number of other issues. From a global
perspective, the developing world's aspirations for a reasonable
level of prosperity will mean that their energy use will grow,
and, in order to allow this without crossing further ecological
thresholds, constraining energy use in the developed world is
imperative. Renewable sources alone are not and cannot be the
answer. Only major success in reducing demand will put us
firmly on the soft path.

Was the original soft path approach and its strategies right
about everything? Of course not. First, the emphasis placed on
finding low-tech and easy-to-understand technologies, as well
as the aversion to *any* technologies involving large-scale, centralized facilities, was overstated. Hydrogen technology, or
even a high-efficiency gas furnace, is not really much simpler
to understand than nuclear power, though a toppled wind turbine is certainly a lot easier and cheaper to fix than a nuclear
unit that is "down." And even though the hard and soft paths
have opposite assumptions and approaches, the real world has
elements of both at the same time.

Second, the soft path strategies were too limited in their
analysis of what drives change. Comparatively high prices for

conventional fuels and rational economic behaviour were presumed to be the main motivators for change in the original studies. Though the right economic signals are essential, it is now apparent that other factors are equally or perhaps even more important. As Ralph Torrie put it, "The demand is for better services, not for more energy-efficient services. The fact that better buildings (and more profitable factories, better vehicles, more compact urban forms, etc.) are also more energy efficient is a good thing, but the benefits, including the financial benefits, are much greater from the way the service is improved than from the fuel and electricity savings they deliver."[14]

Third, some political realities that hold back change needed to be more effectively addressed. Governments, both politicians and the bureaucracy, always prefer a situation where there are no (visible) problems to one where they are expected to solve problems. Not surprisingly, then, the years of energy "normalcy" were unproductive for soft path initiatives, especially those that supported renewable technologies. This inertia was strengthened in Canada by program and staff reductions as governments struggled to get deficits under control, and in the United States by the election of governments unwilling to support pro-environment interventions for fear they would limit business. In addition, apart from times of energy crisis, few politicians worry much about how much energy is being used. Rather, they bias policies to protect industries in their constituencies, including energy supply industries. Revenue stability from taxes and royalties also matter: it's hard to believe that the Alberta government's desire to maintain its substantial revenues from the energy sector did not play a role in its opposition to the Kyoto Accord.

Finally, the concept of sustainable development has highlighted the need to consider equity implications of policies
alongside economic and environmental matters. For example,
incorporating environmental costs into energy prices would
likely raise prices, and the effect of this on particular groups of
consumers and of employees in the energy sector needs evaluation. Low income is not the only factor causing vulnerability.
Rural location, which affects transportation, as well as age,
education, family situation, or even being new immigrants are
other factors that should be examined as creating the conditions for unfairly burdensome impacts.

The world today has also brought a number of changes
that certainly affect what a soft path will look like, but in ways
that are not yet clear. Among the most important are the
deregulation and reorganization of utilities and the electricity
market; the role of exports in countries like Canada that have
or could build the capacity for dedicated energy export facilities; and how key emerging technologies will evolve, especially
in the transportation sector, where change is also closely linked
to changes in settlement patterns, urban and suburban planning, trade, and the structure of industry. But however many
misty patches there are in a re-visioning of the soft path, its
direction remains fixed by the lodestar values of sustainability
— maintaining and improving human well-being and the economic and social structures that support it, and, equally, maintaining and restoring the ecosystems that surround and
support human activities and of which we, too, are a part.

In summary, the general soft energy approach and the specific soft energy study for Canada have both proven to have
lasting, and indeed growing, value. On the one hand, the

Canadian study turned out to be more prescient than even the fifteen or so analysts who worked on it might have expected. On the other hand, both the approach and the study overestimated government's willingness to recognize the value and act on the principles of the soft path. Nowhere is this contradiction better illustrated than in the changing reactions of Canadian energy bureaucrats over the course of the study. In the early days of soft path analysis, the typical response was, "Yes, you have created a very desirable future for Canada, but do you *really* think it is feasible?" After the study was completed, the response changed: "Yes, you have shown that this future scenario is feasible, but do you really think it is *desirable?*"

The Dawn of the Hydrogen Economy

Jeremy Rifkin

Imagining a World Without Oil

Imagine, for a moment, a world where fossil fuels are no longer burned to generate power, heat, or light. A world no longer threatened by global warming or geopolitical conflict in the Middle East. A world where every person on Earth has access to electricity. That world now looms on the horizon.

We are in the early stages of an historic change in the way we organize the Earth's energy. The Industrial Age, which began with the carrying of coal from Newcastle several hundred years ago, is now winding down in the oil fields of the Middle East. Meanwhile, a wholly new energy regime is being readied. Hydrogen — the lightest and most abundant element in the universe — is the key to the next great energy revolution. Scientists call hydrogen the "forever fuel" because it never runs out. And when it's used to produce power, the only by-products are pure water and heat.

It's difficult to comprehend a world beyond oil when so much of the Modern Age has been fueled by the burial grounds of the Jurassic Era. We heat our homes and businesses, run our factories, power our transportation, and light our cities with fossil fuels. We grow our food and construct our buildings with materials made from fossil fuels, treat illnesses with pharmaceuticals made from fossil fuels, and produce our clothes and home appliances with petrochemicals. Virtually every aspect of modern life is made from, or powered by, fossil fuels.

Until recently, experts had been saying that we had another forty or so years of cheap, available crude oil left. Now, however, some of the world's leading petroleum geologists are suggesting that global oil production could peak and begin a steep decline much sooner, as early as 2020, at which point — assuming we don't curb our global appetite for oil — prices will go through the roof. Oil-producing countries outside of the Organization of Petroleum Exporting Countries (OPEC) are already nearing their peak production, leaving most of the remaining reserves in the politically charged Middle East. Increasing tensions between the Islamic world and the West are likely to compound the threat to our access to affordable oil. Rising oil prices will assuredly plunge developing countries even further into debt, ensuring that much of the Third World remains in the throes of poverty for years to come. In desperation, many nations may turn to dirtier fossil fuels — coal, oil from tar sands, and heavy oil — which will only worsen global warming and imperil the Earth's already beleaguered ecosystems. Looming oil shortages will make industrial life vulnerable to massive disruptions and possibly even collapse.

Hydrogen has the potential to end the world's reliance on oil from the Persian Gulf, the most politically volatile region on the planet. Indeed, making the transition to hydrogen is the best insurance against the prospects of future oil wars in the Middle East. Hydrogen will also dramatically cut down on carbon dioxide emissions and mitigate the effects of global warming. And because sources of hydrogen are so plentiful, people who have never before had access to electricity will be able to generate it.

In October 2002, the European Union became the world's first superpower to announce a long-term plan to make the transition out of fossil fuel dependency and into a renewable-based hydrogen economy. Romano Prodi, the president of the European Commission, said at the time that weaning Europe off Middle East oil and making the shift to a hydrogen future would be the next great integrating task for Europe after the introduction of the Euro, and he compared the ambitious effort to the American space program in the 1960s to put a man on the moon.

How Hydrogen Power Works

Hydrogen is found everywhere on Earth, yet rarely exists in nature as a free-floating gas. Instead, it has to be extracted from either hydrocarbons or water. Today, the most cost-effective way to produce commercial hydrogen is to harvest it from natural gas via a "steam-reforming" process. However, greenhouse gas emissions are produced as a by-product of steam reforming. Moreover, the supply of natural gas is finite just like our oil supply, and therefore is not a dependable long-term source. There is, however, another way to produce hydrogen, one that uses no fossil fuels. Renewable sources of energy — photovoltaic cells (solar), wind, hydro, geothermal, and biomass — are increasingly being used to produce electricity.

That electricity, in turn, can be used in a process called electrolysis to split water into hydrogen and oxygen. Once produced, the hydrogen can be stored and used, when needed, to generate electricity.

Storage is the key to making renewable energy economically viable. That's because when renewable energy is harnessed to produce electricity, the electricity flows immediately. But if the sun isn't shining or the wind isn't blowing or the water isn't flowing, electricity isn't generated and economic activity relying on that electricity grinds to a halt. Which is why it is important to store electricity in the form of hydrogen. To do that, some of the electricity generated from solar or wind must be used for extracting hydrogen from water. That way, society will have a continuous supply of power.

While the costs of harnessing renewable technologies and extracting hydrogen are still high, new technological breakthroughs and economies of scale are dramatically reducing these costs every year. Moreover, hydrogen-powered fuel cells are two and one-half times more efficient than internal combustion engines. Meanwhile, the direct and indirect costs of oil and gas on world markets will continue to rise. As we approach the nexus between the falling price of renewables and hydrogen and the rising price of fossil fuels, the old energy regime will steadily give way to the new energy era.

The Future Is Now

Stationary commercial fuel cells powered by hydrogen are just now being introduced for home, office, and industrial use. Portable fuel-cell cartridges will be on the market in a few years. Consumers will be able to power up their cell phones,

laptops, computers, and other appliances for forty days or
more with a single cartridge. The major automakers have
already spent over US$2 billion developing hydrogen cars,
buses, and trucks, and the first mass-produced vehicles are
expected to be on the road beginning in 2009.

The hydrogen economy will make possible a vast change in
the way power is distributed, with far-reaching consequences
for society. Today's centralized, top-down flow of energy, controlled by global oil companies and utilities, could become
obsolete. In the new era, every human being with access to
renewable energy sources could become a *producer* as well as a
consumer of his or her own energy, using so-called distributed
generation. When millions of end-users connect their fuel cells
into local, regional, and national hydrogen energy webs
(HEWs), using the same design principles and smart technologies that made possible the World Wide Web, they can begin to
share energy — peer to peer — creating a new, decentralized
form of energy generation and use.

In the new hydrogen fuel-cell era, even the automobile
itself will become a "power station on wheels," with a generating capacity of twenty kilowatts. The average house requires
only two to four kilowatts of power. Since cars are parked most
of the time, owners will be able to plug them into the home,
the office, or the main interactive electricity network, during
non-use hours, selling the electricity they produce back to the
grid. If just 25 percent of drivers used their vehicles as
mini–power plants, we could eliminate all the giant, environmentally polluting power plants on which we now depend.

The Marriage of Software, Communications, and Hydrogen

The truly great economic revolutions in history occur when new communication technologies fuse with new energy regimes to create wholly new economic paradigms. The introduction of the printing press in the 1400s, for example, established a new form of communication that, when later combined with coal and steam technology, gave birth to the Industrial Revolution. Print provided a form of communication that was information intensive and quick enough to co-ordinate a world propelled by steam power. It would not have been possible to co-ordinate the increase in speed, pace, flow, density, and interactivity of commercial and social life — made possible by steam power — by relying on script or oral communication technologies. Similarly, the telegraph and, later, the telephone provided forms of communication that were fast enough to accommodate the quickened pace, flow, density, and interactivity made possible when coal gave way to an even more agile hydrocarbon, crude oil.

Today, hydrogen and the new fuel-cell, distributed-generation technology are beginning to fuse with the computer and communications revolution to create a wholly new economic era. Before the distributed generation of hydrogen can be fully achieved, however, changes in the existing power grid will have to be made. That's where the software and communications revolution fits in. Connecting thousands and then millions of fuel cells to main grids will require sophisticated dispatch and control mechanisms to route energy traffic during peak and non-peak periods. A U.S. company called Encorp has already developed a software program for remote monitoring and control that would automatically switch local generators onto the main grid during peak loads, when more auxiliary energy was required. Retrofitted existing systems are estimated to run at about US$100 per kilowatt-hour, which is still less costly than building new capacity.

An inherent problem with the existing power grid is that it was designed to ensure a one-way flow of energy from a central source to all of the end-users. It is no wonder that Kurt Yeager, president of the Electric Power Research Institute (EPRI), recently remarked that "the current power infrastructure is as incompatible with the future as horse trails were to automobiles." In many ways, the current grid resembles the state of the broadcast industry before the advent of the World Wide Web, when connections flowed in only one direction, from the media source to the viewing audience. Today's transmission systems are not set up to direct specific quantities of energy to specific parts of the grid. The result is that power flows all over the place, often causing congestion and energy loss. A new technology developed by EPRI called FACTS — short for Flexible Alternative Current Transmission System — gives transmission companies the capacity to deliver measured quantities of power to specified areas of the grid.

The integration of state-of-the-art computer hardware and software transforms the centralized grid into a fully interactive intelligent energy network. Sensors and intelligent agents embedded throughout the system can provide up-to-the-minute information on energy conditions, allowing current to flow exactly where and when it is needed and at the cheapest price. For example, Sage Systems, in the United States, has created a software program that allows utilities to "shed load instantly" if the system is at peak and stressed to the limit, by "setting back a few thousand customers' thermostats by 2 degrees . . . [with] a single command over the Internet." Another new product, Aladyn, allows users, with the aid of a Web browser, to monitor and make changes in the energy used by home appliances, lights, and air conditioning.

In the very near future, sensors attached to every appliance or machine powered by electricity — refrigerators, air conditioners, washing machines, security alarms — will provide up-to-the-minute information on energy prices, as well as on temperature, light, and other environmental conditions, so that factories, offices, homes, neighbourhoods, and whole communities can continuously and automatically adjust their energy requirements to one another's needs and to the energy load flowing through the system.

The People's Energy

Whether hydrogen becomes "the people's energy" depends to a large extent on how it is harnessed in the early stages of development. The first thing to keep in mind is that with distributed generation, every family, business, neighbourhood, and community in the world will be potentially both a producer and a consumer of its own hydrogen and electricity. Because fuel cells will be located at the sites where the hydrogen and electricity are going to be produced and partially consumed, with the surplus hydrogen sold as fuel and the surplus electricity sent back onto the energy network, the ability to aggregate large numbers of producer-users into associations will be critical to energy empowerment and the advancing of the vision of democratic energy.

Like with the struggle to control the World Wide Web, we are likely to see a hard-fought and protracted battle for control over HEWs. End-users have long argued that information ought to run free over the Web. Time Warner, Microsoft, and other global software and content companies, on the other hand, have fought hard to control access to the portals of cyberspace. Expect global energy companies like BP and Royal Dutch/Shell and the world's leading power and utility companies to attempt to exercise similar control over almost every aspect of the emerging HEWs.

The aggregation of distributed generation has much in common with the aggregation of labour in the early union movement at the beginning of the twentieth century. Industrial workers, individually, were too weak to negotiate the terms of their labour contracts with management. Only by organizing collectively as a block within factories, offices, and whole industries could labour amass enough power to bargain with management. The ability to withhold labour collectively by using "the strike" gave labour a powerful tool in its campaign to shorten workweeks, improve the conditions of work, and increase both pay and benefits.

Similarly, empowering individuals and democratizing energy will require that public institutions and non-profit organizations — local governments, co-operatives, community development corporations, credit unions, and the like — jump in at the beginning of the new energy revolution and help to establish distributed-generation associations in every country.

Eventually, the end-users' combined generating power via the energy webs will exceed the power generated by the utility companies at their central plants. When that happens, it will constitute a revolution in the way energy is produced and distributed. Once the customer, the end-user, becomes the main producer and supplier of energy, power companies around the world will be forced to redefine their role if they are to survive. A few power companies are already beginning to explore new roles as bundlers of energy services and co-ordinators of energy activity on the energy web that is forming. In the new scheme of things, power companies would become "virtual utilities," assisting end-users by connecting them with one another and helping them to share their energy surplus profitably and efficiently. Co-ordinating content rather than producing it will become the mantra of power companies in the era of distributed generation.

Utility companies, interestingly enough, serve to gain — at least in the short term — from distributed generation, although, until recently, many have fought the development. Because distributed generation is targeted to the very specific energy requirements of the end-user, it is a less costly and more efficient way of providing additional power than relying on a centralized power source. It costs an American company between US\$365 and US\$1,100 per kilowatt-hour to install a six-mile (ten-kilometre) power line to a three-megawatt customer. A distributed-generation system can meet the same electricity requirements at a cost of between US\$400 and US\$500 per kilowatt-hour. Generating the electricity at or near the end-user's location also reduces the amount of energy used, because between 5 and 8 percent of the energy transported over long-distance lines is lost in the transmission.

U.S. power companies are anxious to avoid making large financial investments in capital expansion because under the new utility restructuring laws they can no longer pass the costs of new capacity investment on to their customers. And because the field is now very competitive, power companies are reluctant to take funds from their reserves to finance new capacities. The result is that they put stress on existing plants beyond their ability to keep up with demand, leading to more frequent breakdowns and power outages. The major East Coast blackout of August 14, 2003, is the most illuminating recent example of this. That is why a number of power companies are looking to distributed generation as a way to meet the growing commercial and consumer demand for electricity while limiting their financial exposure.

Toward a Third Industrial Revolution

The harnessing of hydrogen will alter our way of life as fundamentally as did the introduction of coal and steam power in the nineteenth century and the shift to oil and the internal combustion engine in the twentieth century. Championing a fifty-year plan to build a hydrogen economy is a grand economic vision on the scale of the first and second industrial revolutions in North America. By taking a commanding lead in building a hydrogen infrastructure for Canada and by developing renewable resources and hydrogen technologies and related products and services, the Canadian economy can help to set the twenty-first-century economic agenda for the rest of the world.

Investing in a hydrogen economy will reinvigorate capital markets, spur productivity, create new export markets, and increase the GDP of Canada. According to a recent study by Price Waterhouse Coopers, the hydrogen economy could generate US$1.7 trillion in new business by the year 2020. It should be emphasized that no other single economic development will have as great an effect on the global economy over the course of the next several decades.

The transition from a fossil fuel energy regime to the hydrogen age will require a dynamic partnership between Canadian business and local, provincial, and national governments. Business will provide the entrepreneurial know-how to create the software and hardware of the new hydrogen era and redesign and manage the decentralized hydrogen energy grid. Government, at every level, will need to ease the transition by partnering with business. In the early stages of creating a new energy regime and laying out a new energy infrastructure, government assistance, in the form of research and development funds, tax credits and incentives, early technology adoption agreements by government agencies and their contractors, and favourable regulatory changes will all be critical to making the transition workable.

A government–business partnership will quicken the pace of the change by helping industry to underwrite the large direct and indirect costs involved in getting to the kind of economies of scale and speed that will make the new technology and infrastructure commercially viable. All earlier energy revolutions were similarly underwritten by the forging of government–business partnerships. Canada has traditionally supported public–private partnerships and, therefore, is ideally suited to steward a new working relationship between government and industry to make the transition to the hydrogen era.

Organized labour will also benefit from the shift to the hydrogen economy. While new "smart" technologies are moving the global economy away from mass labour and toward small, professional workforces over the long term, in the short term — the next thirty years — millions of new jobs will be required to install renewable technologies in every community, reconfigure the nation's power grids, and create a hydrogen energy infrastructure. Qualitative leaps in employment always occur during periods in history when new energy regimes are being established and the accompanying infrastructures are being laid out. The harnessing of coal and steam power and the laying down of continental rail infrastructures between the end of the American Civil War and the beginning of World War I created millions of jobs in North America, as did the harnessing of oil, the introduction of the internal combustion engine, the laying down of roads, and the electrification of factories and communities in the first sixty years of the twentieth century. Once operational, these new energy regimes — the first and second industrial revolutions — spawned great leaps in productivity and made possible new kinds of goods, services, and markets, resulting in the creation of still more jobs.

The key point is that fundamental changes in energy regimes and accompanying infrastructures are traditionally the source of new employment opportunities. And because the installation of renewable technologies and the establishment of a hydrogen infrastructure as well as the reconfiguration and decentralization of the nation's power grid are geographically tied, the employment generated will all be within Canada. If both the technologies and technical know-how that comprise the hydrogen economy are also produced by research institutes and Canadian-based companies, additional domestic employment will be generated.

Making the transition to the hydrogen era provides a unifying vision for the environmental movement and offers the first real hope of creating a truly sustainable global economy for future generations. By eliminating carbon dioxide altogether from the economic equation, the hydrogen economy leaps ahead of the current paltry and piecemeal efforts to reduce greenhouse gas emissions. The shift to hydrogen is a bold plan to confront, head-on, global warming, the single most dangerous problem facing humanity and the Earth in the coming century. The ambitious and uncompromising nature of the plan will reinvigorate the green spirit, especially among the young, who will likely identify with both the high-tech and the democratic vision of peer-to-peer energy sharing.

The hydrogen economy will also improve the lot of Canada's most disadvantaged citizens. The rising price of oil and gas in the years ahead will fall disproportionately on the poor. Already, the poor, many of whom have lost part-time minimum-wage jobs in the recent downturn of the global economy, are increasingly unable to pay their electricity, gas, and heating bills and cannot afford the rising price of gasoline at the pump. A Canada-wide hydrogen game plan that emphasizes the installation of renewable technologies and a hydrogen fuel-cell infrastructure in poor urban and rural communities can help to create energy independence among Canada's most vulnerable populations.

Empowering the Developing World

Incredibly, 65 percent of the human population has never made a telephone call, and a third of the human race has no access to electricity. Today, the per-capita use of energy throughout the developing world is a mere one-fifteenth of the consumption enjoyed in the United States. Narrowing the gap between the haves and have-nots means first narrowing the gap between the connected and the unconnected. Lack of access to electricity is a key factor in perpetuating poverty around the world. Conversely, access to energy means more economic opportunity. Electricity frees human labour from day-to-day survival tasks. It provides power to run farm equipment, operate small factories and craft shops, and light homes, schools, and businesses. Making the shift to a hydrogen energy regime, using renewable resources and technologies to extract the hydrogen, and creating distributed-generation energy webs that can connect communities all over the world, together hold great promise for helping to lift billions of people out of poverty.

As the price of fuel cells and accompanying appliances continues to plummet with new innovations and economies of scale, these products will become far more broadly available, just as was the case with transistor radios, computers, and cellular phones. The goal ought to be to provide stationary fuel cells for every neighbourhood and village in the developing world. Villages can install renewable energy technologies — photovoltaic, wind, biomass, etc. — to produce their own electricity and then use it to separate hydrogen from water and store the hydrogen for subsequent use in fuel cells. In rural areas where expensive commercial power lines have not yet been extended, stand-alone fuel cells can provide energy quickly and cheaply. After enough fuel cells have been leased or purchased and installed, mini–energy grids can connect urban neighbourhoods as well as rural villages into expanding energy networks. The HEW can be built organically and spread as the distributed generation becomes more widely used. The larger hydrogen fuel cells have the additional advantage of producing

pure drinking water as a by-product, a not-insignificant consideration in village communities around the world where
access to clean water is often a critical concern.

Distributed-generation associations need to be established
throughout the developing world. Civil-society organizations,
co-operatives (where they exist), micro-credit lending institutions, and local governments ought to view distributed-generation energy webs as the core strategy for building sustainable,
self-sufficient communities. Breaking the cycle of dependency
and despair, becoming truly "empowered," starts with access to
and control over energy.

National governments and world lending institutions need
to be lobbied or pressured to help provide both financial and
logistical support for the creation of a hydrogen energy infrastructure. Equally important, new laws will need to be enacted to
make it easier to adopt distributed generation. Public and private
companies will need to be required to guarantee that distributed-
generation operators have access to the main power grid and
the right to sell energy back or trade it for other services.

The fossil fuel era brought with it a highly centralized
energy infrastructure, and an accompanying economic infrastructure, that favoured the few over the many. Now, on the
cusp of the hydrogen age, it is possible to imagine a decentralized energy infrastructure, the kind that could support a
democratization of energy, enabling individuals, communities, and countries to claim their independence.

In the early 1990s, at the dawn of the Internet era, the
demand for "universal access" to information and communications became the rallying cry for a generation of activists,
consumers, citizens, and public leaders. Today, as we begin our

journey into the hydrogen era, the demand for universal access to energy ought to inspire a new generation of activists to help lay the groundwork for establishing sustainable communities.

If all individuals and communities in the world were to become the producers of their own energy, the result would be a dramatic shift in the configuration of power: no longer from the top down but from the bottom up. Local peoples would be less subject to the will of far-off centres of power. Communities would be able to produce many of their own goods and services and consume the fruits of their own labour. But, because they would also be connected via the worldwide communications webs, they would be able to share their unique commercial skills, products, and services with other communities around the planet. This kind of economic self-sufficiency becomes the starting point for global commercial interdependence, and is a far different economic reality than that in colonial regimes of the past, in which local peoples were made subservient to and dependent on powerful forces from the outside.

By redistributing power broadly to everyone, we can establish the conditions for a truly equitable sharing of the Earth's bounty. This is the essence of the politics of reglobalization from the bottom up.

Two Approaches to a Hydrogen Future

While the European Union understands that in the immediate future much of the hydrogen will have to be extracted from fossil fuels, its long-term game plan is to rely increasingly on renewable sources of energy to extract hydrogen. (The E.U. has set a target to generate 22 percent of its electricity and 12 percent of all of its energy from renewable sources of energy by 2010.)

Now, the U.S. business community is worried that it might fall behind Europe in reaching a hydrogen future and has begun to put pressure on the Bush administration to spearhead a similar effort. Even though the American president embraced the hydrogen future in his 2003 State of the Union address, in reality the energy bill he sent to Congress for deliberation focuses almost entirely on subsidizing research and development aimed at extracting hydrogen from fossil fuels and by harnessing nuclear power to the task, with little emphasis on developing renewable sources of energy to extract hydrogen. In other words, the White House would like to head into a hydrogen future without ever leaving an old-fashioned fossil fuel and nuclear energy regime. Its failure to imagine a new energy era and to take the steps to get there could put the United States significantly behind Europe as a world power by mid-century.

Laying the Groundwork for the Hydrogen Economy in Canada

In order to jump-start the hydrogen economy in Canada, the federal government should consider adopting a number of high-visibility initiatives. First, create a high-level working group to draft a blueprint for Canada to become an integrated hydrogen economy by the year 2050. Second, assemble a consortium of universities, technical institutes, and government laboratories to help facilitate research and development of hydrogen technology and related products and services. Third, create a working group of software, chemical, automotive, energy, and power companies to co-ordinate joint efforts to produce and market hydrogen technologies. Fourth, prepare a fiscal plan for using government funds to stimulate research and development programs — in partnership with the private sector — and to provide tax incentives for companies and consumers to produce and use hydrogen-based technologies. Fifth, establish a working group of financial institutions to work with the federal government to jointly underwrite new venture opportunities. Sixth, establish several strategically located hydrogen technology parks and provide tax credits and incentives to lure businesses from around the world that are engaged in hydrogen technology products and services to set up shop in Canada. These hydrogen technology parks can create a "synergy effect" and spur quicker development, much like Silicon Valley did in the 1980s and 1990s. Seventh, set up a task force made up of representatives of the country's main labour unions and businesses, as well as government officials, to explore ways to ensure maximum participation of organized labour at the local, provincial, and national levels in the planning, building, running, and servicing of the new hydrogen energy infrastructure. Eighth, work with local and provincial governments, public and private utilities, and civil-society organizations to set up prototype distributed-generation associations and HEWs in the poorest urban and rural communities, with the goal of creating universal energy independence. Ninth, establish a working committee made up of provincial education ministries and the leading technical schools, colleges, and universities to design curriculum and provide course instruction to train the next generation of workers in hydrogen-related technical skills. Tenth, assemble an intellectual advisory board to address the many social, cultural, and political ramifications and consequences of making the transition from a fossil fuel–based economy to a hydrogen-based one.

The opportunity to make a fundamental change in energy regime, remake the underlying technological infrastructure, and spur wholly new types of commercial activity occurs only occasionally in history. This is one of those occasions. We find ourselves at the dawn of a new epoch in history. Hydrogen, the very stuff of the stars and our own sun, is now being seized by human ingenuity and harnessed for human ends. Charting the right course at the very beginning of the journey is essential if Canada is to make the great promise of a hydrogen age a reality for its children and a worthy legacy for the generations that will come after them.

NOTES

FOOD
SAVING AGRICULTURE FROM ITSELF

1. As cited in *Beyond Factory Farming: Corporate Hog Barns and the Threat to Public Health, the Environment and Rural Communities*, ed. Alexander Ervin et al., Centre for Canadian Policy Alternatives, 2003.
2. Wendell Berry, *What Are People For?* (New York: North Point Press, 1990), 123.
3. Richard Manning, *Against the Grain: How Agriculture Has Hijacked Civilization* (New York: North Point Press, 2004), 89–91.
4. Stuart Laidlaw, *Secret Ingredients: The Brave New World of Industrial Agriculture* (Toronto: McClelland & Stewart, 2003), 129.
5. Manning, *Against the Grain*.
6. Bob Stirling, "Work, Knowledge and the Direction of Farm Life" in *Writing Off the Rural West: Globalization, Governments and the Transformation of Rural Communities* (University of Alberta Press: Edmonton, 2001), 257.

7. Leo Horrigan, Robert Lawrence, and Polly Walker, "How Sustainable Agriculture Can Address the Environmental and Human Health Harms of Industrial Agriculture," *Environmental Health Perspectives* 110, no. 5 (May 2002): 445.

8. National Farmers Union, *The Farm Crisis, Bigger Farms, and the Myths of "Competition" and "Efficiency,"* November 2003.

9. First recounted in Laidlaw, *Secret Ingredients*, 81–82.

10. Horrigan, Lawrence, and Walker, *Sustainable Agriculture*, 446.

11. Interview, January 29, 2004.

12. Manning, *Against the Grain*.

13. David Tilman et al., "Agricultural Sustainability and Intensive Production Practices," *Nature* 418 (August 8, 2002): 671–77.

14. Horrigan, Lawrence, and Walker, *Sustainable Agriculture*, 446.

15. Laidlaw, *Secret Ingredients*, 66.

16. Ibid., 63–81.

17. Bill Weida, "The ILO and Depopulation of Rural Agricultural Areas: Implications for Rural Economies in Canada and the U.S.," in *Beyond Factory Farming*, 114–16.

18. Ibid., 136.

19. Ibid., 129.

20. Ibid., 127.

21. Richard Manning, "The Oil We Eat," *Harper's Magazine*, February 2004.

22. Brian Halweil, *Home Grown: The Case for Local Food in a Global Market*, WorldWatch Institute Paper no. 163 (November 2002).

23. Manning, "The Oil We Eat." Energy statistics also taken from Tilman, et al., "Agricultural Sustainability."

24. Michael Pollan, "When a Crop Becomes King," *New York Times*, July 19, 2002.

25. Manning, "The Oil We Eat."

26. Vandana Shiva, *Stolen Harvest: The Hijacking of the Global Food Supply* (Cambridge, MA: South End Press), 62.

27. Michael Pollan, "Power Steer," *New York Times Magazine*, March 31, 2002.

28. Taken from transcript prepared by Van Acker. Talk given October 29, 2003, in Dauphin, MB.

29. Halweil, *Home Grown.*

30. Russell Shorto, "A Short Order Revolutionary," *New York Times Magazine*, January 11, 2004.

31. Ibid.

32. Interview, March 18, 2004.

33. Interview, March 30, 2004.

34. Interview, March 18, 2004.

35. Interview, April 14, 2004.

36. Taken from transcript prepared by Van Acker. Talk given October 29, 2003, in Dauphin, MB.

37. http://www.organicvalley.coop/ (accessed June 23, 2004).

38. Telephone interview, June 24, 2004.

39. Quotes taken from transcript prepared by Van Acker. Talk given October 29, 2003, in Dauphin, MB.

40. Telephone interview, June 24, 2004.

BETTING THE FARM: FOOD SAFETY AND THE BEEF COMMODITY CHAIN

1. Verna Mitura and Lina de Piétro, *Canada's Beef Cattle Sector and the Impact of BSE on Farm Family Income 2000–2003*, Statistics Canada Agriculture Division Working Paper no. 69 (Ottawa, June 2004): 5.

2. Statistics Canada, Census of Agriculture, 2001.

3. Statistics Canada, Agriculture Division, special tabulations from "Cattle Statistics" Catalogue, July 2003, 23–012.

4. Temple Grandin, "Conveyor Restrainer," http://www.grandin.com/restrain/new.conv.rest.html.

5. Experimentation showed that material from tuberculous lesions in the viscera (notably in the lungs, lymphatic glands, and liver) could contaminate otherwise wholesome meat by the hands, knives, and clothes of the butcher during the processes of flaying and dressing the carcass. See *Royal Commission Appointed to*

Inquire into the Effect of Food Derived from Tuberculous Animals on Human Health, P.P. 1895, xxxv, 14.

6. The Honourable Donald H. Oliver, Q.C., Chairman, Senate of Canada, The Standing Committee on Agriculture and Forestry, *The BSE Crisis — Lessons for the Future*, Interim Report (April 2004): 10.

7. Canadian Food Inspection Agency, "Transmissible Spongiform Encephalopathies (TSEs) Questions and Answers," February 5, 2001, http://www.inspection.gc.ca/english/anima/heasan/disemala/spong/tse_e.shtml.

8. Kevin Grier and Larry Martin, *Cattle Pricing and Other Contentious Industry Issues*, Special Report (Guelph: George Morris Centre, 2004), http://www.georgemorris.org/PDF%20Files/GMCSpecialReport-BeefPricing031604.pdf.

9. Anthony S. Wohl, *Endangered Lives: Public Health in Victorian Britain* (London: Dent, 1983), 130.

10. Keir Waddington, "The Science of Cows," *History of Science* 39 (2001): 355–81.

11. Barry Wilson, "Eliminating Bovine TB Said Next to Impossible," *The Western Producer*, March 10 2003, http://www.producer.com/registered/articles/2003/0306/livestock/20030306ls05.html; and Canada House of Commons Standing Committee on Agriculture and AgriFood, *Bovine Tuberculosis in the Immediate Area of Riding Mountain National Park in Manitoba* (April 2003), http://www.parl.gc.ca/InfoComDoc/37/2/AGRI/Studies/Reports/agrirp01-e.htm.

12. F. D. Menzies and S. D. Neill, "Cattle-to-Cattle Transmission of Bovine Tuberculosis," *The Veterinary Journal* 160 (2000): 92–106.

13. Nobel e-Museum, "Stanley Prusiner," http://www.nobel.se/medicine/laureates/1997/prusiner-autobio.html.

14. Variant CJD (vCJD) is a rare degenerative brain disease that is invariably fatal with no known treatment. It is associated with the consumption of tissue contaminated by the active agent that causes BSE in cattle. The vast majority of cases have been in the United Kingdom and the average age at mortality is

under 30. Classic Creutzfeldt-Jakob disease (CJD) is an invariably
fatal degenerative brain disease of the elderly and is endemic
worldwide. See http://www.hc-sc.gc.ca/english/diseases/
cjd/bg4.html and http://www.cdc.gov/ncidod/diseases/cjd/
cjd_fact_sheet.htm.

15. Patrick Van Zwanenberg and Erik Millstone, "BSE: A Paradigm
of Policy Failure," *The Political Quarterly* 74 (2003): 30.

16. United Kingdom, *The BSE Inquiry Report*, vol. 6, chap. 7, 740–742,
http://www.bseinquiry.gov.uk/index.htm.

17. National Creutzfeldt-Jakob Disease Surveillance Unit, University
of Edinburgh, CJD Statistics, http://www.cjd.ed.ac.uk/figures.htm.

18. Health Canada, *First Canadian Case of vCJD* (May 2003),
http://www.hc-sc.gc.ca/english/diseases/cjd/index.html.

19. Merle Jacob and Tomas Hellström, "Policy Understanding of
Science, Public Trust and the BSE–CJD Crisis," *Journal of
Hazardous Materials* 78 (2000): 309.

20. Keir Waddington, "Safe Meat and Healthy Animals: BSE and
Bovine TB," *History and Policy*, http://www.historyand
policy.org/archive/policy-paper-04.html.

21. Oliver, *The BSE Crisis*, 14.

22. Health Canada Food Directorate, *Policy on Specified Risk Materials
(SRM) in the Food Supply* (2003), http://www.hc-sc.gc.ca/
food-aliment/fpi-ipa/e_policy_srm.html.

23. Canadian Food Inspection Agency, "Risk Assessment on Bovine
Spongiform Encephalopathy in Cattle in Canada, Part C: Risk
Estimation," Section 3.1 Probability that the Imported Bovine
Animal is BSE-Infected, December 2002, http://www.inspection.
gc.ca/english/sci/ahra/ bseris/bserisc1e.shtml#Cfig2.

24. Ibid., Section 6.1 Risk Estimate, http://www.inspection.gc.ca/
english/sci/ahra/bseris/bserisc2e.shtml#Cfig5.

25. William Leiss, "A Closer Look at CFIA's BSE Risk Estimation,"
BSE Risk in Canada, Part 4, 2004, http://www.leiss.ca/bse/155?
download.

26. Health Canada Food Directorate, *Policy on Specified Risk Materials
(SRM) in the Food Supply* (2003), http://www.hc-sc.gc.ca/ food-
aliment/fpi-ipa/e_policy_srm.html.

27. Canadian Food Inspection Agency, "Canada: A Minimal BSE
Risk Country," December 2003, http://www.inspection.gc.ca/
english/anima/heasan/disemala/bseesb/minrisexece.shtml.

28. In Canada the term "specified risk materials" (SRM) is now
used to denote an expanded list of bovine by-products that
contain the infective agent of BSE and are restricted from entering the human food supply. SRM include skull, brain, trigemi-
nal ganglia of the skull, eyes, tonsils, spinal cord, and dorsal
root ganglia of the spine from cattle aged 30 months or older;
and the distal ileum (the end of the small intestine) from cattle
of all ages. Because complete removal of the dorsal root ganglia
is impractical, the Meat Inspection Regulations require removal
and disposal of the vertebral column from all cattle aged thirty
months or older and it cannot be used in the preparation of
mechanically separated meat or finely textured meat. To ensure
the complete removal of the distal ileum, the entire small intestine of all cattle, regardless of age, must be removed and dis-
posed of as inedible product. See Health Canada, "Regulations
Amending the Food and Drug Regulations," July 2003,
http://www.hc-sc.gc.ca/food-aliment/friia-raaii/ food_drugs-
aliments_drogues/part-partie_11/e_1389.html; and Canadian
Food Inspection Agency "Report on Actions Taken by Canada
in Response to the Confirmation of a Case of Indigenous BSE,
http://www.inspection.gc.ca/english/anima/heasan/disemala/bs
eesb/internate.shtml ." In the U.K., specified bovine offal (SBO)
was defined differently in 1989. See United Kingdom, *The BSE
Inquiry Report*, vol. 6, chap. 3, 77–91; vol. 13, chap. 3, 38–44,
http://www.bseinquiry.gov.uk/index.htm.

29. Gary Little, "BSE Surveillance in Canada," *CAHNet Bulletin*,
Canadian Animal Health Network Edition 8, (Winter 2003): 3;
and Alberta Auditor General, *Report of the Auditor General on
the Alberta Government's BSE-Related Assistance Programs* (July
27, 2004): 49.

30. "Farmers Not Meeting BSE Test Quotas," *Lethbridge Herald*,
August 5, 2004, 1.

31. Alberta Auditor General, *Report on Alberta Government's BSE-Related Assistance Programs*, 48.

32. Upton Sinclair, *The Jungle*. (New York: Bantam Books, 1906; Bantam Classics Edition, 1981). For an account of the effect of Sinclair's novel in Canada, see Ian MacLachlan, *Kill and Chill: Restructuring Canada's Beef Commodity Chain* (Toronto: University of Toronto Press, 2001), 128–31.

33. U.K. Food Standards Agency, *Report on the Review of Scientific Committees* (2002), http://www.food.gov.uk/multimedia/pdfs/CommitteesReview.pdf.

34. Anne Hardy, "Animals, Disease and Man," *Perspectives in Biology and Medicine* 46 (2003): 200–15.

35. D. S. Edwards, A. M. Johnston, and G. C. Mead, "Meat Inspection: An Overview of Present Practices and Future Trends," *The Veterinary Journal* 154 (1997): 136.

36. Ibid., 136, 138.

37. Ibid., 135–36.

38. Tag is manure that has caked-up in a thick layer and becomes matted in the hide.

39. Canadian Cattle Identification Program, http://www.canadaid.com/.

40. Canadian Cattlemen's Association, "Quality Starts Here," http://www.cattle.ca/QSH/.

41. John Spriggs, Jill Hobbs, and Andrew Fearne, "Beef Producers Attitudes to Coordination and Quality Assurance in Canada and the U.K.," *International Journal of Food and Agribusiness Management Review* 3 (2000): 98; and Farm Assured British Beef and Lamb, http://www.fabbl.co.uk/.

42. Eunice Taylor and Joanne Zaida Taylor, "Perceptions of 'the Bureaucratic Nightmare' of HACCP," *British Food Journal* 106 (2004): 65–72.

43. Reported slaughter for federally and provincially inspected plants does not include unreported domestic slaughter on the farm. Agriculture and Agri-Food Canada, Annual Livestock and Meat Report, 2003, http://www.agr.gc.ca/misb/aisd/redmeat/almr2003.htm.

44. Saskatchewan, *Final Report of the Live Stock Commission of the Province of Saskatchewan*, (Regina: King's Printer, 1918): 20.

45. Temple Grandin, *Report on Handling and Stunning Practices in Canadian Meat Packing Plants*, prepared for Agriculture Canada, Canadian Federation of Humane Societies, Canadian Meat Council and Canadian Poultry and Egg Processor's Council (Fort Collins, CO: Grandin Livestock Handling Systems, 1995).

46. Gordon Doonan, Martin Appelt, and Alena Corbin, "Nonambulatory Livestock Transport: The Need for Consensus," *Canadian Veterinary Journal* (August 2003), http://www.inspection.gc.ca/english/anima/heasan/transport/consensuse.shtml.

47. Canadian Food Inspection Agency, "Interim BSE Export Restriction," January 2003, http://www.inspection.gc.ca/english/anima/meavia/commun/20040113come.shtml.

48. Grandin, *Report on Handling and Stunning Practices*, 13.

49. Ontario Office of the Provincial Auditor, 2001 Annual Report, chap. 3.01, http://www.auditor.on.ca/english/reports/en01/301e01.pdf.

50. Dead stock refers to any food animal that has died due to disease or accident sometime prior to processing. In Ontario, it is illegal to sell or process meat from dead animals for human consumption. For details of the various allegations involving Aylmer Meat Packers, see Canadian Food Inspection Agency, "Update — Health Hazard Alert," September 2003, http://www.inspection.gc.ca/english/corpaffr/recarapp/2003/20030916e.shtml, and The Honourable Roland J. Haines, *Farm to Fork: A Strategy for Meat Safety in Ontario*, Report of the Meat Regulatory and Inspection Review (Toronto, 2004): Appendix B.

51. Haines, *Farm to Fork*, 247–51.

52. The notable exception is Quebec, which recently established the *Centre québécois d'inspection des aliments et santé animale*, which enjoys a level of independence similar to the CFIA.

53. Haines, *Farm to Fork*, 245.

54. Ontario Ministry of Agriculture and Food Inspection Programs, June 2004, http://www.gov.on.ca/OMAFRA/english/food/inspection/.

55. Anthony Giddens, "Risk, Lecture 2," *BBC Reith Lectures*, 1999, http://www.lse.ac.uk/Giddens/reith_99/week2/ week2.htm; Anthony Giddens, *The Third Way and Its Critics* (Cambridge: Polity Press, 2000), 135–39; and Michael Jacobs, "Environment, Modernity and the Third Way," in *The Global Third Way Debate*, ed. Anthony Giddens (Cambridge: Polity Press, 2001), 325–26.

56. United Nations Conference on Environment and Development, "Rio Declaration on Environment and Development," Principle 15, 1992, http://www.un.org/documents/ga/confi51/aconfi5126-1annex1.htm.

57. Tony Van der Haegen, "EU View of Precautionary Principle in Food Safety," European Union in the U.S., October 2003, http://www.eurunion.org/news/speeches/2003/031023tvdh.htm.

58. Canada Privy Council Office, "Framework for the Application of Precaution in Science-Based Decision Making About Risk," July 2003, http://www.pco-bcp.gc.ca/default.asp?Language= E&Page=publications&Sub=precaution&Doc=precaution_ e.htm#1.0.

59. William Leiss, "BSE Risk in Canada: Finally the Penny Drops," July 22, 2003, 14–15, http://www.leiss.ca/chronicles/125.

FISH OR CUT BAIT: SOLUTIONS FOR OUR SEAS

1. Fred (Fritz) Goldstein, personal communication, May 2004.

2. Ibid.

3. Ibid.

4. Carl Safina, *Song for the Blue Ocean* (New York: Henry Holt, 1998).

5. Food and Agriculture Organization of the United Nations (FAO), "The State of World Fisheries and Aquaculture," 2002.

6. Ibid.

7. Ibid.

8. Ibid.
9. Reg Watson and Daniel Pauly, "Systematic Distortions in World Fisheries Catch Trends," *Nature* 414 (November 2001): 29.
10. Dayton L. Alverson et al., Food and Agriculture Organization of the United Nations, *A Global Assessment of Fisheries By Catch and Discards*, FAO Fisheries Technical Paper no. 339, (Rome, 1996), http://www.fao.org/docrep/ 003/t4890e/t4890e00.htm.
11. Dayton L. Alverson, personal communication to Mercedes Lee, Blue Ocean Institute, 2004.
12. Inter-American Tropical Tuna Commission (IATTC), *Annual Report of the Inter-American Tropical Tuna Commission 2001* (2002), ISSN: 0074-1000.
13. Lance E. Morgan and Ratana Chuenpagde, *Shifting Gears: Addressing the Collateral Impacts of Fishing Methods in U.S. Waters*, Pew Science Series (Washington, DC: Island Press, 2003).
14. Larry B. Crowder and Ransom A. Myers, *A Comprehensive Study of the Ecological Impacts of the Worldwide Pelagic Longline Industry*, First Annual Report to the Pew Charitable Trusts (2001).
15. National Marine Fisheries Service (NMFS), "Stock Assessment and Fishery Evaluation for Atlantic Highly Migratory Species," 2003, http://www.nmfs.noaa.gov/sfa/hms/.
16. Western Pacific Fishery Management Council (WPFMC), "Western Pacific Council Announces Opening of Model Swordfish Fishery," 2004, http://www.wpcouncil.org/press/ pressreleasemodelswordfishfishery.pdf.
17. Dayton L. Alverson et al., Food and Agriculture Organization of the United Nations, *A Global Assessment of Fisheries By Catch and Discards*.
18. Environmental Justice Foundation, "Squandering the Seas: How Shrimp Trawling Is Threatening Ecological Integrity and Food Security Around the World," London, U.K., 2003.
19. Randall Arauz, Sea Turtle Restoration Project, personal communication, 2004.
20. Ransom A. Myers and Boris Worm, "Rapid Worldwide

Depletion of Predatory Fish Communities," *Nature* 423 (May 15, 2003): 280–83.

21. Ibid.

22. Daniel Pauly et al., "Fishing Down Marine Food Webs," *Science* 279 (February 6, 1998): 860–63.

23. Daniel Pauly et al., "Towards Sustainability in World Fisheries," *Nature* 418 (August 8, 2002): 689–95.

24. Ibid.

25. "No Seafood Grille, 2050," *Hollywood Ocean Night: A Town Hall for the Oceans,* DVD, produced and directed by Randy Olsen (2004; The Groundlings).

26. Food and Agriculture Organization of the United Nations (FAO), "The State of World Fisheries and Aquaculture," 2002.

27. Fred (Fritz) Goldstein, personal communication, May 2004.

28. Rebecca J. Goldburg, Matt S. Elliot, and Rosamond L. Naylor, *Marine Aquaculture in the United States*, prepared for the Pew Oceans Commission (2001).

29. Food and Agriculture Organization of the United Nations (FAO), "The State of World Fisheries and Aquaculture," 2002.

30. Carrie Brownstein, Mercedes Lee, and Carl Safina, "Harnessing Consumer Power for Conservation," *Conservation in Practice,* Fall 2003.

31. Carl Safina, "What's a Fish Lover to Eat? The Audubon Guide to Seafood," *Audubon* 100 (1998): 63–66.

32. Carrie Brownstein, Mercedes Lee, and Carl Safina, "Harnessing Consumer Power for Conservation."

33. Julian R. Ashford et al., "Seabird Interactions with Longlining Operations for *Dissostichus Eleginoides* at the South Sandwich Islands and South Georgia," *CCAMLR Science* 1 (1994): 143–53.

34. Susan Boa, Seaweb, personal communication, 2003.

35. International Commission for the Conservation of Atlantic Tunas, *Report of the Standing Committee on Research and Statistics* (Madrid, Spain: SCRS, 2002).

36. Matthew Scully, "The Last Gasps of the Fur Trade," *Humane Society of the United States News*, Fall 1998.

37. Andrea Cimino, Humane Society of the United States, personal communication, 2004.
38. Matthew Scully, "The Last Gasps of the Fur Trade."
39. Aldo Leopold, *Sand County Almanac* (New York: Ballantine Books, 1966).
40. Neil A. Campbell, *Biology*, third ed. (New York: The Benjamin/Cummings Publishing Company, Inc., 1998).
41. NOAA Fisheries, *The Status of U.S. Fisheries*, 2002 Report to Congress (May 2003).
42. National Research Council, *Sustaining Marine Fisheries* (Washington, DC: National Academy Press, 1999).
43. Larry B. Crowder and Ransom A. Myers, *A Comprehensive Study of the Ecological Impacts of the Worldwide Pelagic Longline Industry*.
44. Australian Government, Great Barrier Reef Marine Park Authority, "Explanatory Statement for Great Barrier Reef Marine Park Zoning Plan 2003," 2003, http://www.reefed.edu.au/rap/.
45. Pew Oceans Commission, *America's Living Oceans, Charting a Course for Sea Change* (2003).

DIET FOR A SMALLER PLANET: REAL SOURCES OF ABUNDANCE

1. See Frances Moore Lappé and Anna Lappé, "Maps of the Mind," in *Hope's Edge: The Next Diet for a Small Planet* (New York: Tarcher/Penguin, 2002). Statistics from United Nations FAO.
2. According to Food Research and Action Center. For more information visit http://www.frac.org.
3. Malnutrition in India statistics from the World Bank Group.
4. See Lappé and Lappé, "Seeding Annapoorna," in *Hope's Edge*. Quote from Shanta Kumar, then minister of Consumer Affairs and Public distribution.
5. Estimates of the percent of world grain fed to livestock vary. We are relying here on Vaclav Smil, *Feeding the World: A Challenge for the Twenty-first Century* (Cambridge, MA: The MIT Press, 2000). After considerable research he arrives at 45 percent but cautions that it is impossible to know precisely.

6. Data supplied by the Economic Research Service, Department of Agriculture, and correspondence, December 2000. See also Frances Moore Lappé, *Diet for a Small Planet* (Ballantine Books, 1971, 1991), 445n13.

7. For more information see http://www.rprogess.org. Other alternative indicators include the United Nations Human Development Index (UNHDI), http://www.un.org; the Gross Sustainable Development Product (GSDP) developed by the Global Community Assessment Center and the Society for World Sustainable Development in the U.K.; and the Calvert-Henderson Quality of Life indicators, http://www.calvert-henderson.com.

8. See Gary Gardner and Brian Halweil, *Underfed and Overfed: The Global Epidemic of Malnutrition*, WorldWatch Institute Paper no. 150 (March 2000).

9. See, for example, Eric A. Finkelstein, Ian C. Fiebelkorn, and Guijing Wang, "State-Level Estimates of Annual Medical Expenditures Attributable to Obesity," *Obesity Research* 12, no. 1 (2004): 18–24; and Eric Finkelstein, Ian Fiebelkorn, and Guijing Wang, of the U.S. Centers for Disease Control and Prevention, "National Medical Spending Attributable to Overweight and Obesity: How Much, and Who's Paying?" *Health Affairs*, http://www.healthaffairs.org.

10. Centre Europe-Tiers Monde (CETIM), http://www.cetim.ch.

11. CETIM, "Land Concentration in Brazil: A Politics of Poverty," *Human Rights Sub-Commission 1999*.

12. Statistic from the Brazilian Embassy.

13. Export figures based on statistics from the U.S. Economic Research Service.

14. Brazilian Constitution, 1988, "Chapter III Agricultural and Land Policy and Agrarian Reform, Article 184." The full text reads: "It is within the power of the Union to expropriate on account of social interest, for purposes of agrarian reform, the rural property which is not performing its social function, against prior and fair compensation in agrarian debt bonds with a clause

providing for maintenance of the real value, redeemable within a period of up to twenty years computed as from the second year of issue, and the use of which shall be defined in the law."

15. See Lappé and Lappé, "The Battle for Human Nature," in *Hope's Edge*, 67.

16. Ibid., 80.

17. Ibid., 89.

18. See the Community Environmental Legal Defense Fund, http://www.celdf.org.

19. Dr. C. Robert Taylor, Auburn University, personal communication.

20. Environmental Working Group Farm Subsidy Database, http://www.ewg.org/farm.

21. National Campaign for Sustainable Agriculture, Update, June 2001.

22. For more information see http://www.etcgroup.org.

23. Hope Shand, ETC Group, personal communication.

24. For more information see http://www.primalseeds.org.

25. See ETC Group, "Globalization, Inc. Concentration in Corporate Power: The Unmentioned Agenda," no. 71, July/August, 2001.

26. Ibid.

27. See, for example, John Tuxill, *Nature's Cornucopia: Our Stake in Plant Diversity*, WorldWatch Institute Paper no. 148 (September 1999).

28. Cary Fowler and Patrick Mooney, *Shattering: Food, Politics, and the Loss of Genetic Diversity* (Tucson, Arizona: University of Arizona Press, 1990).

29. See Jeffrey Smith, *Seeds of Deception: Exposing Industry and Government Lies About the Safety of Genetically Engineered Foods*, (Fairfield, Iowa: Yes! Books, 2003).

30. The International Service for the Acquisition of Agri-biotech Applications publishes these statistics and others on the global production of GMOs, http://www.isaaa.org.

31. See Clive James, ISAAA Board of Directors "Global Status of Commercialized Transgenic Crops: 2003," http://www.isaaa.org.

32. A. F. Jeu, "Organic Agriculture Can Save the World," *Well- Being Journal* 13, no. 2 (March/April 2004).
33. UNFAO, *The State of Food and Agriculture 2004* (United Nations: May 2004).
34. Smith, *Seeds of Deception*.
35. Margaret Mellon and Jane Rissler, *Gone to Seed: Transgenic Contaminants in the Traditional Seed Supply* (Cambridge, MA: Union of Concerned Scientists, 2004).
36. Definition of hybrid seeds can be found at Genetics Resources Action International (GRAIN), http://www.grain.org.
37. Norman Borlaug (lecture, Earth Institute at Columbia University, 2003).
38. Lappé and Lappé, "Seeding Annapoorna," in *Hope's Edge*, 143.
39. Ibid., 156.
40. See Third World Network, http://www.twnside.org.sg.
41. Lappé and Lappé, *Hope's Edge*, 161–62.
42. Jules Pretty and Rachel Hine, "Empirical Findings of SAFE-World Project," in *Reducing Food Poverty with Sustainable Agriculture*, Center for Environment and Society (University of Essex, U.K., February 2001).
43. Pretty and Hine, see "Empirical Findings," in *Reducing Food Poverty*.
44. Lappé and Lappé, *Hope's Edge*, 286.
45. Margot Roosevelt, "The Coffee Clash," *Time* online edition, March 1, 2004.
46. For more information see TransFair USA, http://www.transfairusa.org.
47. For studies on the productivity of sustainable agriculture, see, for example, Pretty and Hine, *Reducing Food Poverty*; Jeu, "Organic Agriculture"; and Nicholas Parrott and Terry Marsden, Department of City and Regional Planning, Cardiff University, "The Real Green Revolution" (Greenpeace Environmental Trust, February 2002). See in particular Table 4.1 — Examples of yield increases attributable to adoption of OAA.
48. Jules Pretty quoted in *New Scientist*, "An Ordinary Miracle:

Bigger harvests, without pesticides or genetically modified crops? Farmers can make it happen by letting weeds do the work" (February 3, 2001).

49. Quoted in Jeu, "Organic Agriculture." From Remarks by the President at the Bio 2003 Convention Center and Exhibition, Washington Convention Center, Washington, DC, June 2003.

OVERFEEDING THE FUTURE

1. Shengxu Li et al., "Childhood Cardiovascular Risk Factors and Carotid Vascular Changes in Adulthood: The Bogalusa Heart Study," *JAMA* 290 (2003): 2271–76.

2. World Health Organization, *Obesity: Preventing and Managing the Global Epidemic* (Geneva, Switzerland: World Health Organization, 1998).

3. World Health Organization, "Global Strategy on Diet, Physical Activity and Health," http://www.who.int/dietphysicalactivity/publications/facts/obesity/en/ (accessed July 14, 2004).

4. R. Sturm, "The Effects of Obesity, Smoking, and Problem Drinking on Chronic Medical Problems and Health Care Costs," *Health Affairs* 21 (2002): 245–53; and R. Sturm and K. B. Wells, "Does Obesity Contribute as Much to Morbidity as Poverty or Smoking?" *Public Health* 115 (2001): 229–95.

5. Eric A. Finkelstein, Ian C. Fiebelkorn, and Guijing Wang, "State-Level Estimates of Annual Medical Expenditures Attributable to Obesity," *Obesity Research* 12, no. 1 (2004): 18–24.

6. S. Musich et al., "Association of Additional Health Risks on Medical Charges and Prevalence of Diabetes Within Body Mass Index Categories," *American Journal of Health Promotion* 18 (2004): 264–68.

7. Table adapted from information on American Obesity Association website, http://www.obesity.org/subs/fastfacts/Health_Effects.shtml (accessed July 17, 2004).

8. Rebecca Puhl and Kelly D. Brownell, "Bias, Discrimination, and Obesity," *Obesity Research* 9, no. 12 (2001): 788–805.

9. S. A. Richardson et al., "Cultural Uniformity in Reaction to Physical Disabilities," *American Sociological Review* (1961): 241–47.

10. Janet D. Latner and Albert J. Stunkard, "Getting Worse: The Stigmatization of Obese Children," *Obesity Research* 11, no. 3 (2003): 452–56.

11. Adapted from Kelly D. Brownell and Katherine Battle Horgen, *Food Fight: The Inside Story of the Food Industry, America's Obesity Crisis, and What We Can Do About It* (New York: McGraw-Hill/Contemporary Books, 2004).

12. Barry M. Popkin, "An Overview on the Nutrition Transition and its Health Implications: The Bellagio Meeting," *Public Health Nutrition* 5 (2002): 93–103; Barry M. Popkin, "The Nutrition Transition and Obesity in the Developing World," *Journal of Nutrition* 131, no. 3 (2001): 871S–73S; and A. Drewnowski and Barry M. Popkin, "The Nutrition Transition: New Trends in the Global Diet," *Nutrition Reviews* 55 (1997): 31–43.

13. See M. J. Friedrich, "Epidemic of Obesity Expands Its Spread to Developing Countries," *JAMA* 287, no. 11 (2002): 1382–86.

14. Michael Pollan, "This Steer's Life," *New York Times Magazine*, March 31, 2002.

15. Saritha Rai, "Protests in India Deplore Soda Makers' Water Use," *New York Times*, May 21, 2003.

16. Table adapted from Michael Browner and Warren Leon, *The Consumer's Guide to Effective Environmental Choices: Practical Advice from the Union of Concerned Scientists* (New York: Three Rivers Press, 1999).

17. M. Story and S. French, "Food Advertising and Marketing Directed at Children and Adolescents in the U.S.," *International Journal of Behavioral Nutrition and Physical Activity* 1, no. 3 (2004): 3–20; Kaiser Family Foundation, "The Role of Media in Childhood Obesity," publication no. 7030, http://www.kff.org/entmedia/7030.cfm (accessed July 12, 2004); American Psychological Association Taskforce, "Television Advertising

Leads to Unhealthy Habits in Children," February 23, 2004, http://www.apa.org/releases/childrenads_summary.pdf (accessed July 12, 2004); Brownell and Horgen, *Food Fight*; and World Health Organization, "Marketing Food to Children: The Global Regulatory Environment," http://www.who.int/ dietphysicalactivity/publications/en/ (accessed July 14, 2004).

18. P. Rozin et al., "The Ecology of Eating: Smaller Portion Sizes in France Than in the United States Help Explain the French Paradox," *Psychological Science* 14, no. 5 (2003): 450–54.

19. Barbara J. Rolls et al., "Increasing the Portion Size of a Packaged Snack Increases Energy Intake in Men and Women," *Appetite* 42 (2004): 63–69; and Barbara J. Rolls, Erin L. Morris, and Liane S. Roe, "Portion Size of Food Affects Energy Intake in Normal-Weight and Overweight Men and Women," *American Journal of Clinical Nutrition* 76, no. 6 (2002): 1207–13.

20. Marion Nestle, *Food Politics: How the Food Industry Influences Nutrition and Health* (Berkeley: University of California Press, 2002).

21. Kelly D. Brownell and Marion Nestle, "The Sweet and Lowdown on Sugar" (OpEd) *New York Times*, January 23, 2004, A23.

22. David A. Kessler, *A Question of Intent: A Great American Battle with a Deadly Industry* (New York: Public Affairs, 2002).

23. K. D. Brownell and K. E. Warner, *The Perils of Ignoring History: Big Tobacco Played Dirty and Millions Died; How Similar Is Big Food?* Paper submitted for publication.

24. Courtney Kane, "TV and Movie Characters Sell Children Snacks," *New York Times*, December 8, 2003.

25. World Health Organization, "Marketing Food to Children," http://www.who.int/dietphysicalactivity/publications/en/ (accessed July 14, 2004).

26. American Psychological Association, *Psychological Issues in the Increasing Commercialization of Childhood*, report of the APA Task Force on Advertising and Children, http://www.apa.org/ releases/childrenads_summary.pdf (accessed July 14, 2004).

27. American Academy of Pediatrics, "Prevention of Pediatric Overweight and Obesity," *Pediatrics* 112 (2003): 424–30.

28. Kaiser Family Foundation, "The Role of Media," http://www.kff.org/entmedia/entmedia022404pkg.cfm (accessed July 14, 2004).

29. Story and French, "Food Advertising and Marketing," 3–20.

30. Comments of William McLeod at public meeting of the Kaiser Family Foundation on food advertising directed at children, http://www.kaisernetwork.org/health_cast/uploaded_files/ 022404_Media_and_Obesity1.pdf (accessed July 14, 2004).

31. Comments of Shelley Rosen of McDonald's in response to a *Reveries Magazine* survey, http://www.reveries.com/reverb/ revolver/obesity_marketing/ (accessed July 14, 2004).

32. David S. Ludwig, Karen E. Peterson, and Steven L. Gortmaker, "Relation Between Consumption of Sugar-Sweetened Drinks and Childhood Obesity: A Prospective, Observational Analysis," *Lancet* 357, no. 9255 (2001): 505–08.

33. George A. Bray, Samara Joy Nielsen, and Barry M. Popkin, "Consumption of High Fructose Corn Syrup in Beverages May Play a Role in the Epidemic of Obesity," *American Journal of Clinical Nutrition* 79, no. 4 (2004): 537–43.

34. S. Nielsen and B. M. Popkin, "Changes in Beverage Intake Between 1977–2001," *American Journal of Preventive Medicine*, 2004.

35. National Soft Drink Association, http://www.nsda.org/soft-drinks/CSDHealth/Nutrition/NutritionPR/Consumption43. html (accessed July 14, 2004).

36. K. Severson, "L.A. Schools to Stop Soda Sales: District Takes Cue from Oakland Ban," *San Francisco Chronicle*, August 28, 2002, A1.

37. Brownell and Nestle, "The Sweet and Lowdown," A23.

38. Report on letter for William Steiger from the U.S. Department of Health and Human Services to the World Health Organization, http://bmj.bmjjournals.com/cgi/reprint/ 328/7433/185-a.pdf (accessed July 14, 2004).

39. T. J. Muris, "Don't Blame TV," *Wall Street Journal,* June 25, 2004, A10.
40. Kelly D. Brownell and Marion Nestle, "Are You Responsible for Your Own Weight?" *Time,* June 7, 2004.
41. Brownell and Horgen, *Food Fight.*
42. Brownell and Warner, *The Perils of Ignoring History.*
43. M. F. Jacobson and K. D. Brownell, "Small Taxes on Soft Drinks and Snack Foods to Promote Health," *American Journal of Public Health* 90, no. 6 (2000): 854–57.
44. Brownell and Horgen, *Food Fight.*
45. Frances Moore Lappé and Anna Lappé. *Hope's Edge: The Next Diet for a Small Planet* (New York: Tarcher/Penguin, 2002); David Suzuki Foundation, "The Nature Challenge," http://www.davidsuzuki.org/ WOL/Challenge/Meals.asp (accessed July 12, 2004); Browner and Leon, *Consumer's Guide to Effective Environmental Choices*; and Cary Fowler and Pat Mooney, *Shattering: Food, Politics, and the Loss of Genetic Diversity* (Tucson: University of Arizona Press, 1996).

FUEL

BRINGING INGENUITY TO ENERGY

1. For a complete discussion, see Thomas Homer-Dixon, *The Ingenuity Gap: Can We Solve the Problems of the Future?* (Toronto: Knopf Canada, 2000), and Thomas Homer-Dixon, "The Ingenuity Gap: Can Poor Countries Adapt to Resource Scarcity," *Population and Development Review* 21, no. 3 (1995): 587–612.
2. Quoted in Gordon Laird, *Power: Journeys Across an Energy Nation* (Toronto: Penguin Viking, 2002), 167.
3. Sheela Basrur, "Air Pollution Burden of Illness in Toronto," City of Toronto (Toronto: Toronto Public Health, May 2000): i–ii.
4. Henry David Venema and Stephan Barg, "The Full Costs of Thermal Power Production in Eastern Canada" (Winnipeg: International Institute for Sustainable Development, July 22, 2003).

5. This research is reviewed in Martin Seligman, *Authentic Happiness: Using the New Positive Psychology to Realize Your Potential for Lasting Fulfillment* (New York: Free Press, 2002), 51–55.
6. Laird, *Power*, 144. The phrases quoted in the last sentence are from Laird's interview with Bryan Young, general manager of the Toronto Renewable Energy Coalition.

AT THE FRONTIER OF ENERGY

1. Carol Howes, "2001: An Ice Odyssey," *Financial Post* (*National Post*), September 2000.
2. Mackenzie Gas Project, Preliminary Information Package, April 2003, vol. 1, Project Description.
3. www.shell.com/home/content/responsible_energy/performance/environmental/energy_intensity/energy_intensity_27032008.html
4. Alberta Energy and Utilities Board (EUB), "Alberta's Reserves 2006 and Supply/Demand Outlook 2007–2016," 2006.
5. L. F. Ivanhoe, "Canada's Future Oil Production: Projected 2000–2020," M. King Hubbert Center For Petroleum Supply Studies, Colorado School of Mines, (Hubbert Center Newsletter #2002/2).
6. "2 Oil Firms Plan Alaska Gas Pipeline," *New York Times*, April 9, 2008.
7. "2 Oil Firms Plan Alaska Gas Pipeline," *New York Times*, April 9, 2008.
8. www.eia.doe.gov/oiaf/aeo/gas.html
9. www.oilnergy.com/1gnymex.htm
10. "Exxon sees energy growth despite downturn," *MarketWatch*, December 4, 2008.
11. Robert G. Bromley, Project Director, "Progress Report: What Is Sustainable Community Energy Project," *Ecology North*, Yellowknife, NT, October 17 2002.
12. "Pipeline Hit by Fresh Delay," *Calgary Herald*, December 6, 2008.
13. Robert G. Bromley, Project Director, "Progress Report: What Is Sustainable Community Energy Project," *Ecology North*, Yellowknife, NT, October 17 2002.

14. U.S. Geological Survey, 2008,
    www.usgs.gov/newsroom/article.asp?ID=1980
15. United Nations Environment Programme (UNEP), June 2001.
16. "CNPC Plans to Build Longest LNG Pipeline," *Shanghai Daily*,
    June 4, 2007
17. "Xinjiang's Oil and Gas Equivalent Ranks Number One in
    China," *People's Daily*, January 8, 2008
18. Geoffrey A. Fowler, "Trouble in Toy Town," *Far Eastern
    Economic Review*, February 6, 2003.
19. "Uighurs on Both Sides of Conflict in China," *New York Times*,
    September 2, 2008
20. Amnesty International, "China," 2003,
    http://web.amnesty.org/report2003/chn-summary-eng, and
    Amnesty International, "China: Torture — A Growing
    Scourge," February 2001.
21. "China's Big Bet on Gas," *Businessweek*, April 29, 2002.
22. "China's 'War on Terror'," BBC NEWS, September 10, 2002,
    and BBC, "US Diplomat Visits China's Muslim Area," December
    18, 2002,
23. Mark O'Neill, "Xinjiang Separatists Called Top Terror Threat,"
    South China Morning Post, November 4, 2002; "Uyghur Leader
    Denies Terror Charges," *Radio Free Asia*, January 29, 2003; and
    Matthew Forney, "One Nation Divided," *Time Magazine*, March
    25, 2002.
24. Stephanie Mann, "China's Report on Xinjiang Region
    Questioned," *Voice of America*, May 29, 2003.
25. "One Nation Divided," *Time Magazine*, March 25, 2002.
26. StratFor, "China: Separatist Crackdown Could Taint Foreign
    Companies," May 29, 2002.
27. AFP, "Anti-American Sentiment Among China's Muslims
    Growing," March 31, 2003, and Reuters, "China Quake
    Highlights Ethnic Rift in Xinjiang," March 25, 2003.
28. China International Finance, Shell Intensifying Investment in
    China, September 3, 2006. www.fdi-hn.gov.cn/english/
    news/2006/3/9/ 1141887447842.shtml

29. AZo Journal of Materials Online, "Shell Eyes Big Opportunities in China," September 22, 2005, www.azom.com/News.asp?NewsID=4002

30. Jasper Becker, "Shell Defends Pipeline Decision," *South China Morning Post*, March 25, 2002, and Ray Heath, "BP, Shell Hope to Fuel China's Growth," *Evening Standard*, London, January 14, 2003.

31. "EU hits out at China's economic nationalism," *Financial Times*, September 25, 2008.

32. National Energy Board, "Energy Brief — Natural Gas Supply Costs in Western Canada in 2007," www.neb.gc.ca

33. David Hughes, "The Energy Sustainability Dilemma: Can Alternatives to Oil Bail Us Out"Geological Survey of Canada, October 18, 2007.

34. International Energy Agency, "World Energy Outlook 2007: Key Strategic Challenges," www.iea.org

35. Claudia Cattaneo and Tony Seskus, "Drop in Oil Exploration Spurs New Supply Fears," *National Post*, April 19, 2003.

BOOM, BUST, AND EFFICIENCY

1. "Clean technologies" refers to appropriately scaled solar, wind, hydro, biomass, and wave/tide energy supply technologies. In a broader sense, it also refers to the wide array of ways to use all forms of energy more efficiently. It does not include nuclear technology, or the centralized renewable technologies.

2. K. Butti and J. Perlin, *A Golden Thread: 2500 Years of Solar Architecture and Technology* (Palo Alto, CA: Cheshire Books, 1980).

3. Energy efficiency means doing the same tasks using less energy. It is not the same as curtailment, which means cutting back activities to use less energy. Conserving energy can be done either by efficiency or by curtailment. Confusion between these concepts is what led Vice President Dick Cheney, architect of the Bush administration's national energy policy, to state that a nation cannot conserve its way to greatness. Expansionists may argue that this is true of curtailment. Only someone profoundly

uninformed of economics would make the same argument of efficiency. Doing more with less, paying less, causing less harm to the environment, and thereby enhancing national security not only constitute an effective foundation for a national energy strategy, they are the cornerstone.

4. A. Lovins and H. Lovins, "Mobilizing Energy Solutions," *American Prospect*, February 2002.

5. Early in his administration Reagan ordered the Department of Energy (DOE) to pulp the Agricultural Yearbook, which taught farmers how to use energy more efficiently. The then executive director of the Daughters of the American Revolution (DAR) went to the DOE warehouse at night and loaded a pickup with as many copies as his truck could carry and distributed them to DAR members at their Continental Congress the next day.

6. A. Lovins and H. Lovins, "Mobilizing Energy Solutions," *American Prospect*, February 2002.

7. According to David Roodman, an analyst at the Center for Global Development, the U.S. government subsidizes automobiles at a rate of US$111 billion a year above and beyond what it reaps in auto taxes and fees — an estimate that does not include the environmental, health, and military costs of burning fossil fuels. One recent example of a subsidy is the provision in the Bush economic plan to increase the amount that business owners can deduct for the purchase of an SUV.

    For example: Dodge Durango sticker price US$27,205; Current law Equipment deduction US$25,000; Total tax deduction* US$25,971. Bush economic plan Equipment deduction US$27,205; Total tax deduction US$27,205. This includes the bonus tax write-off enacted by Congress in March 2002 and a deduction for normal depreciation.

    How the write-off works: Hummer H1 sticker price US$106,185; Current law Equipment deduction US$25,000; Total tax deduction* US$60,722. Bush economic plan Equipment deduction US$75,000; Total tax deduction* US$88,722.

Sources: Detroit News research, IRS, Taxpayers for
Common Sense. Reported in a story by Jeff Plungis / Detroit
News Washington Bureau, January 20, 2003.

8. Reuters, "Environmentalists Criticize Ford Fuel Efficiency," June
5, 2003, http://www.planetark.org/dailynewsstory.cfm/
newsid/21045/story.htm.

9. Transportation Research Board, *Effectiveness and Impact of
Corporate Average Fuel Economy (CAFE) Standards* (Washington,
D.C.: National Academy Press, 2002), http://www.nap.edu/books/
0309076013/html/. This is a conservative analysis.

10. Some analysts doubt that there is any economically recoverable
oil in the Arctic National Wildlife Refuge. The U.S. Geological
Survey conducted a peer-reviewed assessment that concluded
that there is probably *no* oil that would be cost effective to
extract at the moderate oil prices discovered in the futures
market, forecast by industry and government, and relied upon
by the state of Alaska's revenue forecasts. For more details, see
the July–August 2001 *Foreign Affairs* article "Fool's Gold in
Alaska." The published version and a heavily annotated hyper-
text version are both available at http://www.rmi.org/
sitepages/pid171.php.

11. Simon Beavis, "Volkswagen Unveils World's First 1 Litre Car,"
May 24, 2002, http://www.wbcsdmobility.org/news/cat_1/
news_106/index.asp.

12. Hal Harvey, Bentham Paulos, and Eric Heitz, "California and
the Energy Crisis: Diagnosis and Cure," *The Energy Foundation*,
March 8, 2001, http://www.ef.org/california/downloads/
CA_crisis.pdf.

13. *New York Times*, May 6, 2001. Cheney also said, "Conservation
may be a sign of personal virtue, but it is not a sufficient basis
for a sound, comprehensive energy policy."

14. R. Smith, "Power Industry Cuts Plans for New Plants, Posting
Risks for Post-Recessionary Period," *Wall Street Journal*, January
4, 2002. The article reports data from Energy Insight (Boulder,

Colorado), showing that at least 18 percent, or 91 out of a total announced portfolio of 504 billion watts planned for construction, had been cancelled or tabled by the end of 2001. (The 504-billion-watt portfolio included longer-term projects than those summarized at the beginning of this paragraph.) Ms. Smith interprets the reductions as likely to create power shortages; we interpret them as likely to reduce financial losses when demand assumptions prove exaggerated — especially if saving electricity is allowed to compete fairly with producing it.

15. The states most actively supporting energy efficiency programs continue to be primarily in the northeast, the Pacific northwest, and certain parts of the Midwest, along with a handful of other states, including California, Florida, and Texas. The average annual spending across all fifty states is US$3.88 per capita. Connecticut ranks first in per-capita program spending at US$19.48. While this overall national trend is encouraging, the research demonstrates that only about one-third of the states account for nearly all (86 percent) of the spending by utilities and states on energy efficiency programs. The report "State Scorecard on Utility and Public Benefits Energy Efficiency Programs: An Update" is available at ACEEE's web site at http://www.aceee.org/.

16. This and other information about energy efficiency can be found in A. Lovins and H. Lovins, "Mobilizing Energy Solutions."

17. A. Lovins, "Negawatts, 12 Transitions, Eight Improvements and One Distraction" *Energy Policy* 24, no. 4: 331–343. See also World Alliance for Decentralized Energy, "World Survey of Decentralized Energy — 2002/2003," http://www.localpower.org/.

18. Productivity increases when workers can see better what they're doing, breathe cleaner air, hear themselves think, and feel more comfortable. Offices typically pay about one hundred times as much for people as for energy, so 6 to 16 percent higher labour productivity increases profits by about 6 to 16 times as much as eliminating the entire energy bill. See J. J. Romm and W. D.

Browning, "Greening the Building and the Bottom Line," *Rocky Mountain Institute*, 1994, http://www.rmi.org/images/other/GDS-GBBL.pdf.

19. Lester R. Brown, Janet Larsen, and Bernie Fischlowitz-Roberts, *The Earth Policy Reader* (New York: W. W. Norton & Company, 2002). Also available on-line at http://www.earth-policy.org/Books/EPR_contents.htm.

20. Reuters, "New EU Law Aims to Double Green Energy by 2010," July 5, 2001, http://www.viridiandesign.org/ notes/251-300/00254_europe_doubles_green_power. The strategy was first laid out in the European Commission's "Energy for the Future: Renewable Sources of Energy," section 1.3.1, p. 9, http://europa.eu.int/comm/energy/ library/599fi_en.pdf.

21. European Wind Energy Association, "European Wind Energy Capacity Breaks the 20,000 MW Barrier," November 2002, http://www.ewea.org/doc/20gw%20briefing.pdf.

22. Reuters, "German 2002 Wind Power Market Up 22 Pct," January 24, 2003, http://www.planetark.org/dailynewsstory.cfm?newsid=19548.

23. Reuters, "Germany Approves Second Offshore Wind Project," December 19, 2002, http://www.planetark.org/dailynewsstory.cfm?newsid=19129.

24. European Wind Energy Association, "European Wind Energy Capacity Breaks the 20,000 MW Barrier."

25. Reuters, "US Wind Power Growth Waned in 2002," January 27, 2003.

26. Lester R. Brown, "Wind Power Set to Become World's Leading Energy Source," *Earth Policy Institute*, June 25, 2003, http://www.earth-policy.org/Updates/Update24.htm.

27. H. Lovins and W. Link, "Insurmountable Obstacles," (paper presented to the United Nations Regional Roundtable for Europe and North America, Vail, Colorado, 2001).

28. Lester R. Brown, *Eco-Economy: Building an Economy for the Earth* (New York: W. W. Norton & Company, 2001). Also available on-line at http://www.earth-policy.org/Books/index.htm.

29. Shell International, *Exploring the Future: Energy Needs, Choices and Possibilities — Scenarios to 2050* (2001), http://www.shell.com/home/media-en/downloads/scenarios.pdf.

30. M. Mansley, "Long Term Financial Risks to the Carbon Fuel Industry from Climate Change" (London: Delphi Group, 1995).

31. Michelle Nichols, "Solar Power to Challenge Dominance of Fossil Fuels," Reuters, August 9, 2002.

32. Reuters, November 25, 2002.

33. None, the free market will do it . . .

34. C. van Beers and A. de Moor, *Public Subsidies and Policy Failures* (Cheltenham U.K.: Edward Elgar Publishing, 2001). The European Commission took the first step toward possible reform of E.U. energy subsidies by producing an inventory of all forms of state support provided to the fossil fuel, renewable, and nuclear energy sectors. Published in December 2002, the document "Working Paper of the European Commission: Electricity from Renewable Energy Sources and the Internal Electricity Market" says the inventory may determine "whether certain energy sources are . . . given advantages that do not adhere to the objectives of energy policy and combating climate change." In recent years, members of the European Parliament, environmentalists, international bodies such as the OECD, and, increasingly, member state governments have been asking for the support granted to different energy sources to be made more transparent. Furthermore, the E.U. renewable energy directive, adopted in 2002, calls on the commission to propose a harmonized support framework for renewables if a comparison of subsidies identifies any "discrimination" between energy sources. ENDS Environment Daily January 9, 2003.

35. I have sat in meetings with senior energy officials from such European nations as France who have denied that their governments give any subsidies, and when confronted with clear evidence of a variety of subsidies, have refused to reveal the amounts given (for example, to the nuclear programs of Électricité de France, one of the most heavily subsidized electricity programs in the world).

36. R. Heede, "A Preliminary Assessment of Federal Energy Subsidies" (1984), http://www.rmi.org.

37. Ricardo Bayon, *Atlantic Monthly*, January–February 2003, 117.

38. Matthew Wald, "Use of Renewable Energy Took a Big Fall in 2001," *New York Times*, December 6, 2002.

39. Tom Doggett, Reuters, April 2, 2002.

40. Elinor Burkett, "A Mighty Wind," *New York Times*, June 15, 2003, http://www.nytimes.com/2003/06/15/magazine/ 15WIND.html?ex=1057204576&ei=1&en=c6657f4c00300148.

41. British Wind Energy Association brochure, http://www.bwea.com/ pdf/gen.pdf.

42. Howard Geller, *Energy Revolution: Policies for a Sustainable Future* (London: Island Press, 2002).

43. E.U. programs to improve end-use efficiency include the GreenLight Programme, the Standby Initiative, the Motor Challenge Programme, the Luminaire Design Competition, the EuroDEEM database, and initiatives in the appliance, building (e.g., the Thebis database), and industrial fields. See http://energyefficiency.jrc.cec.eu.int/html/readmore.htm.

44. "Energy-Intelligent Europe Initiative," ACEEE, http://www.eceee.org/eceee_forum/EI-Europe.lasso.

45. European Alliance of Companies for Energy Efficiency in Buildings, address to the Parliamentary Hearings on Intelligent Energy for Europe, http://www.europarl.eu.int/ hearings/ 20020911/itre/euroace.pdf.

46. Sacramento Municipal Utility District, "Facts and Figures," *SMUD*, http://www.smud.org/about/facts/index.html.

47. *Public Utilities Fortnightly*, December 1, 1994.

48. Stephen Beers and Elaine Robbins, "Lights Out: The Case for Energy Conservation," *E Magazine*, January 1998.

49. Ibid.

50. Sacramento Municipal Utility District, "Shade Tree Program," *SMUD*, http://www.smud.org/sacshade/ index.html (accessed September 2001).

51. Stephen Beers and Elaine Robbins, "Lights Out: The Case for Energy Conservation."

52. SMUD, http://www.smud.org/hp/index.html (accessed September 2001).

53. Dr. Robert Fountain, Real Estate and Land Use Institute, California State University at Sacramento, "Economic Impact of SMUD Energy Efficiency Programs," March 29, 2000, http://www.smud.org/hp/index.html.

54. *The Electricity Daily*, "Despite the Fuss, Some Things Work in Calif.," August 24, 2000.

55. SMUD, http://www.smud.org/hp/index.html (accessed September 2001).

56. SMUD, "Facts and Figures," http://www.smud.org/about/facts/index.html. The actual decrease was from 2,759 MW to 2,688 MW.

57. San Francisco Business Wire, "First Federal Facility Switches to 100% Renewable Power," July 23, 1999.

58. SMUD, http://www.smud.org/hp/index.html (accessed September 2001).

REVERSE ENGINEERING: SOFT ENERGY PATHS

1. Robert Stobaugh and Daniel Yergin, eds., *Energy Future: Report of the Energy Project at the Harvard Business School* (New York: Vintage Books, 1983), 4.

2. We will sometimes use the term "energy conservation" simply because people use it and understand it, even though it is not precise in terms of the principles of physics.

3. Amory B. Lovins, *Soft Energy Paths: Toward a Durable Peace* (New York: Harper & Row, and Toronto: Fitzhenry & Whiteside, 1979), 38–39.

4. David B. Brooks, John B. Robinson, and Ralph D. Torrie, *2025: Soft Energy Futures for Canada*, vol. 1, *National Report of Friends of the Earth Canada to the Department of Energy, Mines and Resources and Environment Canada* (Ottawa: 1983), italics added. Note to the reader: Robert Bott, David Brooks, and John

Robinson, *Life After Oil: A Renewable Energy Policy for Canada* (Edmonton: Hurtig Publishers, 1983) is the most accessible of the several versions of the Canadian soft energy path study.

5. David B. Brooks, *Another Path Not Taken: A Methodological Exploration of Water Soft Paths for Canada and Elsewhere, Report to Environment Canada* (Ottawa: Friends of the Earth Canada, 2003).

6. Brooks et al., *2025: Soft Energy Futures for Canada.*

7. Stobaugh and Yergin, *Energy Future.* The original study was reported in the Demand and Conservation Panel of the Committee on Nuclear and Alternative Energy Systems, "U.S. Energy Demand: Some Low Energy Futures," *Science,* April 14, 1978.

8. See, for example, Brooks et al., *Another Path Not Taken.*

9. Ralph Torrie and David Brooks, with Ed Burt, Mario Espejo, Luc Gagnon, and Susan Holtz, *2025: Soft Energy Futures for Canada — 1988 Update* (Ottawa: The Canadian Environmental Network, 1988).

10. $30 per barrel in 2000 and $55 per barrel in 2025.

11. Janet Shawin, "Charting a New Energy Future," *State of the World: 2003* (Washington, D.C.: The Worldwatch Institute, 2003).

12. Ralph Torrie, Richard Parfett, and Paul Steenhof, *Kyoto and Beyond: The Low Emissions Path to Innovation and Efficiency* (Vancouver: The David Suzuki Foundation, and Ottawa: Climate Action Network Canada, 2002).

13. E. U. von Weizsäcker, A. B. Lovins, and L. H. Lovins, *Factor Four: Doubling Wealth, Halving Resource Use* (London: Earthscan, 1997). See also Paul Hawken, Amory Lovins, and Hunter Lovins, *Natural Capitalism: Creating the Next Industrial Revolution* (New York: Little, Brown and Company, 1999).

14. Ralph Torrie, personal communication, 2003.

Acknowledgements

We would like to acknowledge the contributions of those at House of Anansi Press who were instrumental in making this volume happen, including Lynn Henry, Janie Yoon, Matt Williams, Sarah MacLachlan, Scott Griffin, and all those who have worked to prepare this book. It's also important to note the excellent work of those who were instrumental in the original volumes *Fueling the Future* and *Feeding the Future*, including Kevin Linder, Martha Sharpe, and Kevin Siu.

Finally, to our families, Tammy Quinn, Maizie and Gideon Solomon, and Roz, Theodore, and Molly Heintzman who are the inspiration behind the project.

INDEX

Aboriginal peoples, and Arctic energy production, 158–70, 180, 182; early history of, 158–60, 166–67, 168; and land claims/self-government, 166–68, 180; and Mackenzie River Valley gas pipeline project, 158–61, 165–70, 180

agribusiness, xiii–xv, 5, 27; as oligopoly, xiv–xv; and overconsumption, 119–22; subsidies for, xiv, 9, 12, 13, 92–93, 121–22. *See also* agriculture, industrial; beef industry; food industry; meat processing industry

agriculture, industrial, 3–18; and artificial fertilizers, 7–12, 14, 15, 24, 27, 99, 120; in Brazil, 89; capital investment required for, 11–12, 22, 100; and corn/grain as animal feed, 16–17, 32, 85–86, 120, 121; energy expended by, 15–17, 85–86, 119–21; environmental impact of, 8–9, 13, 14, 24, 27, 119–21; and factory farms, 3, 13–18; and fossil fuel use, 15–16, 17, 18, 19, 27, 120; and hybrid corn, 6–7; and impact on farmers, 11–12, 22, 99, 100, 103; jobs created by, 15; and mechanization, 7–8, 15, 99, 100; and outside suppliers, 15; and overconsumption, 119–22; and pesticide/herbicide use, 12–13, 14, 99, 100, 120; and rural depopulation, 3–6; as unsustainable, xvi, 5–6, 8, 18, 106–7. *See also* agribusiness

agriculture, industrial, alternatives to, 18–28; co-operatives, 3, 4, 23–26; local food, 18–21; local infrastructure, 21–23, 26, 56; organic farming, 10, 11, 19, 23–26, 27–28, 56; subsidies for, 26–38

agriculture, traditional: and crop rotation, 7, 10; and fair trade movement, 106; jobs created by,

315

energy policy, U.S., 209–16; under
Bush, 213, 227–28, 280, 310n3,
311n7; under Carter, 210–12; and
fossil fuels, 209, 212, 213, 227–28;
and hydrogen energy, 280; under
Nixon, 209–10; under Reagan,
212, 310–11n5. *See also* soft path
approach, to energy policy
ethanol, vi–ix
European Union, 31, 41, 58, 256, 265,
279; efficiency/renewables strategy of, 229–31; hydrogen energy
strategy of, 265, 279–80; renewable energy in, 220, 256; wind
energy in, 220–22, 256

factory farms, 3, 13–18; and corn as
animal feed, 16–17; and corporate
land ownership, 92; economic
impact of, 13–14; and economies
of scale, 18; and fossil fuel use,
15–16, 17, 18; jobs created by, 15
fair trade movement, 104–6
Fallboard, Dean, 23, 25–26
Farmers Diner (Barre, Vt.), 20–21,
27
"farm to fork" programs, 30, 50, 60
fast-breeder nuclear reactors, 194,
197–98, 202
fast food industry: and children, 110,
111, 122–23, 124, 130; and portion
sizes, 121–24, 133, 141; and pricing
incentives, 123–24; and trans fats,
110–11, 133. *See also* food industry; obesity; overconsumption
fertilizers, artificial, 7–12, 14, 15, 24,
27, 99, 120. *See also* nitrogen
Finland, 136, 139, 190, 199, 200
fishing: and bycatch, 66–68; by
country, 64, 65–66; and ecosystem damage, 69–70; illegal,
unregulated, and unreported, 78;

over-reporting of, 65–66, 78; and
postwar technology, 62–63, 65.
See also aquaculture; oceans;
seafood industry
Flexible Alternative Current
Transmission System (FACTS),
269
Food and Agriculture Organization
(FAO), 64, 65, 66, 70, 85, 97–98
Food Guide Pyramid (USDA), 111,
125
food industry, 125–34; and appearance of social responsibility, 110,
125–26, 127–28, 132; and children,
110, 111, 122–23, 125, 128–34,
136–37, 140–41; and collusion
with government, 133, 143; environmental impact of, 119–22;
major players in, 125; playbook of,
127–28, 137–38; and portion sizes,
111, 121–24, 132, 141; and promotion of unhealthy eating, 110, 111,
116–17, 122–24, 125; and public
change, 134–37; recommended
actions for, 137–43; and subsidized corn, 93, 121–22; and
tobacco industry, 126–28, 134;
and trans fats, 110–11, 133; and
USDA, 111, 125, 133; and WHO,
132–33. *See also* agribusiness;
obesity; overconsumption
food prices, viii–ix
food production. *See* agribusiness;
agriculture, industrial
food safety: and bovine tuberculosis, 38–39; in Britain, 46–47; and
BSE, 39–46; and meat inspection,
46–57; and quality assurance
protocols, 30, 48–51; and risk
management, 30, 40–46, 48, 49,
53, 57–60; and scientific auton-
omy/freedom, 46–47

food taxes, 138–39, 140, 142
Ford, Henry, vi–vii
Forgues, Travis, 24, 28
fossil fuels: costs/effects of, in
    Arctic, 164, 165; and electricity
    demand, 184–85; and industrial
    agriculture, 15–16, 17, 18, 19, 27,
    120; and modern lifestyle,
    263–65; and nuclear energy, 185,
    186, 187–89; uncontrolled
    demand for, 157–59; and U.S.
    energy policy, 209, 212, 213,
    227–28. *See also* natural gas; oil
    sands project (Alberta)
France, 124, 190–91, 198, 200, 203
Fresh From the Farm (Toronto),
    20, 27
fuel-cell technology, 161, 224,
    266–68, 276, 277–78
fuel efficiency, 212–15, 255–56

genetically modified food (GMOs):
    and contamination of other vari-
    eties, 96, 98; and control of seeds,
    96–98; and cost of food, 98–99;
    and non-food production, 97;
    and scarcity scare, 84
Genuine Progress Indicator (GPI), 87
Germany, xvi–xvii, 186, 198, 200,
    221, 226
Giddens, Anthony, 57, 58
Goldstein, Fritz, 61–62, 63, 70, 81–82
Grandin, Dr. Temple, 52–53
Great Barrier Reef Marine Park
    (Australia), 80–81
green/renewable energy: Arctic
    projects involving, 164–65; in
    China, 224–25, 226; and energy
    efficiency, 219–26, 229–35; in
    Europe, 220–22, 256; in Germany,
    221; and hydrogen, 161, 265–66; in
    India, 225; obstacles to, 150–57;

trends in, by source, 220; in U.S.,
    227. *See also* soft path approach,
    to energy policy; *see also specific
    types of energy*
green/renewable energy, obstacles
    to: consumption, 150, 153–55;
    costs, 150–53; political/bureau-
    cratic systems, 155–56; small-
    scale/local advocacy of, 156–57
Green Revolution, 9, 11–12, 28,
    99–100, 103
Grocery Manufacturers of America,
    130
Gross Domestic Product (GDP),
    86–88, 273
growth hormones, 31, 58, 120

Haines, Roland, 55
Halweil, Brian, 16, 19, 21, 22, 26
Hazard Analysis Critical Control
    Points (HACCP), 48–51
heart disease, 113, 114
high-temperature gas (HTGR)
    nuclear reactors, 196–97, 202
hog and poultry barns. *See* factory
    farms
hunger, and absence of democracy,
    83–109; in Brazil, 88–91; and
    control of arable land, 88–93; and
    control of seeds, 94–104; and fair
    trade movement, 104–6; and
    GDP, as flawed measurement,
    86–88; and
    overconsumption/obesity, 88; and
    scarcity scare, 83–84, 108–9
hybrid crops, 6–7, 99
hydrogen energy, 161, 184, 224, 226,
    259, 263–82; benefits of, 264–65;
    in Canada, 273, 274, 275, 276,
    280–83; and consumers as pro-
    ducers, 267, 270, 271–72, 279; cost
    of, 272; and developing world,

Agriculture (USDA), 93, 101, 111,
125, 133, 141
uranium, 188, 193–94, 197, 198,
201–3, 238
Urumqi (China). *See* Uighurs of
Xinjiang, China; Xinjiang
Province (China)

Van Acker, Rene, 4, 18
Via Campesina (international
peasants' organization), 104

Wallace, Henry, 6–7
WhaTi, N.W.T., 165
wind energy projects, 220–24, 256;
in Arctic, 164, 165; and Cape Cod
proposal, 228; in Germany, 221; in

India, 225; resistance to, 228–29;
in Sacramento, 232; in Toronto,
155–56
World Health Organization
(WHO), 112, 113, 129, 132–33, 140

Xinjiang Province (China), gas
pipeline project in, 170–81; and
economic boom, 171–73, 174–75;
and energy consumption, 173,
175–76, 180–83; and intra-
national conflict, 176–80; and
Uighur majority, 171–75, 176–79,
180–81

Yucca Mountain nuclear waste
repository (Nevada), 189, 192, 200

About the Contributors

DR. DAVID B. BROOKS is a natural resources economist who has recently retired after fourteen years with the International Development Research Centre, a Canadian crown corporation that supports research on international development proposed and carried out by people in developing countries. He is now Senior Advisor of Research for Friends of the Earth Canada (part-time). Among past positions, he was founding director of the Canada Office of Energy Conservation and director of the Ottawa Office of Energy Probe. Among his books are *Zero Energy Growth for Canada, Watershed: The Role of Fresh Water in the Israeli-Palestinian Conflict*, and *Water: Local-Level Management*. He has been elected to the International Water Academy, based in Oslo, Norway.

DR. KELLY D. BROWNELL is an internationally known expert on eating disorders, obesity, and body weight regulation. He is professor and chair of the Department of Psychology at Yale ·

University, where he is also professor of Epidemiology and Public Health and the director of the Yale Center for Eating and Weight Disorders. He has been president of several U.S. organizations, including the Society of Behavioral Medicine, the Association for the Advancement of Behavior Therapy, and the Division of Health Psychology of the American Psychological Association. He has received numerous awards and honours for his work, including the James McKeen Cattell Award from the New York Academy of Sciences and the award for Outstanding Contribution to Health Psychology from the American Psychological Association. Dr. Brownell has written eleven books, including 2004's *Food Fight,* and more than 300 scientific articles and chapters. In 2006, *Time* magazine listed Dr. Brownell among "The World's 100 Most Influential People."

CARRIE BROWNSTEIN has a Masters degree in Environmental Management from Duke University, where she focused on ecosystem considerations within fisheries management. Her professional work has focused on merging good science and business to create practical market-based solutions to issues in fisheries and aquaculture. Born to a family whose roots in seafood reach back to 1909, Brownstein continues the long-held tradition by working passionately to make today's seafood industry a more sustainable one. She has worked as an independent consultant for a range of environmental NGOs and is one of the founding members of the Blue Ocean Institute. She is the co-author of *Fish or Cut Bait: Solutions for Our Seas* with Carl Safina. Currently, she works at Whole Foods Market, Inc., where she continues her seafood sustainability work.

SUSAN HOLTZ is a senior consultant who specializes in energy, environment, and sustainable development. She has been a principal in projects on long-term energy planning, electricity rates, municipal energy management, and greenhouse gas reduction. She also served on government hearing panels on electricity regulation in Nova Scotia and on hydrocarbon exploration on Georges Bank. She has been appointed to many advisory bodies and boards, including the Auditor General of Canada's Panel of Senior Advisors and the External Advisory Panel for Canada's Commissioner of Environment and Sustainable Development, and was the founding vice chair of both the Canadian and Nova Scotia Round Tables on the Environment and the Economy.

THOMAS HOMER-DIXON holds the Centre for International Governance Innovation Chair of Global Systems at the Balsillie School of International Affairs in Waterloo, Canada, and is a Professor in the Centre for Environment and Business in the Faculty of Environment, University of Waterloo. His books include *The Upside of Down: Catastrophe, Creativity, and the Renewal of Civilization*, which won the 2006 National Business Book Award, *The Ingenuity Gap*, which won the 2001 Governor General's Award, and *Environment, Scarcity, and Violence*, which won the Caldwell Prize of the American Political Science Association.

WYATT KING is an experienced international project manager and policy adviser to political candidates and elected officials. He is currently a senior adviser on energy and environmental policy to a Member of the U.S. House of Representatives. He has a Bachelors of Arts from Williams College and a Masters in International Relations from the Fletcher School at Tufts University, with concentrations in International Business and International Environment and Resource Policy.

STUART LAIDLAW is faith and ethics reporter at the *Toronto Star,* where he has also covered business and served on the editorial board for three years. He has led the paper's coverage of food and agricultural issues as well as covering the World Trade Organization. Before joining the *Star,* he was a senior news editor with the *Financial Post* and a reporter for the Canadian Press, where he also covered agriculture and world trade talks. He first got to know Canada's farming community early in his career as a reporter for several small-town papers. His coverage of food, agriculture, and trade has taken him across North America and to Europe and introduced him to farmers, activists, scientists, and business people from around the world. His book, *Secret Ingredients: The Brave New World of Industrial Farming,* was based on that experience.

GORDON LAIRD is a journalist and author who has worked on documentary and investigative projects in Canada, the United States, and Asia. His books include *Power: Journeys Across an Energy Nation,* a survey of climate change, energy, and the perils of the industrial age. His next book will be published in 2009 by McClelland & Stewart. His web site is www.gordonlaird.com.

ANNA LAPPÉ is the co-author, with Frances Moore Lappé, of *Hope's Edge: The Next Diet for a Small Planet.* A regular public speaker and commentator on food politics, globalization, and the media, Anna Lappé's articles have been widely published in the United States and Canada, appearing in the *Washington Post, San Francisco Chronicle, Los Angeles Times,* and *Globe and Mail,* among others. She has been a Food and Society Policy Fellow of the Kellogg Foundation and is the co-author of *Grub: Ideas for an Urban, Organic Kitchen,* with Bryant Terry. She is currently working on a book about the link between our diet and climate change.

FRANCES MOORE LAPPÉ is author or co-author of sixteen books, including the three-million-copy bestseller *Diet for a Small Planet.* Her books have been used in hundreds of colleges and in more than fifty countries and have been translated into over a dozen languages. She lectures widely and has received seventeen honorary doctorates from distinguished universities. In 1975, she co-founded one of the U.S.A.'s most respected food think tanks, the Institute for Food and Development Policy (Food First). With her daughter Anna Lappé, she directs the Small Planet Institute. In 1987 she received the Right Livelihood Award in Sweden, considered the "alternative Nobel." Her most recent book is *Getting a Grip: Clarity, Creativity, and Courage in a World Gone Mad.*

L. HUNTER LOVINS is currently a founding Professor of Business at Presidio School of Management, one of the first accredited programs offering an MBA in Sustainable Management. Her areas of expertise include Natural Capitalism, sustainable development, globalization, energy and resource policy, economic development, climate change, land

management, and fire rescue and emergency medicine. She also developed the Economic Renewal Project and helped write many of its manuals on sustainable community economic develop- ment. She is the recipient of numerous honours, including the Right Livelihood Award, the Lindbergh Award and Leadership in Business, and she was named *Time* magazine's 2000 Hero of the Planet. She has co-authored nine books, including *Natural Capitalism,* and hundreds of papers. She has served on the boards of governments, non- and for-profit companies.

ALLISON MACFARLANE is an Associate Professor of Environmental Science and Policy at George Mason University. Previously she was a Senior Research Associate at the Massachusetts Institute of Technology's Security Studies Program. From 1998 to 2000 she was a Social Science Research Council–MacArthur Foundation fellow in International Peace and Security at the Belfer Center for Science and International Affairs at Harvard University. She has also served on a National Academy of Sciences panel on the spent fuel standard and excess weapons plutonium disposition. She received her Ph.D. in geology from MIT in 1992.

IAN MACLACHLAN is a Professor of Geography at the University of Lethbridge but his contribution to this collection was written while he was on leave at the Centre for Canadian Studies at the University of Edinburgh. His book, *Kill and Chill: Restructuring Canada's Beef Commodity Chain*, describes the changing geography of Canada's cattle and meat-packing industries during the twentieth century. His current research is focused on the global livestock revolution associated with rapid growth in meat consumption in developing countries.

JEREMY RIFKIN is the author of many best-selling books, including *The Hydrogen Economy: The Creation of the World Wide Energy Web and the Redistribution of Power on Earth*. He serves as an adviser to Romano Prodi, the president of the European Commission, and provided the strategic white paper that led to the European Union's adoption of a new energy initiative to become the first fully integrated hydrogen superpower in the twenty-first century. He is also the president of the Foundation on Economic Trends in Washington, D.C. Since 1994 he has been a fellow at the Wharton School's Executive Education program, where he lectures to senior corporate management from around the world on new trends in science and technology and their impacts on the global economy, society, and the environment.

CARL SAFINA is president of Blue Ocean Institute, which he co-founded in 2003. He is the author of more than a hundred scientific and popular publications on ecology and oceans, including featured work in *National Geographic* and a new Foreword to Rachel Carson's *The Sea Around Us*. His first book, *Song for the Blue Ocean*, won the Lannan Literary Award and was chosen as a *New York Times* Notable Book of the Year, a *Los Angeles Times* Best Nonfiction selection, and a *Library Journal* Best Science Book selection. His second book, *Eye of the Albatross*, won the John Burroughs Medal for nature writing and was chosen by the National Academies of Science, Engineering, and Medicine as the year's best book for communicating science. He is also the author of *Voyage of the Turtle*, and has been profiled in the *New York Times* and on *Nightline*. He is the recipient of a MacArthur's Foundation "genius" Fellowship, among many other honours.

ERIC SCHLOSSER is a correspondent for the *Atlantic Monthly*. His first book, *Fast Food Nation*, is a *New York Times* bestseller and has appeared on the bestseller lists of the *Los Angeles Times*, the *San Francisco Chronicle*, the *Boston Globe*, the *Washington Post*, *USA Today*, and *Publishers Weekly*, among others. Schlosser has appeared on *60 Minutes*, CNN, *CBS Evening News*, *NBC Nightly News*, FOX News, *The O'Reilly Factor*, and *Extra!*, and has been interviewed on NPR and for *Entertainment Weekly*, *USA Today*, and the *New York Times*. He is currently at work on a book about the American prison system.

About the Editors

ANDREW HEINTZMAN is president of Investeco Capital Corp, a private equity company that invests in for-profit environmental business. He is a director of The Sustainability Network, the Tides Canada Foundation, Triton Logging, and Lotek Wireless. He was the co-founder and publisher of *Shift* magazine and a founder of consulting company d~Code.

EVAN SOLOMON is the co-host of the current affairs shows *CBC News: Sunday* and *Sunday Night* and the host of CBC Newsworld's *Hot Type*. He co-founded and was the editor-in-chief of *Shift* magazine and is the author of the novel *Crossing the Distance*. He is also the co-founder of Realize Media Inc., and he sits on McGill University's Arts Advisory Board.